Plotinus on
Sense-Perception:
A Philosophical Study

Plotinus on Sense-Perception: A Philosophical Study

Eyjólfur Kjalar Emilsson

Member of the Institute of Philosophy of the University of Iceland

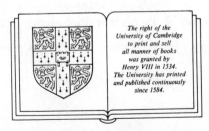

The right of the
University of Cambridge
to print and sell
all manner of books
was granted by
Henry VIII in 1534.
The University has printed
and published continuously
since 1584.

Cambridge University Press

Cambridge

New York   New Rochelle   Melbourne   Sydney

Published by the Press Syndicate of the University of Cambridge
The Pitt Building, Trumpington Street, Cambridge CB2 1RP
32 East 57th Street, New York, NY 10022, USA
10 Stamford Road, Oakleigh, Melbourne 3166, Australia

First published 1988

Printed in Great Britain at
the University Press, Cambridge

British Library cataloguing in publication data
Emilsson, Eyjólfur Kjalar
Plotinus on sense-perception:
a philosophical study.
1. Plotinus
I. Title
186'.4   B693.z7

Library of Congress cataloguing in publication data
Emilsson, Eyjólfur Kjalar
Plotinus on sense-perception.
Revision of thesis (Ph. D) – Princeton University, 1984
Bibliography
Includes index.
1. Plotinus. 2. Perception (Philosophy – History.
I. Title.
B693.Z7E46   1987   121'.3   87-11771

ISBN 0 521 32988 4

This work is dedicated to the memory of my mother,
Kristín Anna Thórarinsdóttir

Contents

Contents

Acknowledgements

This book is a revised version of my Ph.D. dissertation: *Plotinus on Sense-Perception: A Philosophical and Historical Study*, on which I began work in 1980 and which I defended at Princeton University in 1984. Thanks are due to many people who have helped me in my work on Plotinus. In particular I should like to thank, first, my thesis adviser, Professor Michael Frede, who originally suggested Plotinus to me as a dissertation topic, and from whose vast knowledge and acumen I have greatly benefited. My friend and colleague, Professor Mikael M. Karlsson, read the penultimate version of my thesis and vastly improved its style. My discussions with him of philosophical points have also been invariably fruitful for me. Thirdly, I should like to thank Professor Henry J. Blumenthal, who has kindly read my thesis and given me detailed comments on it, which have been of great help in the revision of the work. And in addition to these I am indebted to many others, but especially to Donald Morrison, Peter King, Sigurdur Pétursson, Gunnar Hardarson, and Svavar H. Svavarsson, all of whom have assisted me in various ways at different stages. I also wish to thank the Institute of Philosophy of the University of Iceland, and especially its chairman, Thorsteinn Gylfason, for a grant which has made it possible for me to work full time on the transformation of the thesis into a book. Finally, I wish to thank my wife and my children for all their support and patience, and simply for being there, which has mattered most of all to me.

Acknowledgements

Introduction

The merest glance at a list of the treatises of the *Enneads*, or at an *index verborum*, is sufficient to show that Plotinus took a great interest in sense-perception. Three treatises deal specifically with questions relating to perception, and remarks of varying lengths about perception are to be found throughout the *Enneads*.[1] A philosophically-minded person who bothers to look at some of these passages is bound to find statements and arguments that evoke his curiosity.

Nevertheless, very little has been written about Plotinus' views on perception;[2] none of the classic Plotinian studies, for example, discusses them in any detail.[3] Presumably the main reason for this is that among Plotinian scholars there has been a strong tendency to focus on those aspects of Plotinus' philosophy that are of theological or religious interest; hence, other subjects have tended to receive less attention than they deserve. In any event I shall deal, in the present work, with the subject of sense-perception in Plotinus. In what follows I shall give some account of the nature of this undertaking.

The *Enneads* are held to be unusually difficult to read, even among philosophical works. Indeed it takes considerable effort to acquire sufficient feeling for Plotinus' thought, so as not to be lost most of the time. One – and perhaps the most important – reason for this is the nature of the composition of the *Enneads*: they are a collection of treatises intended for circulation in Plotinus' school and not for publication. Thus we have Plotinus' discussions of set problems and questions, presupposing familiarity on the part of

1

the audience. Plotinus never attempts to set forth the whole of his philosophy in a systematic manner. Porphyry tells us that "when he [Plotinus] had written anything he would never bear to go over it twice".[4] And he goes on to say that "Plotinus worked out his train of thought from beginning to end in his own mind, and then when he wrote it down, since he had set it all in order in his mind, he wrote continuously as if he was copying from a book".[5] This gives some explanation of Plotinus' language, which often is very elliptical and not easy to read.[6]

It goes without saying that these aspects of the material pose certain difficulties for any interpretation of Plotinus' thought. As regards the subject of perception, special difficulties arise from the fact that, despite his obvious interest in the subject, Plotinus nowhere sets out his views on perception as a whole. The treatises mentioned above deal with specific problems relating to perception but do not expose Plotinus' total views on the subject. Thus, these views must be reconstructed from remarks he makes in passing, where the main focus is on something else. It is perhaps typical that the passage in which Plotinus comes closest to giving us a systematic exposition of his views on perception, IV.4.23, was written in order to answer the question whether bodily organs are necessary for perception; and this question in turn comes up in a discussion of what psychic capacities the earth, which in Plotinus' view is a living being, is endowed with.

In my treatment of the subject I do not attempt to comment on every remark Plotinus makes about perception – which in any case would be a hopeless task. My method can be described as follows: I attempt to pin down statements about perception that either recur in the *Enneads* or seem, at least, to be especially emphasized where they occur. Thus, the interpretation is based on statements which we can affirm with confidence genuinely reflect Plotinus' views. I analyse such statements and inquire whether they can be seen to constitute a coherent total view. I am primarily concerned with attempting to understand Plotinus, not with criticizing his views or commenting on their plausibility. Thus I think it is fair to say that I have adopted a sympathetic attitude towards the material. I believe, in fact, that such an attitude is a prerequisite of getting anywhere in the study of Plotinus' thought. It goes without saying, that in order to criticize a view, one must know what the view is one wishes to criticize. But this does not mean that I have adopted a totally uncritical attitude. It means primarily that I take seriously the following assumptions: (a) that Plotinus generally knew what he was saying; (b) as regards our subject, that he did in fact have an overall view of it. As to the latter assumption, it is not something I have taken for granted *a priori*, but rather a position to which I have been led in my reading of the *Enneads*, even though this total view is far from immediately evident from the texts.

There are strong connections between Plotinus' metaphysics and his account of perception. The frequency of remarks about perception in the *Enneads* is in part explained by the fact that Plotinus likes to use perception both as analogy and as a contrast to shed light on other phenomena, in particular the mode of cognition on the level of *nous*, the divine Intellect.[7] But the metaphysics is also relevant to an understanding of Plotinus' views on perception in themselves. In particular the doctrine that, in perception, the percipient receives the form of the object perceived – which is a central theme in this work – is connected with Plotinus' views on forms in general, which in turn are connected with the whole of his metaphysics or ontology. Although I am minimally concerned with the latter as such, I devote the first chapter to Plotinus' metaphysics, since it is necessary as background for my exposition of the main subject.

Chapter II also contains background material. There I give a survey of Plotinus' views on soul in general, and on man and the human soul in particular. These, for obvious reasons, constitute a part of the immediate background for his views on perception. In both these introductory chapters my exposition is inevitably concise and dogmatic: I refrain from going into details and explaining controversial issues.

In general Plotinus' views must be seen in the light of the views of his predecessors. Plotinus was a Platonist. In fact he was so much of a Platonist that he thought that his most important doctrines contained nothing new, that he himself was merely an exegete who unfolds what lies implicit in the doctrines of Plato (cf. v.1.8, 10-14). However, a reader of the *Enneads* will not only find Platonic doctrines there, he will also find many that are recognizable as Aristotelian rather than Platonic. Nevertheless, he will discover that Plotinus was not one of those Platonists who thought that Plato and Aristotle were in perfect agreement, for Plotinus sometimes explicitly adopts a critical attitude towards Aristotelian views. But this is not all. Despite open hostility towards the Stoics, the reader will sometimes encounter views that seem to be almost undiluted Stoicism.[8] In addition to all this he is likely to find a great deal that will strike him as a strange and impure mixture of Platonic, Aristotelian and Stoic elements, and also a portion that he does not readily recognize at all from earlier Greek thinkers.

This situation is not so odd, however, as it may seem at first sight. One should keep in mind that more than five centuries separate Plotinus from Plato and that philosophy did not stand still in the meantime. Thus, just as twentieth-century followers of Kant are liable to draw upon non-Kantian sources, and to implement their Kantianism through contemporary techniques and jargon, so does Plotinus freely utilize that which he finds valuable in post-Platonic philosophy in defending and elaborating what he takes to be the true Platonic views. Further – and no less importantly – it should also be noted that well before the time of Plotinus there was already in existence a shared philosophical vocabulary which derived from all the major schools, and that the Platonic tradition, to which Plotinus belonged, had already adopted a good deal of Aristotelian doctrine and used it for its own purposes.[9]

Neoplatonism can be viewed as a culmination or, to use Hegelian jargon, the logical synthesis of Greek metaphysics. What I have in mind is that there are certain doctrines and, even more importantly, underlying assumptions that are to be found in the writings of earlier Greek philosophers, which Plotinus and the other Neoplatonists take up and in some cases stretch to their extremes. Thus it is hardly possible to give a purely ahistorical account of Neoplatonic doctrines: if we want to make Neoplatonism understandable we must take into account the assumptions and problems of the tradition to which it belongs. This will help us see more clearly the values and shortcomings of the approach whereby, as Rist puts it, "Plotinus is being dissolved into his sources".[10] Given the fact that Plotinus' philosophy is so much concerned with the tradition, it is important to have an accurate as possible knowledge of the sources he employs. Knowledge of such matters can genuinely add to our understanding of the relevant passages, and prevent misunderstanding. The danger involved in this approach is that Plotinus comes to look too much like a merely eclectic thinker, so that we lose sight of the fact that he is continuing the work of such people as Parmenides, Anaxagoras, Plato and his immediate followers, Aristotle, the Pythagoreans and the Stoics, and not merely borrowing ideas from them when it suits him.[11]

The material to be studied here exhibits all these traits. Plotinus' discussion of perception and of the human soul in general has a notoriously Aristotelian air, although influence from certain Platonic passages is also in evidence. For instance, the Aristotelian notions of perception as the reception of the form of the perceived object, and of perceptions as acts pervade Plotinus' account of perception. On fundamental issues in psychology, however, Plotinus' position is unquestionably Platonic: he consistently maintains the immortality of the soul and an essential distinction between the soul and the body along with a doctrine about the soul's kinship with a realm of transcendent forms. Hence, Aristotelian hylomorphism is unacceptable to him, and he has to modify the Aristotelian notions which he employs, to fit his dualistic views. Similarly, though to a lesser extent, Plotinus is influenced by Stoicism. In his account of the soul and perception we find him adopting some Stoic notions, for example the concepts of *sympatheia* and *synaisthêsis*. But the Stoics are more relevant as Plotinus' main antagonists. One can see, for instance, that Stoic physicalist views on the soul and perceptual impressions prompt Plotinus to articulate some novel views on these subjects, and that in general Stoic materialism helps to polish and sharpen Plotinus' dualistic views.

Although the details remain to be discussed, the foregoing should make clear that Plotinus' views on perception are a synthesis of many elements in Greek philosophy. In fact, like many other aspects of his philosophy, they present a paradigm case of how philosophical ideas can be moulded and swayed in the course of history so that in a new context they come to do a different job from the one they were originally intended to do. It is not my primary concern to trace Plotinus' sources, nor do I intend to relate the history of the notion of perception over a period. However, it is often crucial for an understanding of Plotinus' words to pay attention to his sources and to the historical context of his work; and this I attempt to take into account.

Much of what Plotinus has to say about perception is directly connected with the general dualistic view of the relation between the soul and the body that he wants to maintain. Dualism is of course a part of Plotinus' Platonic heritage, but, as we shall see as we go on, Plotinus' formulation of it is sharper and gives rise to questions which Plato never thought of. Plotinus takes it for granted that perception is a phenomenon in which both body and soul are involved. This is of course not at all original: all Greek philosophers would have agreed. What distinguishes Plotinus from most of his predecessors is his view that the soul is neither a body of any kind nor some sort of a principle of the body, but something which is not to be defined in terms of a body at all.

This generates some special problems. For Plotinus it becomes important to distinguish between the soul's part in perception and the part played by the body. It is Plotinus' view that the soul cannot be affected by the body. However, he believes along with everyone else that perception involves an affection of the percipient from the outside. It therefore becomes important to make a sharp distinction between the affection, which is attributed to the bodily organ of sense, and what the soul does. But although Plotinus makes it clear that such a distinction must be made, it is not as clear exactly what the affection is and what it is that the soul does. To find this out is crucial, however, if we are to reach an understanding of Plotinus' views. So much is clear, however, that in Plotinus' view the soul's act in perception, though connected with the percipient's body and with an external object, is itself of a non-bodily nature. Thus we encounter in Plotinus' theory – perhaps for the first time in western philosophy – a view according to which perception is a matter of crossing an ontological rift between the mental and the physical.

I mentioned above that I take as my starting point statements about perception that either recur in the *Enneads* or are somehow emphasized. Some of these have already been mentioned on the preceding pages. But I shall now list the most important of these statements, and comment briefly on each of them.

(1) Vision and hearing do not depend on the affection of a medium between percipient and object. What other philosophers explained in terms of a medium, Plotinus explains in terms of the phenomenon of *sympatheia* (cf. IV.5. 1-4; 8). The notion of *sympatheia* is Stoic in origin, although apparently the Stoics did not use it in their account of perception. While the doctrine of *sympatheia* does not play a central role in Plotinus' theory of perception (in the sense that it is not much in evidence outside IV.5, which specifically deals with it), this doctrine is nevertheless the background to other passages. And since Plotinus' discussion of *sympatheia* and the question of medium in IV.5 brings to light several important aspects of his views on perception, it seems to be a suitable starting point for an account of these views. *Sympatheia* in perception is thus the subject of Chapter III.

(2) If there is to be sense-perception, a bodily sense-organ must be affected by the object perceived.[12] All Greek philosophers who had anything to say about perception gave their assent to this statement or one close to it. Thus Plotinus is in no way saying anything original here. It is, however, doubtful that all Greek philosophers had precisely the same thing in mind when they said

6

that perception must involve the affection of a sense-organ. We will have to try to determine exactly what Plotinus means when he says this and what role this affection plays in his theory as a whole. In Chapter IV I discuss his views on the nature of sensory affections, i.e. I attempt to determine what phenomena Plotinus has in mind when he speaks of affections in connection with perception. In Chapter VIII, section 1, I discuss the role this sensory affection plays in his theory.

(3) In perception the percipient receives the form of the object perceived.[13] This doctrine is Aristotelian, but there has been much disagreement among commentators as to what Aristotle meant by it. In many respects it raises the same questions of interpretation in Plotinus as it does in Aristotle. One line of interpretation of this doctrine in Aristotle is to identify the reception of the form with the affection of a sense-organ: the organ becomes assimilated to the object by becoming physically qualified in the same way as it, i.e. by taking on its form. Another is to interpret the statement that the sense receives the form of the object (without its matter) as a way of saying that the object comes to exist in the percipient as an intentional object of the same sort. Plotinus' version of this doctrine seems to lend itself to various interpretations in a similar way. Perception as a reception of forms is a recurring theme that is connected with almost everything else Plotinus has to say about perception. Discussion of this doctrine is therefore to be found in all chapters.

(4) Certain facts about the unity of perception reveal characteristics of the soul which serve to mark an ontological distinction between the soul and the body.[14] Plotinus' position on the unity of perception is, I think, best understood through a consideration of the views of his predecessors. Hence, in Chapter V, where I discuss the unity of perception, I begin with a survey of earlier views, in particular those of Alexander of Aphrodisias. I argue that Plotinus' position is a natural, but still original and interesting, development of Alexander's views. Plotinus says that perception terminates in the faculty of representation (*phantasia*).[15] This raises certain questions about the distinction and division of labour between perception and the faculty of representation that has a bearing on the interpretation of Plotinus' views on the unity of perception. Thus, in Chapter V, I also discuss the faculty of representation and its relation to that of perception.

(5) Perceptions are a kind of judgement (*krisis*).[16] This doctrine indicates that Plotinus is one of those thinkers who take sense to be a cognitive power in its own right and not merely an instrument

7

of cognitive powers. But if perceptions are supposed to be judgements, we must inquire what distinguishes them from other judgements. This I discuss in chapter VI, section 2.

(6) Perceptions are acts (*energeiai*) as opposed to affections.[17] The view that perceptions are acts is derived from Aristotle, as I noted above. But it is not clear that Plotinus and Aristotle have exactly the same thing in mind when they describe perceptions as *energeiai*. In Chapter VII I compare Plotinus' and Aristotle's views on this matter and argue that they are probably not identical. Plotinus' view that perceptions are acts is closely connected with the view that perceptions are judgements, and both of these are connected with the issue of forms in perceptions.

(7) Plotinus insists that what we perceive is the things themselves.[18] Nevertheless, as we shall see, the question arises whether he held some sort of representational view of perception familiar from modern philosophy, according to which there is a "veil of ideas" between the percipient and the external world. Some such view has in fact been attributed to Plotinus, and, as we shall see later on, there are indeed passages that lend themselves to such an interpretation. However, I do not think that this interpretation is correct. In Chapter VI I discuss the main passages that give rise to this sort of interpretation and argue against it. In Chapter VIII, section 1, I explain what I take to be Plotinus' position on the subject.

The relationship between these themes – external objects of perception, affections, judgements, acts and forms in perception – is discussed in Chapter VIII, where I set forth what I take to be Plotinus' theory of perception as a whole. Finally, in section 2 of Chapter VIII, I discuss Plotinus' version of dualism of soul and body as it emerges from his account of perception. The origin and history of the mind-body distinction is a matter that has received considerable attention in recent years. In particular it has been debated whether dualistic views of the Cartesian type were ever conceived by the ancients. Although Plotinus' views are not exactly Cartesian, they exemplify a sharper and subtler dualistic position than any previous Greek thinker had arrived at.

In general I use the words "perception" and "perceive" to translate the Greek words *aisthêsis* and *aisthanesthai*. It is a well known fact that *aisthêsis* covers both perception and sensation. I think, however, that so far as the *Enneads* are concerned "perception" is on the whole a more appropriate translation. But that does not necessarily mean that it is always so, and there are indeed places where it is debatable which translation should be used.

Nevertheless, I stick to "perception" as a rendering of *aisthêsis* throughout, except when *aisthêsis* – then used with the definite article – clearly refers to the *faculty* of perception. In those cases I either use "faculty of perception" or "sense". This choice is determined solely by a wish to have a uniform translation of this key word: and, as I have said, if one is to choose between the two, "perception" is preferable. On the other hand, following custom, I talk about the senses, sense-organs, sensibles and so on, in rendering words of the same root as *aisthêsis*.

All translations from the Greek are mine, but I have used some published translations as aids. In this connection I would mention particularly A. H. Armstrong's translations of *Enneads* I–V in the Loeb classical series, which I often follow with minor modifications. References to the *Enneads* are to Henry and Schwyzer's Oxford edition. Thus, for instance, the two references "IV.4.23, 1–3; 25, 6" mean "4th *Ennead*, 4th treatise, chapter 23, lines 1 to 3, and same *Ennead* and treatise, chapter 25, line 6".

Sometimes the reader will see a number enclosed in brackets after the treatise number. This is the number assigned to the treatise on Porphyry's chronological list of Plotinus' treatises. I sometimes, but not always, give the Greek of Plotinian passages I quote in the notes. In the selection of these passages I rely on my admittedly subjective feeling as to when it would be especially convenient for those readers who know Greek to have Plotinus' actual words readily available.

I

Plotinus' metaphysics

The most striking feature of Plotinus' philosophy, and of Neoplatonism generally, is its hierarchical picture of reality. This is also the feature that is most baffling for modern readers. In Plotinus' philosophy we come across a hierarchy of three so-called "hypostases" that are called "the One", "Intellect" and "Soul", followed by matter at the bottom. Similar ideas characterize the writings of the other Neoplatonists. We are told that reality is somehow constituted by this hierarchy, an idea which we presumably find quite puzzling. If we look for arguments for it as such, we do not find any: it seems to be taken for granted. And if we encounter something that looks like an argument for some part of the hierarchy, we feel that it invariably presupposes the general picture.

As a first step towards approaching the Neoplatonic hierarchy, let us consider the ideas of a principle and of a hierarchy of principles. Let us suppose that there is a need to explain in general terms some phenomenon that is taken to be a fact of common experience. This may lead to the supposition of a level of entities or properties or forces, that are taken to be "behind" or "above" the ordinary phenomena, such that by supposing these entities, properties or forces to be there, an explanation has been given of the ordinary phenomenon that needed explanation. At this point we have already divided reality into two levels, the level of ordinary experience and a "more basic" level. We may say that this is the limiting case of a hierarchy, if we take a hierarchy to be anything stratified, such that its strata come in an order of dependence. Normally, however, we reserve the word "hierarchy" for structures only that have more than two strata.

To divide reality into different levels in this way is a common practice in the sciences. For instance, the molecular, the atomic and the subatomic levels of chemistry and physics can be interpreted as a kind of hierarchy. The various principles posited by the ancient thinkers – Empedocles' Love and Strife, the Limit and the Unlimited of the Pythagoreans, the Active and the Passive of the Stoics, to name a few – are also good examples of this. The strata in the Neoplatonic hierarchy are principles in the same sense as those just mentioned. Principle (*archê*) is in fact a term that the Neoplatonists used alternatively with "hypostasis" to refer to a stratum in the hierarchy of being. But explanations or principles do not always form hierarchies. The ancient Greek thinkers were often satisfied with an account of the phenomena as a result of the synthesis of two or more independent (and hence not hierarchically ordered) principles. Hierarchies arise if there is a need to account for some features of the principles that have been posited themselves, and this is done by positing new principles. Such hierarchies of explanations are not unfamiliar. In ancient philosophy the most notable pre-Neoplatonic example is to be found in Plato's theory of Forms. The realm of Forms, that is itself a principle or a set of principles postulated to account for the sensible world, is itself stratified: in the *Republic* the Form of the Good functions as a principle of the other Forms. As one might expect, the Neoplatonic hierarchy is a development of that suggested by Plato.

The Neoplatonic hierarchy is a hierarchy of unity. The distinguishing feature of each stratum is its degree of unity and the strata are ordered in terms of increasing degrees of unity. This needs explanation. Let us start by considering the notion of unity as such.

Unity is a key notion in Plotinus' metaphysical tradition.[1] The Pythagoreans, the Eleatics, Plato, Aristotle and the Stoics are all concerned with it. Plotinus' notion of unity draws on all these sources. While it would be wrong to suggest that all these philosophers were always concerned with unity in exactly the same sense or with exactly the same questions about unity, I think that their concerns with unity are not altogether disparate either. Plotinus' stand is to maintain the ultimate unity of the notion of unity while also insisting on keeping its species distinct. Plotinus accomplishes this by holding that all unity except that of the One is by participation in the One while different things participate in

11

the One in different ways.² This enables him to see his predecessors as talking about the same thing when they talk about unity though not necessarily as talking about the same species of unity.

The Greek thinkers tended to take the notion of unity to be intimately connected with that of being. This line of thinking began with the Pythagoreans and the Eleatics and it is firmly ingrained in Plato and the Old Academy and Aristotle.³ Glossing over details and simplifying the matter somewhat, I think it is fair to say that the connection between unity and being is as follows: whatever is said to be must possess some degree of unity. In order to see the point of this we must realize that "being" is here used in a somewhat restricted sense. What is excluded are accidental collections of things. Consider a set consisting of e.g. the Empire State Building, Fidel Castro and the number 2. There is no denial that this set *exists* and hence has being in the sense of existence. But it does not have being in the sense that we are after. It does indeed contain members that have being in this sense but it does not have being as such in itself. It is tempting to express this by saying that merely accidental sets do not make up a *thing*. We are therefore concerned with being in the sense according to which only something which is a thing or an entity has being. Let us be prepared to give a generous interpretation to the word "thing" so that we might count as things not only horses and tables and the like, but also armies, the number 4 and the Beautiful Itself. It is perhaps obvious by now that the criterion of whether something has being in the sense we are after is in fact unity: we are going to count as having being that and only that which is in one way or another unified. This may seem to make the point about the connection between unity and being uninteresting and almost trivial. But that is all right, because the point is fairly trivial and was, I believe, taken to be obvious by the ancient philosophers. However, a lot can be said that is not trivial about how "things" are unified so as to make up beings, and a lot of nontrivial questions can be asked about the subject. For example, there is intuitively a difference between the ways in which an army, a horse and the Beautiful are each one thing. And obviously there arise various questions from the fact that most of the things we treat as unities are in fact also composite and many.

Given that being implies some sort of unity of that of which being is predicated, we can distinguish different entities by the different kinds of unity that they possess.⁴ We have, for instance, as the limiting case "things" like heaps. A pile of stones has unity in a way dispersed stones do not.⁵ The heap has spatially adjacent parts and is therefore spatially continuous. We can therefore say that it is spatially or locally one in the sense that all its parts occupy one continuous part of a space. On the other hand, a heap lacks various other varieties of unity. It is not one in motion, i.e. one part of it may move without the other parts moving, and it lacks definite shape and internal structure. By contrast, an individual stone is one in motion. According to Plotinus the unity of bodies, of which individual stones are a good example, consists in the spatial unity of a set of qualities: a given colour, a shape and a hardness, say, are all together in the same part of space and accompany each other in motion (cf. VI.2.4).

Living beings possess a higher degree of unity than inorganic bodies. The bodies of living beings are organized as if with the accomplishment of certain ends in view.[6] This organization reveals a more perfect unity than that proper to mere bodies. For the functioning of the parts of a living being must be understood with reference to the living being as a whole: the cat's claws, for example, are not merely hard and sharp extrusions from the cat's toes. A full account of the claws must include a reference to the role the claws perform in the cat's life. Thus, in the case of organisms we have a different part–whole relationship: an account of a part must make reference to other parts and to the whole.

An idea that plays a central role in Neoplatonism and which is likely to strike modern readers as highly peculiar is the view that the sensible world as a whole is one spatially finite living being. Such a view is by no means an idiosyncrasy of the Neoplatonists but was widespread in antiquity in one form or other.[7] It is important not to be misled here. The concept of life involved is presumably not quite the ordinary one, though it is not altogether different from it. For example, to say that the visible universe as a whole is one living being is not to suggest that it procreates its own kind or is in all respects just like any ordinary living being. The attribution of life to the cosmos as a whole is grounded in claims about the unity of its parts, i.e. the regular patterns in the visible cosmos were seen to be harmonious and rational in the same way as the activities of the parts of an ordinary living being. This was taken to imply some unifying principle which operates throughout the cosmos and regulates and coordinates the behaviour of its parts.

These considerations show how it could be claimed that in the things of ordinary experience there are various degrees of unity and that to these different degrees of unity there correspond different degrees of being or "thinghood". We have also seen how

13

the sort of unity a thing possesses may serve as the guide or criterion of important distinctions we want to make and do ordinarily make: how unity in general may be taken to be the mark which distinguishes entities from non-entities, how a special sort of unity is a characteristic of bodies, and how another and more perfect sort of unity is a characteristic of living things. Plotinus rejects all attempts to account for the unity of things in terms of the properties of their constituents (see iv.7.1-5). Here he is again in agreement with the mainstream of Greek metaphysics, the atomists being in this respect as in many others a notable exception. Let us consider his reasons. First, for Plotinus such an explanation from the constituent parts would have to be in terms of the four elements or in terms of the atoms of ancient atomic theory. Plotinus finds both unacceptable because there is no way to give a convincing account of how the mere composition of the elements or atoms could give rise to the organic unity living things possess. For in itself the composition would be hazardous and one would have to assume in addition to the elements and their properties some principle explaining how the material is arranged in an organized manner (see iv.7.2-3). Secondly, Plotinus has a more general reason for thinking that organic unity cannot be explained in terms of bodily constituents, namely disbelief in emergent properties. For, as we have seen, it is precisely the feature of a more perfect unity than bodies possess which distinguishes organisms from mere bodies. Plotinus cannot accept that something which lacks the crucial feature to be explained should give rise to this feature: add a body to a body and you will get a body.

The foregoing considerations suggest that Plotinus would propose some sort of transcendent principles to explain the unity that there is to be found in the sensible cosmos. And so he does. But before we consider these higher principles, I want to mention one important aspect of Plotinus' hierarchical explanations.

It is an underlying assumption of Plotinus' thought that the explanation of any feature must be in virtue of something that possesses the feature in question in a "more perfect" way than the thing to be explained. This kind of an assumption is no innovation of his. In Plato's theory of Forms each Form is a supreme example of that of which it is a Form.[8] The same idea is to be found in the ancient theories of the elements, according to which each element possesses some basic properties. Other things' possession of these properties is in turn explained in terms of the presence in them of the elements that *naturally* have the properties in question. Again, the same sort of assumption seems to be implicit in the Aristotelian doctrine that the actualization of any feature must be caused by something that already has the feature actually. Glossing over differences, we can describe the idea common to Plotinus' philosophy, the theory of Forms, the elemental theories and Aristotle's doctrine of actualization by saying that each attempts to explain properties of things by postulating the presence of something that by virtue of itself has the property at issue. In modern parlance: the ultimate explanatory principles necessarily have the properties whose contingent presence in other things they are supposed to explain.

Given this, the unity of individual things and the visible cosmos as a whole must be explained in terms of a principle that has unity as a necessary property. Ultimately this leads to the supposition of a principle characterized as pure unity which Plotinus calls the One or the Good.[9] I say "ultimate" because, as we shall see, there are intermediate principles in between the One and the sensible world.[10]

Let me explain what is meant by pure unity. According to Plotinus every item with the exception of the One is in some respect or other a composite. This means in effect that these other things are characterized by multiplicity as well as by unity. But according to the underlying assumption noted above, the principles of explanation must possess the properties that they explain in such a way that their own possession of them is self-explanatory. In the case of things that are composite and multiple, unity will always appear as an imposed feature: in so far as they are composite their being one is always a case of unity being imposed on something else which is not one.[11] Hence, in every case of a composite thing the fact that it is one has to be accounted for: it is one by virtue of the presence in it of something else which is one, not by virtue of itself. It is evident that if we go along with this line of thinking, we will in the end have to posit a principle that by itself possesses unity; and it follows that this principle cannot be a composite in any respect. This in turn means that the One is not a "one something".[12] Considered in itself it is sheer unity. In so far as the notion of property or attribute presupposes a distinction between the subject that has the property and the property itself, it would even be wrong to say that the One *is one*.[13] Now, what can be said about an "entity" that satisfies such requirements? Quite wisely Plotinus answers "nothing at all".[14] The One cannot be positively described by discourse nor can its nature be apprehended by thought. This is so because thought necessarily involves the union of subject and predicate and as we have seen there cannot be a question of such union in case of the One (see v.3.10).

The One therefore accounts for the unity of things. But the things of ordinary experience are not characterized by unity alone. Since every item other than the One is also characterized by multiplicity, a full ontological analysis must take multiplicity into consideration.

Now, things are multiple in more than one way. An analysis of things in the sensible world reveals that they are composed of forms and matter. The latter does not have any positive features by itself (since in that case it would have form and already be a composite). But it is necessary to posit matter as the receptacle of form and as that which underlies change.[15] Thus, the Plotinian matter is a kind of a combination of the Aristotelian prime matter and Plato's receptacle.[16] Plotinus insists that matter is to be distinguished from magnitude, as magnitude implies determinacy whereas matter is indeterminate (cf. II.4.11-12). Nevertheless it is clear that he thinks matter is responsible for the dispersion of things in space. It is as if the union with matter is responsible for the fact that the forms of sensible things become extended (cf. II.4.12, 1-7). As a principle responsible for the spatial features of things, matter is a principle of multiplicity. For spatiality implies divisibility: any spatial item is made up of infinitely many distinct parts, and it is a characteristic of things in space that each of them occupies a separate place different from that of any other such thing.[17]

The forms that enter into union with matter are already diverse: there are obviously many different *kinds* of things in the world. This diversity is not due to matter but is grounded in the diversity of the forms themselves. In order to distinguish it from the diversity of spatial dispersion, let us call it "diversity of being". As we noted above, every sensible thing is a composite of form and matter. When we say of a sensible thing that it is, say, a man, we are referring to such a composite. In a similar way as in the case of unity above, an account of the property of being a man will in the end be in terms of something which necessarily has this property, something which is a man by virtue of itself. It is a fundamental assumption of Plotinus' metaphysics that nothing which fails to satisfy this sort of requirement can have being in the full sense of that term. For such entities are not really what they are said to be: what they are, they are by participation, and what they are said to be is predicated on something else. Now, it is in virtue of its form that we say of a composite (of form and matter) that it is a man, and hence one might think that this form which enters into union with matter would satisfy the requirement of being a man by virtue of itself. This, however, is not so. For in Plotinus' view the forms in matter are partners in a union with matter and do not have an independent existence (IV.2.1, 47-53; VI.4.1, 17-24). The form of the sensible man, even when considered in itself in isolation from its underlying matter, is nonetheless spatially dispersed and hence is contaminated in the sense that it has features that the union with matter is responsible for. But if we think away these features of the sensible form that matter is responsible for, we are no longer presented with a sensible form but with a form that is an object of thought. Thus, in Plotinus' view the sensible forms as such are not the real things themselves but rather some sort of images or manifestations of the real things that are uncontaminated by union with matter.[18] Therefore, in order to account for the diversity of being as well as for true being itself, Plotinus posits another realm of forms, the model of which is of course the Platonic Forms, whereas historically the forms in matter derive from Aristotle's notion of immanent forms ("Forms" with an initial capital is used to refer specifically to the Platonic forms whether in Plato or in Plotinus).[19] The ultimate elements of this realm are the five greatest forms or kinds (*gene*) of Plato's *Sophist*: being, motion and rest, identity and difference. All other Forms derive from an interpenetration of these.

The realm of Forms differs from the sensible world in that it is nonspatial and atemporal, and as such it is more unified than the sensible world.[20] The realm of Forms is the structure of the universe. It contains the essences of things and shows how these essences are ordered. This order reveals the necessary connections between things. One who has grasped the realm of Forms is in a position to see how every being is a necessary part of the whole and why it is such as it is – in the realm of Forms "the why it is" is the same as "the what it is".[21] He has seen the world from the viewpoint of eternity.

One sign of Aristotelian influence on Plotinus is the fact that Plotinus often refers to the realm of Forms as the Intellect (*nous*) and to the Forms as the intelligibles (*ta noêta*). In Plotinus' view the Forms exist as the objects of thought of a divine intellect (hereafter called the Intellect). The history of how the Platonic Forms came to be identified with the objects of a divine intellect is both complicated and obscure. It certainly started long before Plotinus, whose role in it is to bring to a completion a pre-existing tendency.[22] That such a development took place is however perfectly understandable. In Plato it is a central idea that the Forms are objects of thought rather than of sense-perception. And in the *Timaeus* the Forms are described as the objects of the thought of a divine demiurge. Thus, already in Plato we find the notion of the Forms as the objects of the thought of a divine mind. In Plotinus this idea has been carried a step further. While the *Timaeus* 28 A suggests that the forms exist independently of the demiurge, and that they are something already present that the demiurge can inspect, in Plotinus the Forms are internal to the Intellect. As Armstrong has admirably shown, the crucial antecedent of this idea is to be found in Alexander of Aphrodisias' interpretation of Aristotle's texts on God and the active intellect.[23] In outline: Alexander identifies the God of *Metaphysics* XII – whose activity is described as the thinking of itself and is said to be identical with its objects – with the active intellect of *De Anima*. In Plotinus we find this idea Platonized: the objects of the Intellect's thinking have become the Platonic Forms.

We have now said something about the One, matter, forms in matter and the realm of Forms. There still remains one hypostasis in Plotinus' hierarchy to be commented on, the Soul. In many respects the Soul is the most complex of the Plotinian hypostases. This is due to the multiplicity of its functions. Soul is responsible for a great variety of functions that may seem to have very little to do with one another. In part this is to be explained by the fact that Plotinus and his predecessors saw as kindred some things that we nowadays take to be quite distinct, and partly by the fact that by Plotinus' time the word *psychê* had become an extremely loaded term in the philosophical literature. Plotinus draws on many different sources and tries to extract from them a unified view.

Since I deal with Soul at some length in the next chapter I shall not dwell on it here. Let it suffice to say that as a member of the hierarchy of being, the Soul has the function of linking the Intellect and the sensible world. Plotinus divides the world into two basic categories, the intelligible (*to noêton*) and the sensible (*to aisthêton*). Their names suggest that they are distinguished by their different modes of apprehension. But in effect the sensible is very often equated with the physical, i.e. with bodies and features of bodies. Thus, spatiality is really the formal distinguishing feature: the sensible can be identified with the spatial, the intelligible with the nonspatial. In any event, the One and Intellect are a purely intelligible realm whereas the Soul is described as the last of the intelligibles and as being in touch with the sensible (IV.6.3, 1-12).

Using Aristotelian terminology we can say that the soul is the efficient cause of the sensible world, the Intellect its formal cause (cf. v.9.6).

Plotinus has three main ways to describe priority and dependence in the hierarchy. Two of them are familiar from Plato: participation and the model–image relation. A lower stratum is said to participate in a higher one, and the higher is said to be a model for the lower or to generate the lower as an imperfect image of itself. The third way, emanation (*eklampsis, proodos*), is peculiar to Neoplatonism.[24] Plotinus uses an analogy of the Sun to illustrate it. The One is like the Sun (or any other source of light), the other hypostases are like the rays flowing from it. They are characterized by diminishing power the further they are removed from their source. This analogy is not successful in all respects. But one reason why Plotinus was fond of it is that he took it to be a characteristic of sources of light that they are in no way diminished by the light they emit. It is an important feature of the One and the other hypostases that they lose nothing by emanation.

It must be emphasized that the causal language used to describe the relations between the strata in the hierarchy is not to be taken to imply temporal priority. Rather the acts from the higher to the lower are to be conceived of as contemporaneous and time itself is explained as an aspect of the increasing division or fragmentation as we go further down in the hierarchy. A kindred point to be made is that the language of "higher" and "lower" is purely metaphorical (cf. vi.4 *passim*).

An important aspect of the Plotinian system which has already been hinted at but which deserves special notice is the fact that the same entities may exist on different levels of the hierarchy. For example, the intelligible man is in some sense the same entity as the sensible man. It is true that Plotinus often makes the point that the image is other than the model, thus suggesting a distinction. This however does not alter the point. For while in one sense the model and the image are in fact distinct, in another sense they are not. I shall not here attempt to pin down each of these senses, but shall rely instead on a Plotinian analogy which illustrates the idea clearly enough for the present purpose. Plotinus sometimes compares the relation of the seed and the fullgrown plant to the relation between the being of an entity on lower and higher levels.[25] The idea is that the parts and the properties of the fullgrown plant already exist in the seed but are not yet unfolded: they are there somehow all together, and only later will they develop into distinct parts and properties. We are supposed to think of the relation between the intelligible man and the sensible man in similar terms, except of course in this case the "development" is not a temporal sequence.

When Plotinus is concerned with the levels between the Intellect and forms in matter, the idea that the same things are present on different levels is often expressed in terms of forms existing in different states of division. We have already mentioned two kinds of forms: the Platonic Forms on the level of Intellect and the forms in matter deriving from Aristotle, which are often identified with qualities. Here, Plotinus and his Platonist predecessors are not simply operating with an ambiguity. They take the Aristotelian forms to be images or ontological descendants of the Platonic Forms.[26] On the level of soul in between the transcendent and the immanent forms, there are intermediate forms characterized by intermediate stages of unity. This point will be of great importance to us later, because the notion of form is central to Plotinus' views on perception. We shall therefore have to consider his accounts of perception in the light of the metaphysical doctrine of forms at different stages of unity.

The foregoing indicates that all the Plotinian principles are to be conceived of on a hierarchical model: the One, being the ultimate source of virtually everything else in the universe, is at the top; matter, the unqualified receptacle of sensible forms, at the bottom. Plotinus thus wants to maintain monism: matter too, being the image of intelligible matter, stems from the One (II.4.4, 7-9). But in effect matter functions in Plotinus' system as the principle invoked to account for the opposites of what the One and the higher principles are supposed to account for. Thus one is sometimes under the impression that Plotinus' system is really a dualistic system positing the One and matter as two opposite principles.

Two of the Neoplatonic principles, Intellect and Soul, bear names which may seem to fit only living beings. What lies behind this? Is the Neoplatonic hierarchy at bottom simply an anthropomorphic picture of reality according to which the world at large and its rule is modelled upon a human being? There is no doubt that the notion of a divine intellect is originally anthropomorphic: the regular, rational patterns in nature are explained by presuming a superior mind that designs them as a human craftsman designs his artifacts. But this idea is by no means unique to Neoplatonism; it is a recurrent theme, found, for example, in the views of Anaxagoras, Plato, Aristotle, the Stoics and the whole of Christian theological philosophy. Thus the label "anthropomorphic" does not capture anything specially characteristic of Neoplatonism. Furthermore, even if Plotinus' philosophy and Neoplatonism generally are in their origins and perhaps at heart, anthropomorphic, they are not naively so. First, the psychological notions they employ in describing the principles of the world have been so refined that they are often barely recognizable as notions belonging to human psychology. To take one example, neither the One nor the Intellect deliberates or chooses to make the world in this way rather than that. In this respect traditional Christian conceptions of God are considerably more anthropomorphic than Neoplatonism. Secondly, if the ideas of the principles of Intellect and Soul have their origins in human psychology, in the full-blown system the order of explanation is reversed: human and animal psychic faculties are explained in terms of the principal Soul and Intellect.

One might be tempted to suppose that the Neoplatonic hierarchy is a sort of logical construct, that it represents the relations between the basic concepts these philosophers use to describe the world. While I think that this description is true as far as it goes, it is surely incomplete and misleading. For it is unquestionable that the Neoplatonists thought that their principles exist in the nature of things and not merely as theoretical constructs in the minds of philosophers. Their attitude towards their principles is in this respect more like the modern position according to which the physical sciences deal with a reality that is more real than the reality of everyday experience and which is itself stratified into more and less basic levels.

But of course the Neoplatonic hierarchy is for the most part intended to account for quite different things than modern science. It is not easy to characterize what it is meant to explain without recourse to very abstract, rather unilluminating philosophical jargon. Something has already been said about the Neoplatonists' concern with the notions of unity, multiplicity and being. In part this concern takes the form of a conceptual analysis of these notions and their connections. But the analysis is never a mere disinterested conceptual inquiry into everyday concepts, because the Neoplatonists attempt to present a certain *Weltanschauung* through their analysis. Plotinus' philosophy is an attempt to discuss ultimate questions about the world and man's place in it. What are the reasons for being? How are we, as knowing subjects, related to the world and its causes? The crucial element in Plotinus' answers to these questions is the idea that there is a viewpoint from which the diversity of things – including the distinctions between subject and object, knower and known – do not exist. The hierarchy is supposed to explain how this is possible, and also how diversity and the subject-object distinction arise.

II

Plotinus' views on the soul and man

1 Synopsis of the theory of souls

In order to approach Plotinus' views on man and the human soul it will be helpful to have a synopsis of his general theory of souls. According to Plotinus' orthodox view one must distinguish between at least four kinds of soul.[1]

There is (1) a transcendent soul which is not the soul of any particular thing, either individuals or the cosmos, and is said to remain in the intelligible realm. Although this soul is, presumably, ontologically posterior to the Intellect, it is in fact not clear how they differ as regards internal properties: both are wholly engaged in pure thinking. But the different terms do suggest a difference in function. Plotinus normally chooses to talk about soul when he is concerned with the generation of the sensible from the intelligible, whereas the term "Intellect" is reserved to refer to the life in the intelligible as contained in itself.[2] For clarity I shall write "Soul" with a capital S when I want to refer to this transcendent soul.

There is (2) the World-Soul which is responsible for the life of the visible cosmos. The usual doctrine is that the World-Soul rules the cosmos without descending into it as its body.[3] Often, however, Plotinus distinguishes between two levels of the World-Soul, a higher level, which is the one just mentioned, and a lower, immanent level.[4] Even if this lower level is on any account closely tied with the higher World-Soul by being its direct ontological descendant, it is for various reasons convenient to discuss them

23

under separate headings. So let us distinguish (3) nature or vegetative soul, which is immanent in the cosmos.

Nature, acting as it were as an agent of the unembodied World Soul, is the power immediately responsible for the lowest organic activities in organisms and it is that which informs matter so as to make it determinate. Thus, forms in matter, though not of the order of matter themselves, are the results of the activities of nature. In many ways Plotinus' conception of how nature acts calls to mind the modern notion of a genetic code or a computer programme: nature is that in the organism which instructs it when and how to grow and change. Plotinus, not being familiar with computers, uses as a model the notes of a melody (iii.6.4, 41-53). According to Plotinus nature is a principle of change without being subject to change itself, just as the tune or the programme is not changed by the moves of the instrument or the machine.[5] Plotinus also often talks about formative principles (*logoi* or *logoi spermatikoi*) as performing most of the same functions we have just ascribed to the vegetative soul. It is not clear whether there is some distinction to be made between the two or not, but this is not of great importance in the present context.[6]

Finally, there are (4) individual human souls, which Plotinus often refers to as *hai hêmeterai psychai*, "our souls". I shall return to the notion of the individual soul in my discussion of man. So, for now I will restrict myself to only a few remarks. A person's individual soul is that by virtue of which the person is an individual, not just a nexus in the chain of nature. Often "individual soul" comes close to meaning "self", that with which we identify ourselves. The individual soul is present to a body though not immanent in a body in the way nature is. It is present in that it is set over a particular body which it rules and makes its concern, but as we shall see the association is not essential to it.

An important aspect of Plotinus' psychology that he never doubts but which he finds hard to account for to his own satisfaction is the doctrine of the unity of all souls.[7] Despite the distinctions among souls described above, all souls are supposed to be one, i.e. they are all supposed to be Soul. This may seem to be a strange position to hold, and Plotinus himself is aware that it sounds absurd.[8] Now it is of course possible for the different parts of the same entity to behave in different ways, and one might think that Plotinus could solve his problem by making the so-called individual souls and the World-Soul parts of Soul. However, he considers this alternative and rejects it (iv.3.2-3).[9] Rather, he sees the unity of all souls as an instance of the Platonic notion that the same form can be present as a whole and undivided in many, and thus, for Plotinus, the former problem can be reduced to the latter.[10] It is of course well known that Plato saw serious difficulties in this idea. Plotinus too is aware of how awkward it appears, but he thinks that the problems can be disposed of. In general, he holds that the presence of one in many seems inconceivable only because we tend to conceive of things as bodies. But surely we should not always do that; and once we have seen that there must be entities that are not of the order of body and are not subject to the division characteristic of bodies, the problem will be seen to be surmountable.

The doctrine of the unity of all souls seems to be required by Plotinus' notion of *sympatheia* (cf. IV.3.8, 1-4; IV.9.3, 1-9). I deal with *sympatheia* more thoroughly in the next chapter, so let it suffice to say here that *sympatheia* is a phenomenon that can take place only within things that have organic unity, i.e. have the same soul. And since Plotinus believes that there is *sympatheia* among individual living beings, and between such and the cosmos, all these must in some sense have the same soul. Since Plotinus rejects the Stoic view that individual souls are parts of the World-Soul, the identity of souls has to be accounted for in a different way.

The individual souls are already distinct on the level of Soul (IV.3.5; VI.4.4, 23-4). In fact Plotinus goes even further and suggests that there are Forms of individuals, which implies that in some sense Socrates exists as an individual already on the level of Intellect.[11] In connection with this doctrine there arises the obvious question whether individuality on the level of Soul and Intellect is not inconsistent with the doctrine of the unity of all souls. How can all souls be one, if they are already individuals on the level of Soul? The answer lies in the unity claimed for the levels of Soul and Intellect:[12] in the intelligible world the whole is implicit in each part and can be predicated of each part and *vice versa*, so that on the level of Soul the individuals are not merely individuals (cf. VI.4.14, 17-22); hence, if an individual soul is tied to one intelligible item, it is *ipso facto* tied to the intelligible realm as a whole.

2 An outline of Plotinus' views on man

The most important aspect of Plotinus' views on man is that the word "man" refers to different things according to what level of the hierarchy of being we are talking about. This is of course true of any entity whatsoever. But as will become clear this is true of man in a special and stronger sense. Plotinus rejects the Aristotelian definition of man as a rational animal. For "animal" means "a compound of body and soul" but the body is not an essential part of man. Thus, this definition does not capture the essence of the definiendum (VI.7.4, 10-18). Instead Plotinus proposes to define man primarily as the intelligible man, or the human soul existing on the intelligible level; secondarily "man" may be used of the lower phases of soul that are ontological descendants of the intelligible man (VI.7.6). In a somewhat dogmatic fashion he distinguishes perception and nature as two stages in this descent. Sometimes opinion (*doxa*) is inserted above perception as the first stage.[13]

This picture suggests that Intellect, perception and nature are three phases of the same individual soul. However, Plotinus also says that the lower psychic functions in us are not derived from our individual souls, but from the World-Soul. The idea is that the vegetative functions in man are just an instance of the general pattern of natural events in the cosmos. And it is the business of the World-Soul to inform matter and to regulate the natural organic processes. It does not seem that such processes as they occur in men are different from those in the rest of the world. Plotinus also believes that the higher functions of soul enter the body only after it has been formed in the womb and acquired the vegetative functions. This gives rise to the doctrine that each man has two souls which are indeed united so long as the organism lives but are separated at death.[14]

There are certain inconsistencies in Plotinus' account of the dual origin of the human soul (I use "human soul" to cover all psychic powers at work in a human being). Firstly, as we have noted, Plotinus says both that we get the vegetative functions from the World-Soul and that the vegetative functions are a lower phase of the individual soul. Perhaps this apparent inconsistency can be resolved. It seems to me that if World-Soul can be identified with Soul in those passages where the lower soul is said to be derived from the World-Soul, there may be a way of interpreting Plotinus in such a way that the statements are compatible. But however this may be – and here we come to the second point – Plotinus is not consistent as to what psychic functions in us come from the World-Soul. Sometimes only the vegetative functions are included, sometimes other functions as well. In IV.9.3, 24-7 he says that the "vegetative soul, which is also passively perceptive, is from the World-Soul, whereas the perception which judges with the aid of intellect stems from the individual soul."[15] But in IV.3.27-31 he argues that both the soul derived from the World-Soul and the individual soul have perceptions and memories, though this duality escapes us. Thus, according to this latter passage, more of our psychic functions come from the World-Soul than according to IV.9.3. It is worth noting that, at least according to IV.3.26 ff., the psychic functions derived from the World-Soul do not coincide with those psychic functions in which the body is involved.[16] For in this same discussion Plotinus makes clear that the body is not involved in memory at all, and hence not involved in the memories attributed to the soul that we receive from the World-Soul.[17]

One might suppose that these obscurities are of a great importance for the subject of perception, as perception appears to be on the border between the higher and the lower souls. They are less relevant, however, than it may seem. When Plotinus is concerned with presenting an objective account of human psychology the doctrine of the two origins of the human soul is not much in evidence. Even if he distinguishes between higher and lower levels of the human soul, the two are not presented as two distinct entities. They intermingle, and the picture suggested is that of a continuum rather than of two entities linked together. And as to the question whether the faculty of perception belongs to the soul that stems from the World-Soul, or to the individual soul, or to both, or partly to the one, partly to the other, it is worth bearing in mind that in Plotinus' view souls are flexible in that one kind of soul is in principle capable of performing functions other than those it actually performs: there is no irrevocable specialization.[18] So there is perhaps no one answer to the question. The duality of the human soul tends to be emphasized when the issue is our capacity to dissociate ourselves from the body, or the origin and fate of the soul.

The individual soul, which descends into the body, is different from its corresponding Form, which remains on the level of Intellect, but is an "image" or ontological descendant of this Form. I mentioned earlier that "individual soul" often means the self. While I think this is accurate, it is important to handle the term "self" with care since its meaning is slippery and it has come to have many different connotations. So let me explain what I have in mind.

Plotinus uses the term "we", *hêmeis*, in a special philosophical sense according to which first person pronouns refer to the self.[19]

For him the question, "What are we?" is a primary question, which he answers by presenting a doctrine about man and the individual soul. The primacy of the question of the self can be seen in passages where Plotinus argues for the existence of the individual soul. It turns out that the main reason why there must be individual souls is the fact that there is evidently something which is genuinely *ours*. Thus, to put it briefly, the answer to the question what are we, is "we are the individual soul".[20]

Plotinus conceives of man in the sensible world as a being which is partly within the chain of natural events, partly outside of it. If we so choose, we can assert ourselves as individuals against the happenings in this world, and see ourselves as something other than a link in the chain of nature. It is by virtue of having an individual soul that is something other than the soul which regulates the order of natural events, that we are able to do this. There is a certain conflict, or at least a tension, in Plotinus between this sort of view, in which the individual soul is opposed to World-Soul, and the sort of view represented for example by the doctrine of the unity of all souls, which portrays man as in harmony with the rest of the world. In the conception of the individual soul as that by virtue of which man is outside and above nature we can see a further reason for Plotinus' dissociation of the vegetative soul from the individual soul. For the external impulses against which the higher soul must struggle are primarily the impulses from our own bodies. And although the vegetative soul is not the body, it is by virtue of the vegetative soul that the body is a living body and hence has needs and urges. Plotinus does not deny, however, that we are closely associated with our own body and its nature. Such association is precisely the characteristic feature of the life of the embodied individual soul. One of the roles of the embodied soul is after all to protect and rule over the body. We, i.e. the individual soul, are one with the living body in so far as we attend to it and make its desires and needs our own. However, Plotinus insists that strictly speaking the animated body is only something that belongs to us, not us ourselves (i.1.10, 3-10).

Another reason for identifying the individual soul with the self has to do with the fact that the individual soul is not to be identified with any particular faculty or set of faculties. It is true that Plotinus does attribute the faculty of reason to it and presumably the faculty of sense-perception as well. But the individual soul is not to be identified once and for all with any such faculties. To use Plotinus' metaphorical language, the soul is that on which it sets its regard. This means that the individual soul may direct its regard either to the sensible world and the animated body or else it may concern itself with its intelligible origin and "the world above". In either case *we* are where the individual soul is. When the soul is wholly engaged in contemplation of the Forms the faculties of sense-perception and the mundane reason are inactive (cf. IV.4.8, 14–16). This reveals in what sense the soul may be identified with these faculties and in what sense not. The soul *is* these faculties when it so acts and their actual functioning is identical with its so acting. It is not as if perception and reasoning continue to operate when the soul is directed towards other things. In this way the soul is reason when we are engaged in reasoning. But the soul is not essentially any such faculty, because it is this selfsame soul which may be engaged in contemplation. Thus the soul is a fluctuating entity. This explains in what way "man" is ambiguous according to what level we are talking about. For the individual soul is also that by virtue of which we are human, not merely beasts. Hence in so far as the individual soul fluctuates, so does the man. As said above, man in the primary sense is the intelligible man. But the descendant of the latter, the embodied individual soul, is also man. Depending on what sort of life we choose to lead, we may fall short of or approach the intelligible man. Thus the human soul is mobile in a way that the vegetative soul, for example, is not: the vegetative soul is, to be sure, linked with higher forms of soul and with the Intellect. But as such it cannot choose, as it were, to return to its origin. By contrast, the individual human soul can make such a choice.

Plotinus' concern with the self was a novelty. His predecessors had made remarks to the effect that we are identical with our souls or that we are identical with the faculty of reason.[21] But nobody before Plotinus had put the question of the self in the foreground. It can perhaps be maintained that a good deal of the psychology of Plato, Aristotle, and the Stoics is in effect an attempt to deal with the self; that when they try to pin down and describe what distinguishes us from the brutes, they are in fact trying to answer the question, "What are we?" But it remains true that through his explicit and continuing concern with the question "Which element in the compound of body and soul and the various psychic faculties is we ourselves?" Plotinus brings a new tone to the issue. It is an open question to what extent his theory of the self coincides with those of later philosophers. The concept is however unquestionably the same. Plotinus' attempts to come to grips with it sometimes suffer from vagueness and he is not always consistent. But his keenness and, I am tempted to say, natural talent for gaining insight into this subject have rarely been surpassed.

Plotinus' doctrine of the ascent of the soul cleverly combines his view on the soul as the self, his metaphysical theory of Intellect, and the Platonic doctrine that the contemplation of the Forms is man's proper goal. Plato portrays the purified soul as a happy spectator in the realm of Forms, leaving its exact status in this realm somewhat unclear. Plotinus, on the other hand, provides an ingenious theoretical framework for this doctrine by his theory of the individual human soul's roots in the intelligible realm. On the level of Soul and Intellect the individual human soul is genuinely a member of the intelligible realm: it is a Form, one of the intelligibles. Thus the soul's ascent consists in a reunion with its intelligible source from which it has been separated, though not cut off, by its preoccupation with the body and the sensible world. As the intelligible archetype is presented as the true man and the real self, the elevated state is described as a state of self-knowledge, with an obvious allusion to the Delphic – and Socratic – "Know Thyself". As in Plato's version of this doctrine, the life of the elevated soul consists in pure contemplation of Forms. But for Plotinus this is a logical consequence of his theory of the intelligible realm: as one of the intelligibles the life of the elevated soul will consist in pure contemplation, for this is what life on the intelligible level consists in anyway. And as a participant in the unity that holds for the intelligible realm the elevated soul is not merely absorbed in contemplation of itself but (*ipso facto*) of the whole intelligible realm.

We should finally note that though Plotinus' doctrine of elevation fits together nicely with the doctrine of Forms of individuals, the former doctrine does not require the latter. Plotinus could deny individual differences on the level of Intellect and still maintain his views on the soul's ascent. Socrates would in that case be reunited with the Form of Man rather that with the Form of Socrates. In that case Plotinus' doctrine would be brought into line with Aristotle's views, as interpreted by Alexander, on the active intellect as impersonal and common.[22]

3 Some details of Plotinus' psychology

Here I will address some details in Plotinus' views on the embodied human soul, concentrating upon matters which provide background to Plotinus' treatment of perception.[23] Let us start by considering the notion of an organism.

An important concept in Plotinus' psychology is that of an organism or compound of body and soul. Plotinus uses several terms interchangeably to express this notion: *to synamphoteron* and *to synthêton*, both of which may be translated as "the compound", *to koinon*, which means "the common", i. e. common to body and soul, and also *to zôion* ("the organism", "the animal"). The main Platonic source for this notion is *Alcibiades* I 129 A-130 C (Plotinus did not question the authenticity of the dialogue). The author defines what each of us is as that which uses the body. In the course of establishing the further claim that man is identical with his soul, he distinguishes between the body, the compound (*to synamphoteron*), and the soul. This passage has had a strong influence on Plotinus' psychological views. The Platonic author's explicit identification of man with the soul motivates Plotinus' homologous but more detailed view as considered above: the soul, characterized as that which uses the body, becomes the individual soul in its capacity as the ruler of the body.

Looking at *Alcibiades* 130 C ff., one may think, at first glance, that there are only two entities described, the soul and the body, the compound being just the entity consisting of both in a similar way as the shovel is in a sense nothing but the handle and the blade. However, a more careful reading suggests that the author is really talking about three distinct things, and that the soul which, together with the body, makes up the compound, is not the same as that which is called simply the soul.[24] In any case, such is Plotinus' understanding of the passage. Roughly, Plotinus thinks that the soul which participates in the compound is that which animates the body, makes it be a living body. Thus it is directly involved in the functions of the body and pervades it. The individual soul, on the other hand, is not involved in the same way. It does indeed rule over the body in its capacity as practical reason, but its contact is always through the mediation of the soul which forms the compound.

Plotinus distinguishes between those psychic acts and affections that involve the body and those that do not, and he attributes those that do to the compound (I.1.9, 15-20). Reasoning and imagination do not, in Plotinus' view, involve the body, whereas sense-perception, and all the activities that are associated with the vegetative soul, do. Thus, there is a significant difference between Plotinus' views and those of Aristotle: Aristotle holds that, with the exception of the activities of the active intellect, all psychic

31

activities, including imagination and discursive thought, involve the body.[25] As we shall see in later chapters, noticing this difference is of great importance for an understanding of Plotinus' views on perception and the body–soul distinction.

We should note that in determining which activities belong to the compound and which to the soul alone, Plotinus only seems to consider whether the activity *in itself* involves one or both. Memory of sensible things, for instance, is attributed to the soul alone, even though the memory of such things is necessarily preceded by the perception of them through the senses. Since perception through the senses involves the body, the involvement of the body is necessary for there to be such memory, though it is not actually involved in the act of memory as such (IV.3.26, 8-10).

Plotinus' notion of the organism brings out certain aspects of his psychology of general philosophical significance. Above we pointed out the connection between his notion of an organism, and the question, raised in *De Anima* 403a 4ff., whether there are any functions proper to the soul. Plotinus' attitudes towards the functions of organisms are in important respects similar to Aristotle's general position on psychic functions, but there are also marked differences. Let us first consider what they have in common.[26] Plotinus would, like Aristotle, heartily agree with the modern Wittgensteinian point against soul–body dualism that some of the so called "mental" functions *essentially* involve the body, though of course neither he nor Aristotle state this point in terms of "how sensation words are learnt" or, in general, in terms of the meanings of words.[27] Plotinus' reason for his view is simply that if we consider these common functions, we see that in each case it is necessary to bring in the body in order to give a full account of them. Clearly there is a marked difference between a view of this sort and the position called Cartesian dualism, which denies that there is an essential connection between the mental and the physical even in the case of sensations.[28] Unlike Descartes – at least as he has usually been interpreted – Plotinus does not take scepticism about the objects of our cognition as his point of departure. One arrives at Cartesian dualism by systematically eliminating all one's beliefs about the causes and objects of one's experiences. The mental is defined as that which is left of the experiences when this has been done. The very nature of this procedure makes the connection between the mental and anything else appear contingent. Plotinus' approach is different. His position is the more commonsensical one that for the most part the objects of our awareness are what we ordinarily take them to be.

He sees no reason, methodological or otherwise, for questioning this. Thus it is, for example, no question for him that when we feel pain we are perceiving changes in our bodily condition. This does not mean, however, that Plotinus is unable or unwilling to distinguish between what belongs to the soul and what belongs to the body in the common functions. But because he is not at all tempted by the "sceptical" approach, he can maintain that the psychic or mental elements in the common functions must be understood in their relations to the body and the external world: it is exactly by considering what prompts them and, when it is a question of cognitive functions, their objects that we can formulate what distinguishes, say, pain and seeing from one another, and these from functions that do not involve the body at all. Thus, the body is indispensable in the account of the common functions. If we had no bodies, there *could not* be any pains, perceptions or desires.

Plotinus' position has interesting consequences for his views on punishment after the death of the body: because pain is possible only for organisms, punishment for wrongdoing must be inflicted by a new embodiment followed by bodily suffering (IV.3.24). The thought behind this is obviously the same as the thought behind Aquinas' rather different doctrine that damned spirits suffer through the frustration of their evil will, not physical torture.[29] The preceding considerations also show that Plotinus' belief in the immortality of the soul is immune to objections which consist in pointing out the puzzles and absurdities involved in attributing sensations to disembodied souls: Plotinus would accept such arguments. The only philosophical difficulties that he has to worry about in this respect have to do with psychic functions that do not involve the body: all depends on whether he can make a plausible case for the possibility of such functions.

Let us now turn to the points where Plotinus and Aristotle part company. Despite the differences between Plotinus and the modern dualists, Plotinus' views regarding the organism are dualistic in a way which Aristotle's are not. Or at least this is so if we interpret Aristotle – and this is how Plotinus and most modern scholars interpret him – as maintaining a strict hylomorphism according to which the soul is the actuality of the body, by its nature inseparable from it as the shape of the wax is inseparable from the wax itself.[30] The Plotinian organism, by contrast, is genuinely a compound whose constituent parts are separable not only in thought or in definition but also in reality. Thus, in Plotinus' view no power of the soul is destructible (IV.4.29; IV.9.3,

22-3). Some need the body or a bodily organ to function in the way they do in actual organisms, but it does not follow that such psychic powers are destroyed when the body or their organs are destroyed. Plotinus' notion of the compound can be fruitfully compared with a machine: the body is analogous to the hardware, the soul to the energy by means of which it functions. These are two different things, separable in reality. If the machine breaks down and stops working, that does not prove that the energy has ceased to exist: it is either staying idle in the machine or it has gone elsewhere. So it is also with the soul.

There are important differences between the ways in which qualities, i.e. forms in matter, and embodied souls are present in bodies. As we have pointed out such forms are inseparable from matter. These forms are also more divided than individual souls: each such form is spatially dispersed along with the magnitude in which it inheres and is something of that magnitude. This means that the whites in two glasses of milk and even the whites in two different parts of the same glass of milk are different insubstantial individuals.[31] Souls, even the soul that constitutes the compound together with the body, are quite different in this respect. In iv.3.20-3 Plotinus discusses the question of how the soul is present in the body. He considers several familiar presence relations: the presence of a body at a place, the relation of being-in (as liquid is in a vase), the relation of being-in-a-substrate, the presence of a part in the whole, the presence of the whole in its parts and the presence of a form in matter.[32] None of these are deemed adequate to illustrate the soul–body relation.

Plotinus then goes on to consider the presence of the art of navigation to the ship (chap. 21) and comes to the conclusion that with certain modifications the presence of the soul in the body is similar to this.[33] The problem is that an account is needed of how the art of navigation is present to the ship. More helpful, in Plotinus' opinion is the presence of light in the air (chap. 22), except that it would be more correct to describe the soul–body relation as similar to the presence of air in light, the soul corresponding to the light.[34] For, following *Timaeus* 34 B, Plotinus holds that body is in soul rather than soul in body. The idea is that the body becomes alive by presence to soul as air becomes luminous by being in light. In general however he talks about the soul being in the body rather than the reverse. But despite the fact that Plotinus settles on the presence of air to light as the best illustration of the soul–body relation, the presence of the soul to the body is in effect generally treated as *sui generis*.[35] The main characteristic of this presence is that the soul is present as a whole, one and undivided, at every point of the body it animates.[36]

Another aspect of Plotinus' psychology that should be mentioned in the present context, and to which I shall return, is the doctrine that the soul cannot be affected by the body.[37] The germ of this doctrine can be found in Aristotle, though Plotinus seems to have been the first to maintain it explicitly.[38] Aristotle holds that movement is not an attribute of the soul, the soul being one of those things that may incite movement without being moved.[39] By putting together his description of the soul as a kind of unmoved mover in *De Anima* and his general account of action and affection in *De Generatione et Corruptione* 323a 25 – 324b 24 it follows that the soul is unaffected by acting. But it does not follow that the soul is altogether unaffectable. At any rate, with the exception of the intellect, the soul is perishable according to Aristotle,[40] though as a form it is never in the process of ceasing to exist. Aristotle holds that only things that are separable from matter are unaffectable,[41] and since the soul is inseparable it seems to follow that it can be affected.[42] But Plotinus extends the intellect's immunity to affection to the rest of the soul. This is a natural move for Plotinus, given that he believes as he does that Aristotle is right in holding that separable things are unaffectable, and that all forms of soul are separable from matter. It would be as impossible to affect the soul by affecting the body as it would be to affect a light-ray by affecting the surface it illuminates.

III

The relation between the eye and the object of vision

It is a remarkable fact about vision that the things we see are at a distance from the organs through which we see them. Everyone who gives some thought to the phenomenon of vision is bound to speculate about this fact. It is evident that somehow the eye must be brought into contact with the object, but it is not at all apparent how this contact is established. The ancient Greek thinkers did not fail to apply their imagination and acumen to this matter.[1] We have records of speculation on the subject from the times of Alcmaeon of Croton onwards. Our records suggest that this came to be a subject that every thinker felt obliged to have views about.

The Greek thinkers did not arrive at a solution in terms of light-reflection and light-waves such as that which we now accept, although some of them, Plotinus among others, approached it in some respects. One should not infer from their failure to find the correct solution that all their theories were nothing but idle speculation, that insofar as they hit upon some true insights this was more due to chance and luck than a careful study of the facts. In a way, the opposite is true. If we compare the Pre-Socratics' doctrines about visual transmission with those debated in the first centuries AD, we can notice considerable progress and increasing sophistication. And although systematic experiments are lacking, many good observations were made. The thinkers of the second and third centuries whose discussions on this subject have come down to us – Alexander of Aphrodisias, Galen and Plotinus – all show considerable skill in testing the various theories against known observations.[2] All of them, Alexander being the most thorough and systematic, make much use of the method of showing that the theory under examination has implicit consequences that are contrary to known facts. Each of them, however, fails to subject the theory he adopts himself to the merciless scrutiny that he subjects rival theories to.

Plotinus' main discussion of visual transmission is to be found in "On the Difficulties about Soul III, or On Sight" (IV.5). This treatise is an appendix to the long preceding treatises "On the Difficulties about Soul I and II" (IV.3 and IV.4). In IV.4.23 – a chapter that we shall often return to – Plotinus raises the question whether the object of perception must touch the organ of sense. He proposes to discuss the question elsewhere. This promise is being fulfilled in IV.5. In the first four chapters, Plotinus discusses and criticizes several theories of visual transmission. The question he is primarily concerned with is whether a medium between the eye and object plays a causal role in vision and in particular whether this happens by means of a progressive affection of a medium. His own position is that a medium plays no such causal role. Instead he suggests that visual transmission is effected by means of *sympatheia*. However, he does not explain in sufficient detail how this *sympatheia* is supposed to work. Chapter 5 summarily deals with the analogous question with respect to hearing, and Plotinus arrives again at the same conclusion. Chapters 6 and 7 discuss the nature of light which, as we shall see, has a bearing on Plotinus' view on visual transmission. And in the eighth and last chapter of IV.5 he returns to a certain difficulty concerning *sympatheia* that had come up in chapter 3.

Plotinus' treatment of visual transmission is less thorough and less clear than the more extensive accounts of Alexander and Galen. His manner of expression is, as usual, elliptical and compressed, and the exposition rather disorganized. Bréhier persuasively suggests in his introduction to IV.5 that Plotinus had in his hand some doxographic material on visual transmission such as Aetius' "On vision, how we see".[3] This would nicely account for the list of doctrines at the beginning of chapter 2 as well as for the free flow of Plotinus' exposition. For as Bréhier remarks, "Mais cette discussion se poursuit sans ordre rigoureux, exactement comme si, le lecteur (ou l'auditeur) ayant en mains un tableau des doctrines . . . Plotin pouvait sans risque de confusion s'arrêter sur quelques points en passant fort vite sur d'autres, sans revenir sur les sujets qu'il a traités".[4]

In the remainder of this chapter, I discuss in three sections the material presented in IV.5.1-4. In the first section, I consider

Plotinus' objections against the theories that attempt to explain visual transmission in terms of a progressive affection of a medium given in IV.5.1-3. In the second section, I consider IV.5.4 where Plotinus discusses the various ways in which the intermediate light may be claimed to be a medium in vision. And in the third section, I consider Plotinus' own solution of the riddle of visual transmission in terms of *sympatheia*.

1 Plotinus' criticisms of progressive affection

Let us first consider the notion of a medium, *to metaxy*, which is central to all of Plotinus' discussion in IV.5.1-4. It is important to realize that by referring to something as *to metaxy* it is not implied that it mediates anything. Thus, its customary translation "a medium" is in many contexts misleading.[5] In the context of IV.5, to say that something is *metaxy* or *to metaxy* simply means that this is something located in between the eye and the object of vision. This helps explain Plotinus' position: he has no wish to deny that there is a medium (in the sense just explained), nor even that a medium may be affected by the objects of vision. He only wants to deny that a medium plays a role in visual transmission. Thus, Plotinus is in no way inconsistent, as he may seem to be, when he denies that a medium is necessary for vision, while admitting that as a matter of fact there is a medium and that it may well be affected by the objects of vision.

The theories that most conspicuously claim a medium as a mediator are those that hold that the medium is affected by the object and that this affection is propagated through the medium till it hits the eye. Hence, Plotinus spends most of his efforts in arguing against such theories. The theory he criticizes in chapters 1-3 claims air as the mediator in vision. According to that theory, as Plotinus presents it, the air is affected quite literally: first the part adjacent to the object is affected, this then affects the portion of the air further away, and so forth. He evidently has in mind physical affection of the same sort as heating or cooling. Let me first list Plotinus' objections against this view, then consider against whose theory they are directed, and finally consider their plausibility. The objections are as follows: (1) If visual transmission is effected by means of progressive affection of the air in between the object and the eye, we would not see the objects themselves but rather the air close to the eye as when we perceive the heat from a fire by perceiving the hot air surrounding our skin; but this would make seeing just like touch, which it obviously is not (2, 50-5). (2) Such theories fail to explain how we can see distant lights in the dark without the intermediate air being illuminated (3, 1-15). (3) If the object sets its impression on the air, the impression should be equal to the object in size; but the part of the impression that hits the eye cannot be larger than the eye; hence, such theories cannot explain how we can see large objects as a whole (3, 27-32).[6]

It has been suggested by Andreas Graeser that Plontius is aiming at the Stoic theory of visual transmission. His main justification of this is the occurrence in IV.5.1, 18 of the word *nyttein* (to prick), which he claims to be a Stoic term.[7] But, however Stoic this term may be, its occurrence here fits badly its occurrences in Stoic contexts.[8] For there visual pneuma streaming out of the eyes is said to prick the air, whereas in the context in Plotinus it is the air which pricks the sense. The Stoic theory of visual transmission is very definitely a projection theory, i.e., a theory that supposes that something is projected from the eye to the object. But in Plotinus' description of the theory he is criticizing, there is no indication of any projection from the eye as one would expect if he had the Stoic theory in mind. Moreover, if he was aiming at the Stoics, objection (3) would entirely miss the point of the theory, because it would fail to take into account the projection from the eye. On the Stoic view, the outgoing pneuma creates tension in the air which takes the shape of a cone. At the base of the cone, pneuma coming from the object causes an alteration in the tension of the cone which is propagated back to the eye by some wave-like motion.[9] Whatever difficulties there may be in the Stoic doctrine, it is clear that the very point of the cone is to account for the difficulties that arise from the fact that the objects of vision are normally much larger than the eye, which is precisely what Plotinus claims the theory he is criticizing gives no explanation of. For these reasons, it is most unlikely that the Stoics are Plotinus' target here.

But whose theory then is Plotinus aiming at? Democritus holds, according to Theophrastus, that the air is impressed by the object and that this impression is progressively transmitted to the eye.[10] So it seems that Plotinus' criticisms would hit the mark, if it is Democritus' theory that he has in mind. But let us consider other possibilities. In the opening lines of IV.5 Plotinus says he is going to "consider whether we could see without a medium such as the

air or another of the so-called diaphanous bodies".[11] The reference
to diaphanous bodies leads one to expect that Aristotle's or
Peripatetic views will be found among those he proceeds to
consider. If there is any Peripatetic view among them, it is either
the one we are now considering or the theory mentioned at the
end of chapter 4, which claims light as an affected medium.
Plotinus summarily rejects the latter theory by saying that all the
same objections hold against it as against the present theory.
Plotinus' polemic is focused on the idea that the eye is not directly
acted on by the object but by an intermediary, and Aristotle is the
philosopher who most expressly emphasizes indirect action: "Vision must occur by some affection of the sense, but it is impossible
that it is affected by the seen colour itself. Thus we are left with
affection by the medium [*to metaxy*] so that there must be
something in between" (*De An.* 419a 17-21). This is precisely the
notion to which Plotinus is objecting. However, the theory
Plotinus is criticizing does not seem to be exactly that of Aristotle
and Alexander. For both Aristotle and Alexander hold that the
movement of colours through the diaphanous medium is instantaneous alteration, whereas the theory Plotinus attacks is a theory
according to which an impression on the air is progressively
transmitted.[12] So if Plotinus is specifically thinking of the views of
Aristotle or Alexander, he misrepresents them. But as we noted
Plotinus is probably working from some doxographic material,
where various views on visual transmission are listed. Aetius has
such a list of views on this subject, which may in fact well have
been Plotinus' source. The summary given there of the views of
Strato and his pupil Aristarchus seems to fit the theory Plotinus is
attacking.[13] Given this I think it most likely that the theory in
question here is that of Strato and Aristarchus, while Plotinus'
general attack on the necessity of a medium is without doubt
prompted by Aristotle's strong affirmation of its necessity.

How good are Plotinus' objections? Well, at least (2) and (3) are
fairly reasonable objections against a possible theory of the sort we
have described. Plotinus remarks that if visual transmission takes
place by means of affection of the air, the air must be physically
affected (*sômatikôs paschein*), meaning, I take it, that the air literally
takes on the physical quality of the thing that affects it (IV.5.3,
27-8).[14] It is in line with Strato's materialistic leanings that he held
that the air is affected in this way, and this is also what Aetius'
summary suggests.[15] But given this, one would expect that the
whole air became illuminated by the lights that we can see in the
dark because the air is supposed to take on the quality seen. The

case ought indeed to be similar to the heating or cooling of the air by a fire or a glacier. When Plotinus claims that we see the lights from light-houses in spite of complete darkness of the air in between us and the lights, he is of course wrong if he means to say that these lights do not illuminate the surrounding air at all: they do illuminate the surrounding air, though perhaps only so slightly that we cannot detect it at a distance. But he is however essentially right in that our seeing these lights does not at all depend on the illumination of the air: we know now that light passes through and can be seen in a vacuum. (3) is also a sound objection against the sort of theory that Plotinus is considering: if the object affects the air in the way we are supposing, the affection ought to be equal to this object in size, and hence it is going to be difficult, without some *ad hoc* moves, to explain how we can see large objects as a whole, since only a fraction of the affection can hit the eyes.

As to objection (1), however, the case is more complicated. Plotinus is claiming that it follows from the theory that we should only perceive the air adjacent to the eye, that vision ought to be analogous to the perception of the hot air surrounding a fire. Why should this necessarily be so? If Plotinus is relying on the assumption that we can only perceive what directly affects our sense-organs, there surely seem to be many counter-examples. There is nothing wrong about, say, a blind person's saying that he perceived – "sensed" would perhaps be a more natural expression here – the light of a candle, even if the blind person was only affected by the hot air surrounding the light. But presumably this sort of objection does not really affect Plotinus' point. For we can distinguish between direct and indirect perception. We perceive something indirectly if we perceive it by means of perceiving something else. Clearly, the blind person's perception of the candlelight falls into the latter category: the blind person perceives the light *via* perceiving the surrounding air that affects his body. Now, I take it that Plotinus' point is that vision is a direct apprehension of a distant object. And surely this is what vision seems to be: when I see the colour of the wall directly in front of me, I do not seem to perceive it by means of perceiving something else. However, the question could still be pushed: is it necessary that we perceive directly only what directly affects our sense-organs? I shall not pursue the issue further, but the fact that Plotinus evidently takes it to be so is revealing of an important aspect of his views on perception.

2 *The role of intermediate light (IV.5.4)*

In chapter 4 Plotinus sets out to consider the question of the relation between the eye's internal light and the external light extending from the eye to the object seen. I shall first outline the various views on this matter Plotinus presents and his objections to them, then say a little about the origin of the views in question, and finally discuss Plotinus' objections.

Plotinus distinguishes between three kinds of theories that assign a role to the intermediate light: (1) the soul uses the intermediate light as a vehicle to travel out to the object. Thus, the external light becomes ensouled (*empsychon*) as is the internal light of the eye. On this view, vision would not be through a medium – because there is nothing in between the sense and the object – but would be a kind of touch (10-17). Plotinus raises the question why one would suppose that the soul has to travel out to the object in this way. He discerns two possible reasons why this might be held: (a) because there is an intervening body (presumably the air) and (b) simply because there is an interval (17-19). If the former is the reason, the proponents of this theory would have to admit that we would see if the obstacle were removed (19-20). If the latter, Plotinus thinks it must be supposed that the object is entirely inactive, but this he takes to be evidently false because "the sense of touch not only announces that something is near and that it touches it, but it undergoes and reports the differences in the object touched" (22-4).[16] In general, if there is an object capable of acting and an organ capable of being affected, why ask for something in between on which the action is exercised? This could only be an obstacle (28-31). Further, we sometimes see the light of the sun before it has illuminated the air close to us, so that we see even if that which according to the theory is supposed to be united with the sense has not yet reached it; the same difficulty arises about explaining the sight of the stars and fires in the dark (31-8). According to the second version (2) of the theories that assign a role to the intermediate light, the soul remains in the eye and uses the intermediate light as one uses a staff to touch things. This theory is rejected on the grounds that if vision were like such indirect touch, we would have to have perceived the thing so apprehended before without any intermediary, which, in Plotinus' opinion, is clearly not the case in vision. Finally (3), there is the view that the light around the object is affected by it and this affection then progressively transmitted to the eye. Plotinus summarily refers back to his previous arguments against progressive affection of the air and says that the same holds against the present view (46-9).

Plotinus does not present the views he discusses in chapter 4 as anyone's actual views. The general idea that visual transmission takes place somehow by means of the union of external light with the eyes' internal light is of course to be found in Plato's *Timaeus* 45 E – D. But none of the positions Plotinus describes can be said to be an accurate description of the *Timaeus* view rather than some later modification of it. After all, Calcidius was able to claim, not without plausibility, and wrong though he was about the origin of the Epicurean theory, that the three "current" theories on the subject, the Epicurean, the Stoic and the visual ray theory, are all based on the *Timaeus* doctrine.[17] The mention of internal light at the beginning of the chapter suggests that Plotinus intends only to consider views according to which the eyes are themselves of a luminous nature. This explains why the Aristotelian theory, which assigns a role to the intermediate light but does not posit an internal light, is not among those Plotinus presents. But it seems that he wants to cover all possibilities of relationship between the external light and the internal light.

However, there is no doubt that at least some of the views he discusses were actually held by philosophers and known by Plotinus as such. This is fairly clear in the case of version (2) according to which the soul stays in the organ but uses the light as a staff to touch the object. It was a common Stoic practice to describe vision by analogy with contact through a staff.[18] The reference to tension of the light (41) also indicates that Plotinus is here aiming at Stoic views.[19]

In his book, *Kosmos und Sympathie*, Karl Reinhardt claims to find in version (1) not only Plotinus' own theory, but also Galen's and Posidonius', which he suggests as the origin of both Galen's and Plotinus' views.[20] And Gordon H. Clark also argues that (1) represents Plotinus' own view based on the *Timaeus*.[21] There is, however, an important difference between his interpretation and Reinhardt's: Clark thinks (1) does not represent the *sympatheia* theory that Plotinus subscribes to in the preceding chapters, but is rather a supplement to it, whereas Reinhardt takes (1) to represent the *sympatheia* theory. These claims must be carefully examined because what is at stake is whether Plotinus held a projection theory of vision or not. Let us first consider Clark's interpretation.

Clark's interpretation of course requires that Plotinus holds that a visual ray passes from eye to object. It is rather unfortunate for his view that Plotinus nowhere commits himself to the existence of such rays.[22] Plotinus does indeed believe in the existence of ensouled light internal to the eye and he assigns a function for it in his *sympatheia* theory, which we shall soon consider. But internal light is not the same as a visual ray. In any case, Clark's claim is that Plotinus holds (1) for reason (a), that is to say, because there is air in between the eye and the object, and air being an obstacle to vision, a visual ray must pass through the air to the object. Clark evidently takes it that all the objections to (1) that follow are directed only against those who would hold (1) for reason (b), i.e., because there is an interval between the eye and the object. This seems to me highly doubtful. But, in any case, there is another and decisive reason why Clark's view must be rejected. He correctly understands that the visual ray doctrine is not the *sympatheia* doctrine presented in the preceding chapters. But on his view the latter doctrine has to be supplemented by the former, because *sympatheia*, being action at a distance, is obstructed by the intermediate air, and hence "this insulation must be pierced by the visual ray".[23] In fact, however, the visual ray doctrine that Clark attributes to Plotinus is rather an alternative to the *sympatheia* doctrine than a supplement to it. For as Clark presents the case, visual transmission *would* be effected by means of *sympatheia*, if the obstruction, i.e. the air, were removed. But, since the presence of the obstruction is, as Clark himself points out, "a uniform and regular accident",[24] it follows that visual transmission would normally be effected by means of the visual ray only. In that case, *sympatheia* does not do any job in vision under ordinary circumstances. But it is plain from the preceding chapters that Plotinus wants to maintain that vision quite generally is effected by means of *sympatheia*. Plotinus' remark that, according to (1) when held for reason (a), one would see without the visual ray once the obstacle were removed, in no way commits him to such a theory; he is only considering its implications.

Reinhardt's claim that (1) represents Plotinus' own views will obviously not be refuted by the argument used to refute Clark's interpretation. For as we saw, the latter's view turned out to be untenable because it severs Plotinus' alleged doctrine of visual transmission from the *sympatheia* doctrine. As to Reinhardt's view, we shall see in the discussion of the *sympatheia* doctrine that whatever *sympatheia* in vision exactly is, it does not consist of a visual ray's going out to the object. On the other hand, Reinhardt may be right in thinking that (1) represents the theory of visual transmission set forth by Galen in *De Placitis Hippocratis et Platonis*. Admittedly Galen does not speak of the soul as going out into the intermediate light. But this description of Plotinus' may be explained by his more vivid language, for at any rate, Galen does say that the intermediate light functions as a sense-organ in vision just as the nerves do in the sense of touch.[25] In outline, at least, this comes close to the position described by (1).

Let us now turn to the objections Plotinus raises against the theories brought up in IV.5.4. The objection against (1), if maintained for reason (b), is that it supposes that the object of vision is entirely inactive. But this is impossible, he says, for the sense of touch – it has been stated in 11.14-15 that this theory of vision works like the tactile sense – not only informs us that something is close, but it is also affected by the differences of the object and announces them; if there were no obstacle, it would even perceive at a distance (20-5). Plotinus is evidently assuming that mere resistance is an entirely passive affair with respect to the object. But through the sense of touch, we come to be aware of various qualities, e.g. heat and cold, that cannot be explained by mere resistance, and we must suppose that the object is active in imparting these qualities on the sense. An opponent might, however, admit that the object is indeed active, while insisting that it must touch the sense in order to act on it. But Plotinus, thinking of this possibility, goes on to say that if there were not an obstacle, the object of touch could indeed act on the sense through a distance. He even goes further and suggests that actually the sense of touch is acted on by the heat from a fire before the intermediate air is, and that we thus do preceive heat from a fire without the mediation of the air. This flatly contradicts his statement in chapter 2, 53-5 (see p. 38 above).

Plotinus' point about the vision of the stars and fires at night (36-8) is the same as he brought up against the affection-of-the-air theory in chapter 3. We should note concerning this point that Plotinus is not denying the light is somehow transmitted from the object of vision to the eye. As we shall see in our discussion of the *sympatheia* theory, he must admit that there is some sense in which it is so. What he is denying is that vision depends on the illumination of the intermediate space, not that it depends on the illumination of the object, or that there is no sense in which the light from the object passes through the space from the object to the eye.

Now, let us consider Plotinus' comments on the Stoic theory according to which the soul uses the light as a staff. On this hypothesis the apprehension would be violent, the light being resistant and stretched out and the sensible object, the colour as colour, itself pressing back. For such is indirect touch. And the object must previously have been close to the organ and then without any intermediary. For in this way indirect touch brings about knowledge subsequently – by memory, as it were, or still more, by inference. But in this case [i.e., in vision], this is not so.[26]

What is the point of this objection?[27] Plotinus' expression is ambiguous as to whether he means to say that knowledge gained by means of a staff is *similar* to knowledge acquired by means of memory and an inference, or that knowledge gained by means of a staff is acquired with the aid of memory and inference, which fact would illustrate how such knowledge is "subsequent". Now, it is of course true that memory requires a previous direct apprehension of what is remembered. The same, however, does not hold for what is inferred. This counts against the first alternative. As to the second alternative, it is true that in practice what blind people learn by means of indirect touch often depends on previous direct close exposure. Or think of people with normal sight under unusual circumstances: the electricity goes off and you are walking around in your house in search of a candle; you use a staff to help you from stumbling into walls and pieces of furniture. As you make your way, you are likely to recognize a lot of objects: "Here is the door, there is the kitchen table" and so forth. For us, for whom this way of perception is rare and exceptional, the recognition of objects will depend on previous "direct" perception. We will even infer various properties of the objects from the combination of our memory of previous experience and the information gained by means of the staff. Moreover, Plotinus might claim, in order to judge the distance of objects, we would either have to know – at least ultimately by means of direct perception – how long the staff is, or else be able to go close to the object and touch it directly. However, this argument is not very convincing. For, firstly, there is no reason why a person could not *in principle* learn to recognize things, not merely qualities such as hardness and softness, by the use of a staff only. Such recognition need not depend on previous direct exposure. Secondly, the objection is presumably not quite fair, inasmuch as it takes the staff analogy more literally than it was intended. Whatever precisely was the point of the analogy, the Stoics cannot have meant to suggest that vision *is* knowledge reached by means of a staff. Nevertheless, even if this objection is not all that good, it is revealing of Plotinus' views on vision. We can infer from it that he took visual knowledge to involve some kind of immediate acquaintance with its object that is excluded from knowledge involving memory or reasoning.

3 The *sympatheia* theory of visual transmission

Plotinus' notion of *sympatheia* is a borrowing from the Stoics.[28] Let us therefore begin by briefly considering the Stoics' use of this notion.

If we consider first an ordinary living being, we can see that there are causal connections between happenings in non-adjacent parts of it. As an example of this, we can take the case of an illness that spreads from one part of the body to other, non-adjacent parts, without affecting the parts in between. The Stoic theory of the soul provided an explanation of such phenomena. According to the Stoics, the soul is pneuma, some kind of combination of airy and fire-like stuff, that permeates the body as a whole (*SVF* 2, 773-89). This pneuma is in a state of tension, as a result of which there is continuous wave-like motion back and forth in the organism (*SVF* 2, 448; 450-7). By means of this tensional motion the organism is affected as a whole by an impact that hits only a part. It is worth remarking that the tensional motion is neither movement of physical particles from one place to another nor is it the kind of action–affection relation by which the quality of a thing is imparted upon the things adjacent to it.[29] Rather, it seems to be the transmission of a state through the pneuma as a vehicle; hence when a change occurs at a given place, this is reflected in the tensional motion and may cause a similar or different affection elsewhere in the organism according to the disposition of those other parts. *Sympatheia* is affection depending on the tension of the pneuma.

The Stoics did not limit the principle of *sympatheia* to familiar organisms.[30] They conceived of the whole cosmos as an organism unified by all-pervasive pneuma in a state of tension, and they put the principle of *sympatheia* to various uses on the cosmic scale. They used it, for example, to explain the connection between the moon and the tides, the change of seasons, and the efficacy of so called occult phenomena, such as divination.[31] *Sympatheia* as a cosmic principle thus exemplifies the tendency of ancient Greek thinkers to explain events in the physical world and the cosmos as a whole on the model of an organism.

Our sources do not attest the occurrence of the words *sympatheia* or the corresponding adjective *sympathês* in connection with Stoic doctrines of vision. However, as we have seen, the Stoics' notion of *sympatheia* is linked with the tensional motion which, in turn, plays a significant role in their theory of visual transmission. Whether or not there were particular Stoics who conceived of visual transmission as *sympatheia* we do not know. But the fact that Plotinus speaks of "those who say that vision takes place by means of sympatheia" suggests that hypothesis (IV.5.2, 15–16).[32]

As one would expect, Plotinus' notion of *sympatheia* cannot be identical with that of the Stoics. Like the Stoics, he explains *sympatheia*, whether in the individual or in the cosmos, in terms of unity of soul. So he and they agree that *sympatheia* is possible only within a single organism. But Plotinus' views on the unity of the soul are importantly different from those of the Stoics, and these differences are reflected in his conception of *sympatheia*: since for Plotinus the soul is incorporeal, he has no room for the Stoic physicalistic account of *sympatheia* in terms of the unity of the all-pervasive pneuma and its tensional motion.

Sympatheia is mentioned in the *Enneads* in many different contexts. Plotinus invokes it to account for phenomena as diverse as the efficacy of magic and prayer, the influence of the celestial bodies, and visual and auditory transmission.[33] There can be *sympatheia* between different parts of the same organism and between souls.[34] It seems that any sort of causation and coordination of states and events that is not to be explained as affection through direct physical contact is the working of *sympatheia*. In general *sympatheia* can occur without affection of the parts that stand between those that are in the relation of *sympatheia*, whereas what is in between may reduce its effect, and there are indications that similar things are particularly susceptible to sympathetic influence on one another (IV.4.32). But beyond what has been said, Plotinus says nothing about the mechanism by which *sympatheia* is supposed to work. At any rate I have not been able to gain many insights relevant to the issue of visual transmission from what Plotinus says about *sympatheia* outside IV.5. So let us turn to that account.

Sympatheia in vision depends on similarity. Similar things are capable of sympathetic relation to one another: "If it is in the nature of a given thing to be sympathetically affected (*paschein sympathôs*) by another thing because it has some resemblance to it, the medium is not affected, or at least not in the same way"

(IV.5.1, 35-8). The reason for this connection between *sympatheia* and similarity is not entirely clear. It has already been mentioned that *sympatheia* is also supposed to depend on the organic unity of the cosmos. In IV.5.8 Plotinus considers a hypothetical objection, which aims at showing that the similarity requirement for sympathetic relation is inconsistent with the requirement of organic unity. The objection goes like this: Suppose you are placed at the edge of the cosmos you are a part of and look out towards another cosmos. Since this is another cosmos, it is by definition a different organism, and hence there cannot be organic unity between you and it. But let us assume that the part of this other cosmos in front of you is coloured just like the things in this cosmos. It would be absurd to suppose that you did not see the colour placed directly in front of your eyes.

Plotinus' response to the hypothetical objection is most obscure. The best I can make of it is that he wants to say that the hypothesis itself is inconsistent in that it supposes that things can be similar without belonging to the same organism. For the organ is supposed to be similar to what is perceived. But there is no way for two things to be similar unless they are made to be so by the same soul. Hence, the supposition that we see a different cosmos must be rejected.[35] Though Plotinus does not say so explicitly here, the further justification for the claim that similar things must be made so by the same soul is no doubt the fact that any two similar things participate in the same intelligible Form by virtue of which they come to have the same quality. This being so, it is natural to conjecture that *sympatheia* holds between similar things somehow because they are linked through a common origin and are therefore in a sense "closer" to one another than dissimilar things. It would, however, be idle to speculate further about how exactly this is supposed to work. In any case, the statement that *sympatheia* is between similar things fits together with Plotinus' general teaching about the nature of the eye. Following Plato in *Timaeus* 45 B, he holds that there is ensouled light in the eyes.[36] This is the light we can see if we push on the eye with a finger (V.5.7, 28-9). And the proper object of vision is colour (II.8.1,13), which Plotinus regards as light-like in nature.[37]

The *sympatheia* theory of vision is clearly supposed to explain what the theories that speak of the affection of a medium intend – but, in Plotinus' opinion, fail – to explain. In IV.5.4, 28-30, he asks rhetorically what need there is to suppose that a medium is affected if there is an object capable of acting and an organ capable of being affected by it. As we have noted, in Plotinus' view all sense-perception involves affection of a sense-organ, though there is more to sense-perception than affection. *Sympatheia* is intended to account for how this affection comes about in vision and hearing. Plotinus evidently takes the *-patheia* part of *sympatheia* to indicate *pathos*, affection (cf. iv.5.1, 27-40). Presumably he conceives of the word *sympatheia* as follows: Suppose a given thing is affected in a certain way, has a certain *pathos*; then another (distant) thing may be affected along with it or come to share in its *pathos*; then there is *sympatheia* between these two things.

Given what has been said so far about Plotinus' notion of *sympatheia* and his rejection of a mediator between the eye and the object, one might think that visual transmission is for him not a matter of something's passing from the object to the eye at all. This is however not so. On reflection, it is also hard to see how Plotinus could plausibly avoid the supposition that something passes between object and eye. For this seems to be the obvious explanation of the fact that we see only the things that are in front of our eyes. Any theory that altogether does away with anything going from object to eye or from eye to object must have a hard time explaining this fact. It is evident from Plotinus' discussion of *sympatheia* in iv.5.2-3 that something does indeed pass from the object to the eye. In chapter 2, he claims that the air is not even affected by bodies such as stones that pass through it and asks rhetorically: "Now, if it [the air] is divided by such bodies without being affected, what prevents admitting that the forms pass to the eye without even dividing the air?"[38] And in the next chapter, by way of explaining the difference between his own views and those who proclaim the affection of the air and face the difficulty of explaining how we can see large objects, he says: "But as it is the whole object is seen, and everybody in the air sees it whether he looks at it in front or sideways, from afar or close by or from behind, so long as the sight is not blocked. Thus, each part of the air must contain the seen object, for instance a face, as a whole."[39] Clearly, what is here called "the seen object" is the same as what in the earlier passage is called 'form'. In this latter passage, Plotinus goes on to explain that the form is not present in the air 'as a bodily affection but in accordance with high psychic forces of a unitary sympathetic organism'.[40] Plotinus presumably conceives of these forms as passing in all directions from the object in straight lines. He remarks that *sympatheia* is in general hindered or weakened by intermediate stuff between agent and patient (iv.5.2, 23-6). In the case of vision, this must mean that the transmission of the forms is obstructed by intermediate bodies – entirely obstructed by non-transparent solids, and less entirely by air, which explains why things seen at a great distance appear less clear than those close by (cf. II.8.1).

The preceding point about forms passing from object to eye is extremely important because it provides a clear link, which would otherwise be missing, between the *sympatheia* theory of visual transmission and other important Plotinian doctrines. For, with the exception of one rather obscure remark (IV.4.23, 21-2),[41] *sympatheia* is nowhere explicitly mentioned in connection with visual transmission except in IV.5. But there are many references to the idea that forms (*eidê*, sometimes *morphai* or *typoi*) pass from the object perceived to the eye.[42] Since the passage just quoted clearly links the transmission of the form with the *sympatheia* theory, we can reasonably use these other passages to shed light on the corresponding material in IV.5 and *vice versa*. Given this, let us first consider whether Plotinus' theory of visual transmission is receptive or projective, and secondly, the nature of such transmission.

In the previous section I indicated that Plotinus did not believe in the existence of visual rays going out from the eyes to the objects of vision, and said that such a suggestion is incompatible with the *sympatheia* theory of visual transmission. Let us consider this a bit more closely. Plotinus makes clear in IV.5 that *sympatheia* involves an agent–patient relationship and that in the case of vision the object of vision is the agent and the eye the patient, or, in the terminology we have been using, the affected party. Furthermore, it is the repeated message of IV.5 that this agency can occur at a distance without any intermediaries. All that is required is that a suitable agent faces the eye, that no solid or non-transparent body is in between, and that the agent and the patient belong to the same organism. The supposition that a visual ray must be projected out to the object is clearly at odds with this picture. The passages in IV.5 mentioning the forms that we just considered confirm this. In neither passage is there any hint of a visual ray. Moreover, IV.5.3, 35-8 positively refutes the supposition that visual rays play a role in Plotinus' theory of visual transmission (cf. also VI.4.12, 11-12). For the suggestion is that the forms are as a whole *everywhere* in the air, not only where the eye happens to be located. The omnipresence of the form of the object is clearly supposed to explain how the forms can be received by the eye, because if a form is everywhere it will of course also be where the eyes are. If Plotinus had intended to explain visual transmission in terms of visual rays, he could indeed have incorporated into his explanation the doctrine that forms pass from object to eye. The idea would be that somehow a visual ray would go out to the thing and return with the form. But the notion that the form is present everywhere clearly rules this out as Plotinus' view. Other passages that mention forms coming to the eye from the objects of vision confirm this. Nowhere is there any mention of a visual ray. The process of visual transmission goes in just one direction: from the object to the organ.

In Chapter I we noted how the word *eidos*, "form" is ambiguous in Middle- and Neoplatonism between "Platonic Form" and Aristotelian "form in matter" (sometimes explicitly described as *enulon* to disambiguate the term). We also saw that this is not a case of sheer ambiguity, because the two kinds of form are in a sense the same thing, i.e., they are the same thing but on different levels in the hierarchy of being, the latter being an image or a representation of the former. We shall indeed see in chapter IV that the whole picture of forms in Plotinus' system is even more complex. But for now let us pose the question: what are the forms that pass from the objects of vision through the intermediate space and to the eye?

In the treatise "On How Distant Objects Appear Small" (II.8.[35]) Plotinus talks about forms from the objects reaching the eyes,[43] and also about colours reaching the eyes (chap. 1, *passim*). It is plain from the context that he uses the words "colour" and "form" interchangeably in this passage. Thus, we may infer that the forms that reach the eye are somehow the colours of the objects. This is also in accordance with what Plotinus says elsewhere: we know that colours are an example of the so-called forms in matter or qualities (IV.2.1, 34-9), and he also says that in sense perception the percipient receives the quality of the object perceived and that sense-perception is of qualified bodies rather than of essences (IV.4.2.3, 1-4; II.6.2, 17). In subsequent chapters we shall investigate the philosophical significance of these statements. For now, let us briefly consider Plotinus' notion of colour as such, and its connection with that of light.

Plotinus takes colours to be objective features of bodies. Their differences are not to be accounted for in terms of the nature of our sense-organs or in general in terms of our mode of apprehending them.[44] In things that have a natural colour, the colour is due to the internal and in itself imperceptible formative principle (*logos*) or nature of the thing that has the given colour.[45] The implication is that those colours which are not the natural colours of the thing that has them are also produced by *logos*, but *logos* of some other thing which imparts its natural colour to the thing in question (cf. ii.6.1, 27-8). However, Plotinus also says that colours have something to do with light: in at least two passages he says that colours are a kind of light (ii.4.5, 10-11; v.3.8, 20), and he elsewhere maintains that they are produced by the light of a luminous body (iv.5.6-7). Clearly, the issue needs some clarification: can colours be both the products of the internal *logos* of things and the products of the external light that falls upon them from a luminous body?

We should note, firstly, that the two different sorts of statements about colours issue from entirely different considerations. When Plotinus links colours with the internal nature of things, he is thinking about the ontological status of qualities or about regularities in nature; when he links colours with light he is thinking about the nature of light and visibility. There is no need to suppose that there is a serious contradiction in his two accounts.[46] Indeed, it seems that the two accounts must supplement each other. For even if it is admitted that colour is in a sense produced by the external light falling on the thing, or that a colour is a kind of light, no explanation has been given of why different things have different colours and why the same natural kinds of things have the same or at least a limited range of colours. This is what the account in terms of the internal nature of things is supposed to explain. On the other hand, the latter sort of account leaves unexplained the essential connection between colours and light (which appears for instance in the fact that any colour has, or perhaps even is, a certain brightness), and that is what the other account is supposed to take care of. Thus, the two accounts deal with different aspects of colour: the one in terms of internal nature deals with colours as qualities or accidents of bodies, the one in terms of light with colours as the primary visible feature of things. It is obviously important for Plotinus to be able to say that colours are somehow of the nature of light because, as we remember, the eye has internal light and *sympatheia* is between similar things. Thus, if the eye is to be affected by colours by means of *sympatheia*, colours must somehow be in the class of light-like things.

The question arises precisely how Plotinus wants to account for the transmission of the colours (forms) from the coloured bodies to the eye. We have seen, of course, that he wants to explain this transmission in terms of *sympatheia*, suggesting that it is effected by means of some purely psychic force. But we should not be misled by the term "psychic force": the label "psychic" need not imply anything stronger than a denial of a mechanistic account in terms of bodily pushings and pullings. It is therefore an open question whether the transmission from object to eye in vision is meant to be anything other than ordinary transmission of light as from a source of light to the objects it illuminates. For, as we have seen, colours are in Plotinus' view a species of light and after all, he also thinks that the transmission of light cannot be accounted for in terms of bodies and their qualities (iv.5.6-7). It would be economical to give the same account of the transmission of light. For primary sources of light are among the things we can see, and if the transmission of their forms to the eyes of the percipient is different from their propagation of light to other bodies, we must suppose that there are two different kinds of transmission of light. But however tempting it may be to attribute to Plotinus such a unified account, it seems to me not to work for the following reason: the point Plotinus makes against the first version of the visual ray doctrine, that we sometimes see the sunlight before it has illuminated the intermediate air, presupposes that the transmission of visual forms is different from the ordinary propagation of light (iv.5.4, 31-8). [47] Besides, Plotinus does not refer to *sympatheia* or organic unity in his account of light and its propagation in iv.5.6-7 as one would expect him to do if he meant to suggest that the ordinary transmission of light and the transmission of visual forms depend on the same principle.

Even if Plotinus did not conceive of visual transmission as ordinary transmission of light, and whatever is precisely the nature of the force by which the visual forms are transmitted, his insistence that the colour should be present as a whole at every point of the surrounding space contains a remarkable element of truth. The context shows that Plotinus did not mean that the whole form of the object is at every point of the air in the sense that both the colour of the front and the back are present at every point. That would be a strange doctrine indeed. He must be saying that the part of the colour of the object that is visible from a given place is present as a whole in the air at that place. As we conceive of the matter nowadays, there is a sense in which this turns out to be so: because light is reflected in all directions from every point of the seen object, light-waves from each point of the visible part of the object intersect every point from which the given part of the object is visible. Plotinus does not tell us how he would explain the presence of the forms at every point so that we do not know for sure whether his explanation is in any way analogous to the modern account. It seems reasonable to conjecture, however, that the explanation is that every part of the visible object emanates its colour in all directions. But it is impossible that he had any understanding of light-waves, and hence any resemblance between his and the modern account must be a mere structural resemblance.

We shall now consider how what we have found out about the *sympatheia* theory of visual transmission succeeds in explaining what other theories Plotinus discusses do not, in his view, explain adequately. Plotinus' criticisms ought to show us some of his requirements for an adequate theory, since one would suppose that his own theory is immune to the objections that he sees in the others or, at least, not obviously susceptible to them. This means that Plotinus' own theory ought to satisfy the following requirements:

(1) It should be able to explain how we see the things themselves rather than something in the air; it should not make vision turn out to be a kind of touch. (2) It should be able to account for our ability to see large objects. (3) The objects of vision should be active and act directly on the eye without acting on a medium. If they do act on a medium, that action is quite incidental and does not play any causal role in vision. (4) The theory should be able to explain vision as a direct apprehension of its object; it should be immune to the kind of objection Plotinus raises against the staff analogy of the Stoics. (5) It should be able to account for how we can see lights in the dark without the illumination of the intermediate air.

Plotinus' *sympatheia* theory satisfies (2) and (3) in a fairly straightforward way. We saw that the statement that the form is present as a whole at every point of the air was introduced in connection with the difficulty about the relative largeness of the objects of vision compared with the eyes. And surely it seems to take care of that difficulty as such. By definition the *sympatheia* theory satisfies (3). As to (5), since Plotinus conceives of the transmission of the visual forms as a special kind of transmission unrelated to the ordinary propagation of light, we can say that (5) is taken care of. In the case of (4), we concluded that Plotinus' point against the staff analogy was not altogether clear, and hence it is not clear either what would constitute the satisfaction of this requirement. But it seemed that the objection presupposes that in Plotinus' view vision somehow directly grasps its object. This is an issue I will have something to say about later, in Chapter VI, section 2. Now let us consider (1). One might argue that Plotinus' theory of visual transmission fails to satisfy (1) on the following grounds: Plotinus believes that the eye receives a form that is present in the air adjacent to the eye. Hence, Plotinus is no better off than those he attacks: he criticizes others for holding theories that entail that we should see the air adjacent to the eye because this is what directly affects us. But on his own theory the eye also receives something present in the air adjacent to the eye and seems to be directly affected by it. Why does it not follow, on Plotinus' own terms, that we should see the form in the air adjacent to the eye rather than the distant object?

As a first response to this question, let us note that Plotinus clearly thinks that his own theory of visual transmission does explain how we can directly see distant objects. This is particularly clear from a passage in VI.4.12 where he uses analogies from vision and hearing to explain the notion of participation and the unity of all souls. He says: "Many eyes looking at the same object are all filled with the spectacle even though they are separated from it."[48] And three lines below, he says in explanation of how many eyes can be filled with the same distant spectacle, using words close to those of IV.5.3, 32-7:[49] "As regards vision, even if the air should be affected by having the form, it has it as undivided. For an eye receives the form there where the eye is placed."[50] It is evident from this passage, as it is indeed also from IV.5.1-3, that Plotinus thinks that his account of visual transmission explains how vision can be a direct apprehension of a distant object. Now, the fact that Plotinus thinks so does not by itself prove that his explanation is convincing. Still, this fact is an indication that there is a radical difference between Plotinus' theory and those he attacks. Let us consider what this difference could be.

The following considerations may help us see the crucial difference between Plotinus' theory and the one in terms of affection of a medium. The directness of the object's action on the visual organ is secured by the fact that the object emits its colour (form) which reaches the eye without any intermediaries. It is also evident from the last lines of IV.5.3 quoted on p.50 above that Plotinus conceives of the presence of the form in the air not as the familiar local presence of a body in space or as the presence of a quality in matter. Thus, the red of the apple is not present in the intermediate space in the same way as it is present in the apple itself. The latter sort of presence presupposes an extended magnitude, a body, which is affected by the presence of the quality. This presumably explains why Plotinus thinks that within his own theory the question of seeing something in the air as opposed to in the object does not arise.

As we shall see in the next chapter Plotinus' application of the notion of form in his theory of perception is a modification of Aristotelian views. I believe that the same holds for certain aspects of his views on visual transmission. Plotinus' theory of visual transmission as a whole involves a free use of Aristotelian, Stoic and Platonic elements, which results in a doctrine that is characteristically Plotinian. In the remainder of this chapter I set forth what seems to me to be the most plausible suggestion about Plotinus' use of these sources. At the same time I attempt to shed more light on Plotinus' theory.

We can summarize the Aristotelian element of Plotinus' theory of visual transmission by saying that Plotinus' account of the forms that pass from object to percipient is generally Aristotelian but with the omission of the notion of a medium. And this is an important difference of course. Aristotle holds that light is reflected in all directions (*De An.* 419b 29). Although he does not connect this doctrine explicitly with visual transmission, it is reasonable to suppose that Aristotle would explain the fact that we can see objects much larger than the eye by saying that colours somehow produce their motions in the diaphanous in all directions. When we come to Alexander's version of Aristotle's views on this subject, we find that the affection of the medium is of a special sort, different from the ordinary presence of forms in matter. For instance, the same medium can be the medium of contrary colours at the same time.[51] Now it seems to me we should look at Plotinus' position as follows: a special account of the presence of colours in the space between object and percipient, different from the normal doctrine of physical affection, is already to be found in the Aristotelian tradition. Plotinus carries it one step further by doing away with an affected medium altogether, and replacing the notion of a medium with that of a nonphysical omnipresence of form which depends on the organic unity of the cosmos. As we shall see as we proceed Plotinus incorporates these developments from Aristotle into a doctrine of visual transmission that is based on the doctrine of *Timaeus* 45 B–D.

Without evidence to the contrary one would naturally assume that Plotinus' doctrine of visual transmission is based on Plato and in particular the Plato of the *Timaeus*. Thus, it is perhaps surprising to find that Plotinus' theory is not of the projective type. However, let us note that in *Timaeus* 45 B–D Plato does not explicitly say that the light emitted through the eyes reaches all the way out to the object that is seen, though this may well be what he meant to imply. But Plotinus may not have understood him thus, and may not have thought that he was betraying his master in denying that the eye's proper light goes all the way out to the object. However this may be, Plotinus surely deviates from the *Timaeus* doctrine in denying that the intermediate light of day has a function in vision. For, according to the *Timaeus*, the emitted internal light fuses with the external light with the result that a continuous pencil of light extending from eye to object is formed. As Plotinus' refusal to assign a function to the intermediate light is quite clear, we are here presented with a case where Plotinus deviates from the Plato of the *Timaeus*, and moreover he must be fully aware that he is doing so.

Despite this I think that Plotinus' doctrine can be described as a modification of that of Plato, and I think that this is how he saw it himself. Let us consider how this may be. We have already pointed out that Plotinus holds that the eye contains some sort of light, that hence the eye is similar to the objects of vision, and that it is by virtue of this similarity that the eye can be affected by them. Even if Plotinus' views on *sympatheia* and its relation to organic unity are inspired by Stoicism, this particular detail is without doubt based on the *Timaeus*: it is also Plato's view that vision depends on the similarity between the eye's internal fire and the light of day. So here we have a significant connection between Plotinus' doctrine and that of Plato. But there are other connections as well. Plato regarded the pencil of light that is formed by the merging of the internal light with the light of day as an extension of the percipient's body. But there are at least two different ways of conceiving of such an extension. On the one hand, we can conceive of the extension as an instrument that is attached to the body without belonging to the organism. The Stoic analogy of a staff suggests this conception. On the other hand, one can conceive of the extension as a genuine part of the organism.[52] Galen is one who interprets the *Timaeus* doctrine in this way. Since there is a strong affinity between Plotinus' and Galen's views on visual transmission, let us consider the views of the latter. They are revealing of Plotinus' understanding of the *Timaeus* passage.

We have already noted some views that are common to Plotinus and Galen: the criticism of the Stoic staff analogy and the failure of progressive affection theories to explain how we can see large objects. Indeed they have more in common. In Galen's opinion "it is impossible to perceive the sizes of the visible objects unless we see that which we look at at the place where it is"[53]. And he attacks the Stoics, the Epicureans, and Aristotle and the Peripatetics for failing to give due notice to this fact in their respective theories of visual transmission. It is needless to point out that in this respect Galen's criticisms reveal exactly the same intuitions as we have seen in Plotinus about these matters. It is in fact plausible to conjecture that there is a historical connection between Plotinus' and Galen's views on this subject. Since they are dissatisfied with other people's theories for the same reasons, it seems not unlikely that their positive views have something in common.

Now, Galen's positive views, which can be described as an up-to-date version of the *Timaeus* account, are stated in terms of a visual ray theory.[54] As regards the visual ray, Galen's view is of course unacceptable to Plotinus. However, Galen evidently thinks of his visual ray theory as of a special sort, and different from that of the Stoics. What makes it special is his view of the relation between the outgoing visual ray, the sunlight and the air. The main idea is this: the intermediate air becomes sensitive by virtue of the presence of the outgoing pneuma in the sunlight. To explain this, Galen refers to the relation between the brain and the nerves that lead from the sense-organs to the brain: when the external light, the visual ray and the air intermingle, the intermediate air has the same relation to the eye as the nerve leading from the eye has to the brain (VII.5, 32-3). He also says that vision works like touch, which operates through the nerves from the surface of the body to the brain, the idea being that the sensitive air close to the colour seen is analogous to the nerve-ends in our skin (VII.7, 18). In short, Galen is basically saying that the intermediate air functions as an extension of the nerves. Thus, one might say that in Galen's view the intermediate air becomes in vision an organic part of our bodies.

Now, I am going to suggest that Plotinus' *sympatheia* theory is conceptually kindred to Galen's theory, especially to the aspect of Galen's theory just related. We do know that in Plotinus' view we are parts of the cosmic organism and that *sympatheia* on the cosmic scale depends on this organic unity. More specifically, we are in organic unity with the rest of the cosmos in virtue of the unity of our lower soul, which animates our bodies, with the soul, which animates the cosmos. Still more specifically, this means, in the case of vision, that our eyes are parts of the same organism as the objects of vision. Now, we can take the import of this organic unity to be that essentially the same conditions hold on Plotinus' view as on Galen's and Plato's as read by Galen: we should regard the distant objects as if they were a part of our own bodies. Apart from the role that Galen attributes to the intermediate air, which

59

Plotinus rejects, the difference between their views comes down essentially to this: Galen does not take the organic unity of the percipient's eyes with the objects of vision and the intermediate space to be a permanent condition but rather something that is brought about by the visual pneuma, whereas Plotinus sees it as a permanent condition. This is why Plotinus has no need for visual rays: the state of affairs that the visual rays bring about on Galen's (and Plato's) theory is already there according to Plotinus. Thus, it turns out that we can say, after all, that in substance Reinhardt was right in pointing out the affinity between Galen's and Plotinus' views, although he went too far in identifying their theories (see p. 43 above).

The idea is, then, that the unity of the cosmic organism upon which vision is supposed to depend is to be taken quite literally: vision is to be seen as analogous to internal sensation within an ordinary organism. This idea is to some extent strengthened by a consideration of Plotinus' criticisms of the Stoic theory of internal perception, i.e. perception of pain, itches and the like. The Stoics speak of transmission (*diadosis*) from the affected part of the body to the principal part of the soul (IV.2.2; IV.7.7).[55] Plotinus interprets this transmission as progressive affection with the result that his criticisms of the Stoic theory of transmission of pain are analogous to his criticisms of progressive affection of a medium in vision in IV.5.1-3: he claims that the ruling part of the soul could at most perceive the affection adjacent to itself. Now, we learn from IV.3.23 that Plotinus assigns some function to the nerves in the sense of touch and it seems reasonable to suppose this to include perception of pain. And in the same passage, he says that the brain is the part of the body from which the activity of the perceptive soul has its origin. So one might speculate that he wants to assume some sort of psychic transmission from the aching part of the body through nerves to the brain, analogous to his account of visual transmission. Further, he implies that internal perception depends on something which he calls *homopatheia*, and there are other passages that suggest that *homopatheia* can be synonymous with *sympatheia*.[56] So, one might suppose that in Plotinus' view vision is exactly analogous to internal perception as it seems to be in Galen's theory.

However, it must be admitted that this idea does not work out in all details as an explanation of Plotinus' theory. First, in those passages where Plotinus criticizes the Stoic theory of internal perception, he does not, in his positive account, propose a theory of psychic transmission through the nerves to the brain. What he says instead is that the soul is present as a whole in every part of the body. In later chapters I shall have something to say about the import of this view. For now, let it suffice to say that it does not seem to vindicate the idea of an exact parallelism between internal perception and vision. There are certain common features though: the presence of the soul as a whole at every point of the body inevitably brings to mind the doctrine that the form of the object is present as a whole at every point of the intermediate space. But it seems to me that this common feature does not indicate any further resemblances; the property of being as a whole in many is a general characteristic of soul and the psychic, and as such, it indicates that both phenomena are psychic; but, so far as I have been able to detect, it does not indicate anything special beyond that. This may explain why Plotinus does not explicitly bring up the analogy between vision and internal perception through the nerves.

On reflection, we should not really expect an exact parallelism between vision and internal perception: for there is nothing in the perception of pain that corresponds exactly to the role of the eye in vision. Even if Plotinus believed that perception of pain takes place somehow through the mediacy of the brain and the nerves, neither the brain nor the nerves seem to be affected in the way the eye is. The eye's sensing the colours of a distant object is a relation between two distinct bodily parts of the cosmic organism whereas the brain does not sense pain in the finger in the way the eye senses the colours: as introspection and the history of physiology teach us, it is not at all evident that the brain is in any way involved in the perception of pain. Plotinus suggests that the perception of pain is a relation between a bodily part and the soul as a whole (IV.4.19, 11-19); visual sensation, on the other hand, is a relation between an eye and some other part of the cosmic organism. If we were to have something exactly analogous within an ordinary organism, it would be something like the finger's sensation of what goes on in the toe. So my suggestion is, then, that we should understand the *sympatheia* between parts of the cosmic organism that makes vision possible as if it were such a sensation by part of a part. This analogy, though correct, is however not particularly illuminating, since there is no such thing as a sensation of what goes on in the toe by the finger – or if there is, it entirely escapes our consciousness.

In conclusion, then, I am suggesting that Plotinus sees the idea of organic unity between the eye and the object of vision at work in the theory of the *Timaeus*. But, whereas Plato and Galen arrive at this unity by presupposing temporary extensions of our own bodies, Plotinus takes it to be an instance of the more permanent unity of our own living bodies with the cosmic organism. This means that Plotinus' solution of the problem of explaining how we can directly see a distant colour is supposed to work roughly as follows: The eye senses directly the colour of the object out there where the object is, as it would do if we think of it as extending all the way out to the object. This means, in turn, that the forms in the intermediate space are to be thought of as that which links the eye with the coloured object and not as the sensed item itself. The omnipresent forms in the intermediate space thus replace the stream of light in the *Timaeus* doctrine. So far nothing has been explicitly said about the nature of the affection that arises in the eye when we see. But the interpretation of Plotinus' views on visual transmission that has just been proposed suggests that the affection in vision is some sort of sensation. It would be bad policy, however, to prejudge the issue of the nature of the affection. So in the next chapter I shall attempt to approach the subject without relying on the indications from the account of visual transmission.

IV

Sensory affection

In the previous chapter we saw, in connection with Plotinus' *sympatheia* theory, that vision involves the affection of the eye by the object of vision. It is Plotinus' view that such affection of the sense-organs occurs in sense-perception quite generally. In the present chapter I consider the nature of this affection. In the first section I briefly discuss Plotinus' word for affection, *pathos*, and its appearance in earlier Greek theories of perception. In the second section I consider the passages in the *Enneads* that are most informative concerning the nature and role of affection in Plotinus' theory. This enterprise will reveal significant points about Plotinus' views on sensory affection, points which, however, are subject to radically different interpretations. In the third section I consider in detail one such interpretation, or rather one family of interpretations that share an important common element. I will show that this type of interpretation, in which sensory affections are regarded as physical changes in the sense-organs, runs into serious difficulties when confronted with other aspects of Plotinus' views on perception. In the fourth and last section, I propose a different line of interpretation which seems to me to conform better to the textual evidence, when everything is considered.

Throughout this chapter, the focus is on sensory affection in vision. The reason for this emphasis is that Plotinus himself, like most philosophers of perception, focuses on vision: it is evident that when he talks about sense-perception generally, without specifying a particular sense, vision is as a rule the case that he is thinking of, though he evidently thinks of his theory as applying to the other senses as well. Given this emphasis, it is a reasonable policy to test one's interpretations against the case of vision: if an interpretation of some statement about perception in general does not work with respect to vision, we can be confident that the interpretation does not represent Plotinus' view.

1 Affection and its role in Greek theories of perception

The Greek word we have rendered as "affection" is *pathos*.[1] We also find its near synonymous cognate, *pathêma*, in the same sort of contexts as *pathos*, and I translate it in the same way.[2] The English expression, "x is affected", on the other hand, is normally a rendering of the Greek expression, "x *paschei* ".[3] These words, especially *paschein* and *pathos* were very common and were put to a great variety of uses. We can say that the basic meaning they were used to convey – which the English words "affected" and "affection" capture tolerably well – is that of undergoing a change, or being passively in a certain state. There are, nevertheless, certain special features of the Greek words that are worthy of comment.

First, a point of grammar. In Greek, we find constructions of the following form: "x *paschei hypo y*", which may be rendered "x is affected by y". This English construction is identical to the Greek one in grammatical form. But there is also another kind of construction with *paschein*, where the verb takes a direct object, to which there is no equivalent English construction using the expression "affected". The general form of this construction is "x *paschei* w", where "w" does not refer to the cause of the affection but to the affection itself. There are, however, ways of translating this with a similar English construction, for instance, "x undergoes w". This could be filled out by "x undergoes pain" or "x undergoes heating", for instance. Since it is sometimes desirable in order to preserve the nuances of Plotinus' language and thought, I also use constructions with "to undergo" to render the Greek *paschein* .

There is one very common but distinct use of *paschein* and its derivatives in which *paschein* is a correlate of *poiein*, "to do", "to act", "to effect". When *paschein* is used in this way, it is presupposed that there is a corresponding agent which brings about the affection in question: *paschein* then denotes the result of, or what is brought about by, an action. As a rule, the passive forms of causative verbs denote an affection in this sense, "to be

64

cut" and "to be killed", for instance. The pair *poiein* and *paschein* came to be technical, philosophical terms: they are among the key terms of Aristotle's philosophy, appearing for example on his list of categories where they are discussed as a pair. In Stoicism there is a fundamental dichotomy between the active (*to poioun*) and the passive (*to paschon*) principles in the universe.[4] From Plato on-wards Greek thinkers expressed much of what now comes under the heading of "causation" in terms of *poiein* and *paschein*, though this fact is often neglected in surveys of ancient views on causation, which tend to focus on the notion of *aitia*.[5]

It is this last use of *paschein* and its derivatives that we find in discussions of the senses, not only in Plotinus but throughout most of ancient philosophy: when it is said that a sense-organ or a sense is affected, it is often explicitly stated, and always implied, that the affection is the result of the action, direct or indirect, of the external object of perception on the organ or on the sense.[6] This universal agreement of the Greek thinkers reflects the reasonable assumption that perceptions are caused by the impact of objects on the percipient, rather than, say, by the percipient's impact on the objects. This does tell us something, but not a great deal: just about everyone, philosopher or not, Bishop Berkeley being the notable exception, seems to suppose that perceptions are caused by external objects. Moreover, in the various ancient theories of perception, the words *paschein* and *pathos* denote quite different things, all, however, regarded as the results of the action of an external object on the percipient. Let us consider a few examples of this.

In Plato's *Philebus* 33 D, we find Socrates saying: "You must take it that among the affections (*pathêmata*) in our bodies some are exhausted in the body before penetrating to the soul, thus leaving the latter unaffected, whereas others penetrate both body and soul and set up a sort of disturbance which is both peculiar to each and common to both." This passage provides us with a conspicuous example of the wide scope of "affection" in the context of ancient theories of perception: an affection may be a merely physical and unconscious stimulus, or it may be the feeling aroused by such a stimulus. Aristotle too speaks of affection in connection with perception.[7] Respected Aristotelian scholars have come to vastly different conclusions about its nature: there are those who think that the affection, which Aristotle describes as the sense's recep-tion of the form of the object, is nothing but a literal assimilation of the sense-organ to the quality of the object perceived; and there are those who think the affection is present in the percipient in some nonphysical way.[8] This divergence of opinion at least shows that there is plenty of room for argument and speculation as to what exactly is being referred to. If we turn to Hellenistic philosophy – the Stoics for instance – we find a rather different view of sensory affections: the Stoics speak of representations (*phantasiai*) as affections of the soul, where "representation" clearly means something like "mental representation" or "mental image", though the Stoics hold of course that the mental images are in fact physical phenomena.[9] The Sceptics, though disagreeing with the Stoics on the import of representations in the theory of knowledge, generally entertained a similar notion of sensory affections as representations.

Now this quick look at the views of previous philosophers concerning sensory affections shows clearly that in Plotinus the subject must be approached with extreme caution. Plotinus explicitly makes the point that sensory affections are the effects of the action of external objects on the percipient (IV.4.23, 19-32). As we have seen this is just what one might expect. But we do not know much more: we do not know the nature of this affection, for example whether we would nowadays consider it mental or physical, or precisely what its role in perception is supposed to be. The fact that Plotinus holds that sensory affection is an instance of *sympatheia* does not by itself settle the issue. Sometimes the effects of *sympatheia* are physical changes (IV.4.34, 30-3); at other times physical changes are ruled out, for instance in the case of *sympatheia* between souls: souls are without matter and hence not subject to physical affection. However, as we shall see later in this chapter, there are indications within IV.5 that sensory affections are not mere physical changes.

Somebody might ask whether there is any good reason for pursuing the question whether sensory affection in Plotinus is something merely physical or something we would nowadays call "mental". After all, it might be said, the mental–physical distinction as we know it is a fairly recent phenomenon, and to force upon Plotinus a distinction of which he was not even aware only invites a distorted presentation of his views. The answer to this is twofold. First, the claim that the mental–physical distinction was unknown to the ancients is questionable (see Chapter VIII, section 2). It is in fact one of our tasks to evaluate this claim with respect to Plotinus. Secondly, it is in any case worth the effort to consider whether Plotinus' sensory affections fall into either one of these categories – whether he himself possessed corresponding labels or not – for the answer will add to our understanding of Plotinus' theory of perception.

2 Plotinus on sensory affection

There are several passages where Plotinus says or implies that perception involves an affection.[10] Let us first look at two such passages where the subject is touched upon and then consider IV.4.23 which is the main *locus* for this notion.

In IV.3.26, 1-9, Plotinus says that perception in act is a common function of body and soul. It is like weaving, he says, the soul representing the craftsman and the body his tool: "The body is affected and obeys, the soul receives the impression of the body, or the impression [that comes] through the body or the judgement which it makes from the affection of the body."[11] Plotinus does not elaborate on the alternatives he gives here for the part played by the soul. It is not clear, for example, whether they are supposed to be different descriptions of the same activity, or descriptions of distinct activities, or a combination of both. Other passages do not provide any means of deciding. The passage unambiguously informs us, however, that the body is the subject of the affection, and it is implied that its affection consists of some kind of impression.

In III.6.[26]1, 1-4, which is next before IV.3 on Porphyry's chronological list,[12] we find the following passage dealing with the same subject: "We say that sense-perceptions are not affections but activities concerned with affections and judgements; affections belong to something else, for instance to the qualified body, but the judgement belongs to the soul."[13] As in the first passage we considered, the affections are here attributed to the body and the two passages also agree in holding that perceptions somehow involve affections. But here it is stated quite unambiguously that even if perception involves affection, the perceptions themselves are not to be identified with affections. This permits us to draw one important conclusion: whatever sensory affections are for Plotinus, nothing which we recognize as a complete perception can be one.

Next, we shall turn to IV.4.23. In the preceding chapter, IV.4.22, the question comes up whether bodily sense-organs are necessary for perception, and in answering it Plotinus presents his richest and most continuous account of sense-perception in general. Nevertheless, one cannot help wishing that he had spelled out his views more clearly and in greater detail. But IV.4.23 represents Plotinus' sole attempt to set out his theory of perception as a whole, and for this reason it is extremely important for our purposes. In it, most of the views on perception that we find expressed elsewhere in the *Enneads* – usually in contexts where the main focus is not on perception in general but rather upon some particular aspect of it or upon something entirely different – are stated in a logical order. Its unique status even seems to justify giving a special weight to its evidence. In what follows I will present the substantial points made in this crucial chapter, and then comment on what it tells us about sensory affection.

At the outset of IV.4.23, Plotinus says that "perception of sensibles is for the soul or the organism an apprehension in which it grasps the quality inherent in bodies and impresses their forms into itself" (1-4).[14] He then goes on to say: "Now this grasp will be accomplished either by the soul alone or with the help of something else. But how could the soul do this when it is alone and by itself? For when it is by itself, it grasps only what it has in itself and is pure thought. If it is to grasp other things as well, it must first acquire these either by being assimilated to them or by being together with something so assimilated" (4-8).[15] In the lines which follow Plotinus argues that the soul could not be assimilated to the sensibles while remaining in itself: he takes this to be as inconceivable as the assimilation of a point to a line or fitting the intelligible line to the sensible line (8-10). The final argument offered in order to show that the soul could not be assimilated to sensible things while remaining by itself is rather obscure. Nevertheless, as we shall see later on, it is unambiguously revealing of an important aspect of Plotinus' view, so I will quote it in full:

But when the soul is alone, even if it is in a position to direct its regard at the sensible, it will end with grasping the intelligible; the sensible escapes it as it does not have anything by which to reach it. For also when the soul sees a visible object at a distance, though it may well be the case that a form comes to it, nevertheless, what begins in the soul and is, as it were, without parts, ends in the underlying colour and figure, which the soul sees with the size they have out there.   (13-19)[16]

From these considerations, Plotinus concludes that

these – the soul and the external thing – cannot be alone [i.e. as participants in perception]; for the soul would not be affected. But what is affected must be a third thing, and this is what receives the form. It must be sympathetic and similarly affected, and of one matter [with the external object].[17] And the one must be affected, while the other must know; and the affection must be such as to preserve something of the agent, though not being identical with it. But since it stands in between the agent and the soul, it must have an affection that is intermediate between the sensible and the intelligible. It is a proportional middle in contact with both by its extremities, both receptive and informative, capable of being assimilated to both: to the external by being affected, to the internal by its affection becoming a form. (19-32)[18]

From this, Plotinus concludes that the only reasonable position is that "perceptions occur by means of bodily organs" (32-3). The last point of interest is the analogy that Plotinus makes in iv.4.23 between a craftsman's tool and sense-organs:[19]

Also in case of the tools of craft can we see that the tools stand in between the judger and the judged and announce to the judger the characteristic of the substrate: for the straight-edge is a link between the straightness in the soul and that in the piece of wood; being placed in between them, it enables the craftsman to judge the piece to be worked. (37-43)[20]

The way Plotinus sets up his problem in lines 1-18 is quite remarkable. As he presents the case, there is an essential difference between the soul and sensibles such that it becomes a problem to explain how the soul can come to know sensibles at all, though it is taken as evident that it does. This is the first time this problem appears in the history of western philosophy, or at least the first time we find it so clearly stated. Indeed, previous philosophers also thought that the soul comes to know sensibles through intermediaries. But in their case, the reason for this is not, as it clearly is here, that the soul is an entity of an ontologically different nature, but rather some more commonsensical observations about the mediacy of the sense-organs.[21] That this becomes a problem for Plotinus is easily explicable in terms of the dualism that he inherited from Plato: he is merely taking seriously and sharpening Platonic ideas about the individual human soul's independence of the sensible and what we have now been presented with is simply a logical consequence of doing so. But, as for instance the passage quoted from the *Philebus* above shows, Plato has no qualms about saying that affections penetrate through the body to the soul. On the other hand, even if Plotinus occasionally uses similar language, his notion of the soul has been refined in such a way that he cannot take action on the soul by the sensible for granted.

To be sure, Plotinus does not think that this is an insurmountable problem: he rather quickly disposes of it by introducing the sense-organs and their affection as something intermediate be-

tween the sensible and the intelligible natures. The bodily nature
of sense-organs serves as a link with the sensible, whereas the
soul-power that resides in them provides a link with the intelligible. It is worth emphasizing that the intermediateness of the
sensory affection cannot be mere spatial intermediateness: Plotinus
is not just saying that the sense-organs and their affections are
spatially in between the soul and the object. That would indeed be
a rather poor doctrine, because if it is a problem to begin with to
explain how soul, which by its nature only knows intelligibles,
can know sensibles, that problem would not be removed merely
by bringing the sensibles spatially closer to the soul. Rather,
Plotinus is saying that the affection of the sense-organ somehow
has an ontologically intermediate position between the sensible
and intelligible. It will be our task in the fourth section of this
chapter to explain exactly what this amounts to.

When Plotinus introduces sensory affection in line 20, he does
not first explicitly argue that something has to be affected in order
for there to be a perception. He simply says that the soul would
not be affected by sensibles, and hence something else is needed as
the recipient of the affection. Now, since virtually everybody in
antiquity who had something to say about perception assumed
that perception either is, or involves, affection, this claim was
seen, perhaps, to need no substantiation. In any case, it is evident
in the context that Plotinus supposes that the theses (1) that the
soul would not be affected by sensibles, and (2) that the third thing
which is needed in addition to the soul and the external object is a
recipient of affection, are established in the preceding passage,
wherein it is claimed that the soul, remaining by itself, could not
be assimilated to sensibles. The implication of this is that Plotinus
takes the assimilation, which is said in line 7 to be necessary for the
perception of sensibles, to be the affection. In other words, an
argument to the effect that an assimilation is necessary and that the
soul by itself cannot be the subject of it, is taken to constitute an
argument for the necessity of affection. This is not at all surprising, for he explicitly says later in the chapter (31), that the organ is
assimilated to the external thing by being affected by it. We also
saw in our discussion of the *sympatheia* theory in the preceding
chapter that in vision the eye and the object of vision are supposed
to become similarly affected. This is naturally understood as a
different way of saying that the organ is assimilated to the quality
of the object. Furthermore, a consideration of grammar also
makes this transition from assimilation to affection quite understandable: Plotinus' word for being assimilated is *homoiôthênai*,

which is a passive form of the causal verb *homoioun*, "to assimilate", "to make alike".

So sensory affection, according to Plotinus, is an assimilation. Let us consider the notion of assimilation more closely. Firstly, we may note that the statement that sensory affection is an assimilation is easily seen to be compatible with the view expressed in IV.3.26, 1 ff. that the affection is an impression (*typôsis*) on the body. For, to say that the organ of sense is impressed by the object suggests that in some sense, literal or nonliteral, the organ takes on something from the object as a result of the object's acting on it. Secondly, we have pointed out that the idea of assimilation is at work in IV.5, where Plotinus implies that in some sense the effect of *sympatheia* is the organ's undergoing the same affection as the object. And in IV.5.4, 23-4, he says about the sense of touch – implying that the same holds for vision – that it undergoes the differences of its object. This implies that in some sense qualitative differences in the object are reflected in the sense of touch, i.e., that the organs of touch somehow take on the different qualities of the object. Something like this is what one would naturally understand by "the organ becomes assimilated to the object". Thirdly, we see in IV.4.23, 20-1 that Plotinus explains the affection of the organ by saying that the organ is that which receives the form. This Aristotelian idea of reception of forms is recurrent in Plotinus' account of perception. We have already come across it in connection with the *sympatheia* theory and we shall return to it repeatedly. Here, I will simply give a preliminary account of what I take to be crucial for an understanding of this idea as it is used by Plotinus, and explain its relation to sensory assimilation.

Sometimes the organ is said to be the recipient of the form, sometimes the soul is said to be the recipient.[22] In itself this need not be an inconsistency: why could not the organ be the first recipient and then in turn transmit the form onwards to the soul? In a sense this is what happens, according to Plotinus; yet this statement omits an important part of the story. We noted earlier that "form" may mean either "quality" or "Form". In the context of perception, "form" sometimes means "quality", sometimes something closer to "Form", and perception in fact involves the process, or is the process, of transforming the form from the former state to the latter (cf. IV.4.23, 31-2). I say "something closer to 'Form' ", rather than simply "Form", because there are two stages of the intelligible form, one which is involved in pure intellection at the level of Intellect and another which is involved in discursive thought.[23] The former is what really has the right to

71

be called "Form" in the strict sense. In any case, it is correct to say that in perception the form is transformed into an intelligible entity. Now in IV.4.23 we find "form" used in both of these senses. In lines 20-1 it is said that the organ is that which receives the form (*morphê*) and this reception is identified with the organ's affection.[24] Other passages show that he also uses *eidos* to refer to that which the organs receive from the outside. But in lines 30-2, we find Plotinus saying that the organ's affection becomes a form (*eidos*) in the soul. It is clear that here the form is contrasted with the affection, and that "form" here designates a specifically intelligible entity. Presumably, this distinction between the intelligible form and the affection is also at work in the opening lines of IV.4.23, where Plotinus talks on the one hand about the grasp of qualities inherent in bodies and on the other hand about the soul's marking itself with the forms of bodies.

Now, how is all this related to the view that sensory affection is an assimilation? Well, assuming that sensory affection is an assimilation of some sort, the question is: how can we understand the expression "the organ receives the form of the object", where "form" means "quality", as describing an assimilation? Abstractly, this is fairly easy. We know from the preceding chapter that the forms received by the eyes are colours, and colours are primary examples of forms in matter. Since Plotinus employs the notion of special sensibles and since he makes clear that what the organ receives in vision is specifically the colours of things, we can confidently affirm that what the other sense-organs receive is their special sensibles.[25] This leaves us with the following general picture: sensory affection is an assimilation of the sense-organ to the object perceived, more specifically, to the quality of the object perceived; this means that in some sense the organs receive and assume the quality of the object, each organ the quality which is its proper sensible. This taking on of the quality is, I take it, what Plotinus is alluding to in IV.4.23, 24 where he says that the affection must preserve something of the agent. The upshot of the foregoing considerations is that sometimes, viz., when applied to the organ, reception of the form is the same as what Plotinus also calls an affection or assimilation; sometimes reception of the form describes the subsequent process as a result of which the form becomes an intelligible entity in the soul. In subsequent chapters I will have more to say about the latter. A correct understanding of Plotinus' views demands that the different uses of "form" in the context of perception be kept very much in mind.

So far our account presents what must be Plotinus' line of

thought, stated in general terms, but only in general terms. It still contains a lot of "somehows" and "in-some-senses", and there remains the task of filling out the details so that we can get rid of at least some of these qualifiers. As we shall soon see, it actually makes all the difference in the world, so far as Plotinus' theory of perception is concerned, how these details are filled out.

Plotinus evidently regards the assimilation of the organ to the quality of the object as a crucial feature of his theory. The fact that assimilation rather than mere affection is the notion he sets out from in IV.4.23 shows that it is important to him that the affection is an assimilation: evidently not just any affection caused by the object would do; it must be such as to render the organ qualified in the same way as the agent. One might suppose that the preceding point could be used to rule out certain kinds of theories of perception, according to which perceiving is a matter of there being a certain causal chain leading from the object perceived to the percipient's sense-organs and finally to the acquisition of a belief in the percipient.[26] It would seem that, inasmuch as theories of this sort do away with the idea of any kind of similarity between percipient and object in favour of a purely causal account, they do away with assimilation while upholding the notion of affection. However, let us not be overhasty. We should note that even if the modern proponents of theories of this sort typically try to avoid the notion of similarity between percipient and object, they do generally assume that there is a correspondence between the changes in the organs and the different features of the object. Thus, such theories are similar in spirit to assimilation theories, positing, as they do, isomorphism between features of the affection and features of the object, even though it may be denied that there is any straightforward similarity involved. Given a generous interpretation of the term "assimilation" such theories might even pass as assimilation theories. Theories of a quite different nature, say, theories that take the affection to be a mental image or picture that arises in the percipient as a result of the object's action on him can also pass as assimilation theories. The assimilation in this case consists of the mental picture. For, if the object somehow produces a mental picture of itself in the percipient, there is surely something that may be called assimilation involved: a picture of x must be similar to x in some respects. The preceding considerations show us that assimilation allows for vastly different interpretations. So, let us consider all plausible possibilities and try to determine which of them Plotinus had in mind.

3 Assimilation as physical change

In this section I consider the hypothesis that, according to Plotinus, sensory affections are merely physical changes in the sense-organs. We may express this hypothesis in a different way by saying that the affections in question are such that they could in principle be had by non-sentient beings: there is no essential difference between sensory affections *qua* affections and, say, affections of books and stones. Thus, the assimilation in question is an assimilation of bodily qualities of the same sort, say, as heatings or coolings of bodies. One can conceive of significantly different accounts of such affections. It depends on which of these alternatives is adopted whether the assimilation must be supposed to be quite literal – by "quite literal" I mean, for instance, that something in the eye is supposed to become literally red when a red thing is seen – or whether some structural similarities between the affection and the object would be sufficient. Since, however, literal assimilation will in all cases satisfy the requirements of the theories we consider, we can assume that the affection is a literal assimilation.

I have already indicated that I do not think that Plotinus conceives of sensory affection as mere physical change. However, I shall discuss this hypothesis that the affection is mere physical change at some length and in some detail. There are two reasons for this. First, the hypothesis is plausible *prima facie* and it is accepted by respected scholars.[27] Secondly, the discussion of the present hypothesis brings forth in a very conspicuous way certain central aspects of Plotinus' views. Thus, even if this interpretation is eventually rejected, the time spent on it is not at all wasted.

One could conceive of a theory that is essentially a version of the causal theory we mentioned at the end of the last section: a perception is an acquisition of a belief about an external object caused by the affection of a sense-organ by the object which the belief is about. Insofar as this may suggest that the soul is a merely passive recipient which is caused to have a certain belief by the sensory affection, we will have to rephrase the theory. For as we saw in the passage we considered from III.6.1, Plotinus emphasizes that the soul is somehow active in perception. So, we might say instead that perception is a judgement of the soul about an external object, rather than the acquisition of a belief, since the latter may suggest that the soul is merely passive. When Plotinus says in III.6.1, 1-2 that perceptions are not affections but activities concerning affections and judgements (*kriseis*), we need not take him to be implying that the *kriseis* are about the affections: there is no need to understand "concerning affections" as an implied complement of *kriseis*.[28] We could then state the outline of Plotinus' whole theory of perception as follows: The sense-organs are affected by the external objects perceived. The affection is an assimilation in the sense that the organ literally takes on the quality of the object. The point of holding that the affection is an assimilation is to provide an isomorphism between features of the object and the input in the percipient. The reason for assuming that there is such an isomorphism is that without it we could not give a reasonable account of how perceptual judgements – by "perceptual judgements" I mean the judgements with which Plotinus identifies perceptions – accurately describe features of the external object. The affection is then somehow transmitted to the soul. We do not know how this happens, but we know that the result of the process is something like a proposition about the external object entertained by the soul and that this proposition is taken to be an intelligible form or representation.

Many details would, of course, have to be added to this outline of a theory. I think that if we spend some effort filling in these details, we might come up with a rather attractive theory. But, before we proceed to do so, it would be wise to consider as carefully as we can whether there are any serious difficulties involved in attributing such a theory to Plotinus.

We have made this sketch of a theory mainly on the basis of IV.4.23 and III.6.1. There may be other views compatible with these passages, but the view described does seem to be compatible with the bulk of what Plotinus says there. The only apparent problem is Plotinus' statement in IV.4.23 that the organ's affection is intermediate between the sensible and the intelligible. On the present theory, the affection as such is assumed to be a mere physical change and hence it must be classified as a sensible rather than something intermediate between sensible and intelligible. This is indeed a difficulty, but perhaps not one that would carry all that much weight, were there nothing else that counted against attributing this theory to Plotinus. As it turns out, however, there is more that counts against it. I shall first mention two points that speak against literal assimilation, though perhaps without being decisive, and then present what I take to be a decisive objection.

In his short treatment of transmission in hearing in IV.5.5 Plotinus comes to a conclusion that he states as follows: "Let this suffice about the difficulties concerning [hearing]; the question here has turned out to be similar to that of the case of vision inasmuch as the affection in hearing is also a kind of community of affection (*synaisthêsis*) that can exist within an organism."[29] The word *synaisthêsis* replaces here *sympatheia* in the previous chapters in such a way that we are given to understand that visual transmission too is a matter of *synaisthêsis*. This word, *synaisthêsis*, often means "consciousness" in the *Enneads*. It then denotes the state of being aware of one's own mental acts.[30] But *synaisthêsis* may also refer to the sensation an animal has of the affections of its own body.[31] It is presumably from this sense of the word that there developed the sense "awareness of mental acts".[32] The fact that Plotinus is ready to describe the *pathos* in hearing and vision as a kind of *synaisthêsis* surely speaks against mere physical alteration. For, to judge from other instances of Plotinus' use of *synaisthêsis*, it never denotes a mere physical alteration.

The second point is that Plotinus says that the subject of sensory affection is the qualified body, *to toionde sôma*.[33] The qualified body is a body that is alive, ensouled. However, the qualified body is not identical with the compound of body and soul, which is the living body together with the soul power that animates it.[34] The fact that it is specifically the qualified body that is the subject of sensory affection suggests that the affection is not just physical change, because any body, ensouled or not, is capable of that.

After IV.4.23, the passage that deals most thoroughly with perception in general, is the short treatise, "On Perception and Memory" (IV.6.[41]). At first glance at least, this passage seems to have surprisingly little in common with IV.4.23. Plotinus' main concern in IV.6 is whether memory is the preservation of sense-impressions (*typoi*) in the soul. The whole treatise is directed against a passage in Aristotle's *De Memoria* 450a 27 – 450b 1, where Aristotle raises the question of how it can be that when the affection is present in us but the object absent, we nevertheless remember the absent thing?[35] Aristotle answers that "it is clear that we must regard the affection (*pathos*) that arises through perception in the soul and in the part of the body where it resides as a kind of picture whose permanence we call memory. For the movement that occurs stamps a kind of impression (*typos*) of the percept (*aisthêma*) just like seal rings in stamping." Now, Plotinus evidently takes the impression referred to here to be literally a physical impression. Despite Alexander's claim that the sealing analogy should be taken merely as a metaphor, Plotinus' understanding is quite natural.[36] For Aristotle says nothing to preclude such a literal interpretation, whereas the reference to the part of the body where perception resides as the place of the picture, as well as Aristotle's subsequent explanation of why the very young and the old have a bad memory, suggests a physical impression.

Plotinus proposes in IV.6.1 the following strategy against this account of memory: since perception does not, in the first place, consist in having impressions in the soul, *a fortiori* memory is not a matter of retaining such impressions (cf. IV.3.26). In chapter 1, he offers an argument for the claim that perception does not consist in having impressions in one's soul. In chapter 2, he attempts to say something positive about what perception is. And in chapter 3, he finally turns to memory itself, presenting his own view and offering further arguments against the impression theory. In what follows, I focus on Plotinus' argument in chapter 1 that perception is not a matter of having impressions in one's soul. The positive account of perception in chapter 2 is so obscure at crucial points that it can scarcely be used as a key to the interpretation of other passages.

Having explained his strategy against the impression theory of memory in chapter 1, Plotinus proposes first to consider "the clearest perception", vision; the conclusions reached about it can be transferred to the other senses (11-14). He then proceeds as follows:

> It is presumably clear that whatever we perceive through sight, we see it out there and we direct our vision there where the object of vision (*to horaton*) is located in a straight line [in front of us]. As the apprehension (*antilêpsis*) evidently takes place there and the soul looks out towards the external and, seeing that no impression (*typos*), I believe, has arisen or is arising in it, as yet it receives no signet-impression like seals on wax.[37] For it would not have had to look outwards, since it would already have in itself the form (*eidos*) of the object as it saw by virtue of the impression's entrance into it. And when the soul adds the distance to the object of vision (*horama*) and announces how far away it is, could it be looking in this way at what is in it and at no distance from it as if it were at a distance? Again, as to the size of the object which it has out there, how could the soul tell how large it is or that it is large, for instance the sky, when there could not be an impression of so large an object in it? And, most importantly, if we receive impressions of the things we see, we could not look at the things themselves that we see, but at images and shadows of visual objects, so that the things themselves (*auta ta pragmata*) would be one thing, what is seen by us something different. (IV.6.1, 14-32)

To start with, let us make two general comments on this passage. First, we noted earlier that Plotinus himself speaks of *typôseis* and *typos* in the soul.[38] But here he emphatically denies that there are any such things. There is a simple explanation of this: he explains elsewhere that when he uses the word *typos* in the context of perception and memory, he does not have in mind anything like the seals (III.6.1, 7-14; IV.3.26, 26-33). Thus, we should take his rejection of *typoi* in the soul here only to extend to physical impressions conceived on the model of seals on wax. Secondly, Plotinus takes physical impressions to be affections, and his denial that perception is a matter of having an impression in the soul is thus in line with his statements in III.6.1 and elsewhere that the soul is not affected in perception. But, as we have also seen, he does elsewhere hold that perception involves an affection, not of the soul, but of the organ. What is surprising about the passage we are now considering is that there is no mention of any affection. And not only is there no mention of it, it is not obvious how an affection of the eye can fit into the story he tells us here. Let us consider this more closely with respect to the hypothesis about the nature and function of sensory affection that we are presently considering.

We are supposing that the affection in perception generally is a physical change such that the organ takes on, in a literal sense, the quality of the object perceived. Now, Plotinus evidently thinks that those who claim that vision is a matter of having one's soul stamped cannot explain how vision could be a perception of distant objects, and moreover that their doctrine implies that we only see "images and shadows". But if Plotinus himself thinks that the eyes receive physical impressions, how can he escape the same conclusion concerning his own theory? It would seem that if those who want to speak of an affection of the soul cannot explain how we see the objects of vision at a distance as large as they are out there; those who want to speak of an affection of the eye are no better off.

One might try the following way out: Plotinus' theory differs from the one he is criticizing in that he takes the organ to be what is affected, rather than the soul itself; on his theory, the soul's function is to judge, and the judgement is about the external object, though the affection plays an intermediary role in supplying the soul with the information necessary to make the judgement. There are two points to be made in response to this. Firstly, it is not clear why Plotinus' opponent, Aristotle, could not make a similar move or even why he should not be assumed to hold a similar view, which in his case would consist in saying that the soul is enabled to judge the external things by having their images impressed on the organ. Secondly, it seems that not only

Plotinus' critical remarks in IV.6.1, but also what he shows there of his positive views, are hard to reconcile with the present view of the affection and the function of the soul in perception. Plotinus asserts in IV.6.1, 16-17 that the apprehension of the object in vision takes place out there where the object is. It is not quite clear how literally we are supposed to understand this statement. But in any event this is in line with the conclusion we arrived at in the previous chapter, that Plotinus conceives of vision as a direct apprehension of the quality of a distant object, though he does not say explicitly in IV.5 that the apprehension takes place there where the object is. Now, it is evident that the affection, understood as a physical change in the eye, does not as such provide any explanation of vision's capacity to apprehend a distant object. Therefore, if this view of Plotinus' is to be incorporated into the present theory, it must somehow be done through an account of the soul's function in perception. We have been supposing that this consists in a judgement, for instance, the judgement expressed by Plotinus as "I see that Porphyry is pale". Now, if perceptions are, according to Plotinus, judgements of this sort, the fact that the judgements are about external objects entitles Plotinus to a place among realists about perception, and IV.6.1 surely shows that this is where he would want to place himself. However, IV.6.1 commits him to some stronger version of perceptual realism than the mere fact that perceptual judgements are *about* external things can give him. This may be illustrated by the following example: suppose I entertain the judgement, "The name of the physician who attended Plotinus was Eustochius", by applying my memory to something I have read. This judgement is about external objects just as much as Plotinus' seeing that Porphyry is pale. But behind Plotinus' claims that the apprehension in vision takes place out there where the object is, that what is seen is the things themselves, and the suggestions of the directness of vision in IV.5, lies something more than the realism contained in the notion that perceptual judgements are about external things. For perceptual judgements are not distinguished from other sorts of judgements merely by virtue of their being about external things; and whatever may turn out to be the correct way of describing what Plotinus has in mind, it is clear that he wants to say that perception in some sense involves "direct contact" with a distant object, a contact that is something more than the judgement's being about the external object.

But perhaps we can amend the present theory by refining our notion of the judgements that constitute perception. It seems reasonable to suppose that these judgements are intrinsically different from, say, memory judgements and other non-perceptual judgements. We might tell a story along the following lines for the case of vision: Suppose that in vision the soul, utilizing the merely physical affection that contains the relevant qualitative features of the object, somehow causes the object to appear before the eye. This may sound a little mystical. Still, this is roughly the story that traditional psychology tells. In any case, we may suppose that such a "production" of appearances accomplished by the soul can also be described as a kind of judgement, because the appearances as such, let us suppose, involve interpretation, i.e. beliefs about what sort of things there are around us.

The first difficulty to be noted about attributing a theory of this sort to Plotinus is that he nowhere says anything like what we have just said, and he nowhere gives the slightest hint that he has anything of this sort in mind.[39] But there are further and stronger reasons for rejecting the present hypothesis than this argument from silence. As we are now looking at the matter, we are explaining the direct apprehension of a distant object entirely in terms of the function of the soul as opposed to that of the organ and its affection. If we look back at iv.4.23, 15-19, we can see that such an explanation is untenable: "For when the soul sees something at a distance, though it may well be the case that a form reaches the soul, nevertheless, what begins in the soul and is, as it were, without parts, ends at the underlying substratum, and the soul sees the colour and the figure with the size which they have out there." We remarked earlier that this passage is fairly obscure. We can nevertheless note two obvious and indisputable facts about it: first, it is evident from the following lines that what is said in this passage is supposed to be an argument for the claim that something in addition to the soul and the external object is needed to account for sense-perception and that this third thing is a sense organ that is affected, i.e., assimilated to the object perceived; secondly, it is clear that Plotinus means to say that if we only posit the soul and the external object, we cannot explain the fact that the soul sees the form of the object, the colour and shape, with the size it has out there where the object is. It is implied that the organ and its affection are needed to explain this fact. Thus the explanation of this must lie in the account of what the organ does in perception. I take this to provide us with a decisive reason to reject the account under consideration.

I cannot think of any other versions of the view that affection is physical change that are plausibly attributable to Plotinus. The one which Blumenthal seems to favour can be stated as follows: visual affection is a physical assimilation in the eye; the soul sees directly only this affection in the eye and thus acquires information about the external object by "seeing" this likeness of it in the eye just as when we acquire information about a person's looks by seeing a photograph of the person.[40] This so blatantly contradicts IV.6.1 and other passages emphasizing the externality of the objects of perception and the directness of perception, that one would need very compelling reasons, which are not forthcoming, to accept it as an interpretation of Plotinus.

We noted above that the passage from IV.6.1 we have been considering is strange and uncharacteristic in that there is no suggestion that perception involves an affection at all; and it seems to portray vision in such a way that it is difficult to see how an affection could be incorporated into the view presented. The question is therefore worth raising whether IV.6.1 should perhaps be discarded as an authoritative source of Plotinus' considered views. Might not Plotinus, in the heat of his polemics against the impression theory, have been led to say things that his considered views would force him to qualify or reject? To this it might be added that, after all, there are two passages, I.1.7 and V.5.1, where Plotinus seems to say, and in fact has been taken to say, that perception is not of the sensibles themselves. Thus, it might be suggested that, on Plotinus' considered theory, we do not see the things themselves. The doctrine clearly expressed in IV.4.23, that perception is via the mediacy of affection of the sense-organs, might be cited in support of this.

For various reasons, this is not an attractive alternative. I shall discuss the two passages just mentioned in Chapter VI. Let it suffice to say here that I do not think that there are any compelling reasons for interpreting these passages as a denial of perceptual realism. Secondly, as a general principle, one does not attribute contradictory views to an author without very strong reasons for doing so. In cases such as the present one, where contradiction would be quite manifest and concerning an issue with which the author is explicitly concerned, a contradiction could only be attributed as a last resort. Thirdly, the remarks in IV.6.1 that we used to dispose of the physical affection hypothesis, express the view that vision is somehow a direct apprehension of a distant object. Though this is nowhere emphasized as much as in IV.6.1 and nowhere expressed as clearly, this view is nevertheless to be found elsewhere, for instance in IV.5.1-3 and IV.4.23, which we have considered. And since both these latter places also speak of perception as involving affection, we must conclude that Plotinus does not think that his doctrine of the mediacy of affection in perception causes any difficulties for the direct realism he also wants to maintain. On the contrary, as we have seen, IV.4.23, 15-18 suggests that Plotinus' notion of sensory affection, so far from precluding that perception can be a direct apprehension of a distant object, is actually supposed to account for how this can be so. Besides it should be noted that after all there may be an implicit reference to sensory affection in IV.6.1: in lines 37-9 Plotinus says that "that which sees must be one thing and the impression (*typos*) must lie elsewhere and not in that which sees". This implies that even here in IV.6 Plotinus allows that vision involves an impression, which in the context is presumably the kind of impression that is an affection. But this impression must not be in the soul, and we have argued that given Plotinus' objective in IV.6.1 he would be no better off making it a physical affection of the eye.

Thus, we shall continue to search for a notion of sensory affection that does justice to Plotinus' intuitions about the directness of vision as well as the other requirements that we have seen his notion of sensory affection must satisfy.

4 Affections as sensations

In the preceding sections we have seen that, according to Plotinus, an affection must satisfy the following conditions: (1) it must be an assimilation to the quality of the object perceived; (2) this assimilation is distinct from perception proper which is a judgement (*krisis*) and an act (*energeia*) concerning affections; (3) affections are attributed to the animated body and more specifically to the sense-organs: in vision to the eyes, in hearing to the ears, and so forth; (4) the affection is neither identical with the knowing subject nor with the external object that causes it, but is intermediate between the sensible and the intelligible; (5) in the case of vision, the eye's affection is supposed to explain how we can see the colour and shape of things out there where the external object is, as large as they are there. Now, let us consider whether there is anything that plausibly satisfies these requirements.

Plotinus' notion of assimilation implies that the organ of sense takes on the qualities of the perceived object and that this is what the affection consists in. We also saw that by "qualities" he means the special sensibles: what the eyes take on is colours, the ears sounds, and so on. Further, we have seen that the hypothesis that this assimilation is a mere physical change, that the eye becomes literally red when something red is seen, runs into serious difficulties. Let us first consider this question: is there some other sense than the sense of physical change according to which it is at all plausible to say that the sense-organs take on the qualities of the object perceived? Let us discuss this with respect to vision since this is Plotinus' primary example. So, in what sense could an eye be said to take on the colours of the objects seen?

As a first approach to this question, we shall consider an ordinary case of seeing. Suppose, for instance, that I see a green field and then raise my eyes so as to see a blue sky. Obviously, some sort of change in my experience occurs when I cease to see the field and come to see the sky. One way to describe this change is to say that it is a change from seeing a field to seeing the sky. The expressions "seeing a field" and "seeing the sky" normally express perceptual judgements, i.e., if I describe my experience by saying "I see the sky" this implies in normal contexts that I believe that what is in front of my eyes is the sky. Thus the change so described involves a change from one perceptual judgement to another.[41] But it might be claimed that underlying this change of perceptual judgement is another change which is not a change in judgement or belief, but rather a change in which I am a purely passive recipient. This more basic change can, it might also be claimed, be brought out by thinking away all belief-content in our visual experiences. Thus, suppose that I strip my visual experience of the judgements "this is a field" and "that is the sky", and also of the judgements "this is something green" and "this is something blue"; in short, suppose I strip it of all conceptual content. Arguably, there will still be something left of my experience when this has been accomplished, namely, the same sort of experience that an infant would, according to some, undergo when moving his eyes in the same way as I did in the same situation. This sort of experience might be called "a pure colour experience", since, presumably, it amounts to a mere sensation of colour. It might be said as well that in this purely passive part of visual experience the colours of things come to exist phenomenally in our eyes or that our eyes take on the colours of things phenomenally.

It can be objected that even if the above is in some sense true, it does not follow that our eyes really *take on* the colours seen or, if they do, only in a trivial sense; the expression "phenomenal existence of colours to the eyes" must be understood as a curious way of describing the simple fact that we see the colours of things through our eyes. I think, however, that this objection is not quite fair. To be sure, we see the colours of things, and we see them through our eyes. But what we are trying to do is to analyse what such seeing involves, and it does not seem to me to be totally empty to say that the eyes are phenomenally coloured when we see. Let me try to make this a bit clearer. By saying that the eyes become phenomenally coloured, I do not wish to imply that the colours that pertain to the eyes are something other than the colours of the things themselves. I am simply alluding to the evident fact that a being capable of vision undergoes experiences of the colours of things that are before his eyes. These experiences are specific to sentient beings: without a sentient being no such experiences would occur. Furthermore, it seems that such experiences of colour are a necessary prerequisite of vision, and that they cannot be analysed in terms of acquisition of beliefs that the colours of things are such and such: I may come to believe that something is white by tasting it, for instance, and that is surely not a case of seeing. It is thus not unreasonable to suggest that a salient feature of seeing is that it involves what we may describe as the presence of phenomenal colours to the eyes.

Another way to spell out this idea is in terms of a percipient's visual field: a visual field is that which subjectively appears before the eyes of a seeing being. Thus, a visual field is something that a percipient has. A visual field is something which contains items of various sorts: it may contain trees, houses, people and so forth, but also and even primarily it contains colours. Among the items in a visual field colours have a very special status: in some sense every other item is also a colour or a combination of colours, and moreover the colours in it seem to be passively received in a way that the rest is not. However, I shall not pursue these suggestions now. The important fact to note for the moment is that a visual field contains colours and is at the same time a state of, or something that belongs to, the percipient. Thus, this notion provides us a way of seeing how a percipient may be said to take on the colours of things.

Now, the idea is that Plotinus' notion of assimilation of the eyes to the quality of the thing seen is to be understood along the lines suggested above: the sense in which the eye becomes qualified in the same way as the object is the sense in which there is something blue, say, in our visual fields when our eyes are exposed to something blue. In what follows, I shall show how this line of interpretation fits the textual evidence better than the ones we considered in the last section, and how certain statements of

Plotinus' are naturally interpreted as suggesting something along these lines. First, however, it is necessary to warn against certain ways of misunderstanding and over-interpreting the position that I suggest we attribute to Plotinus.

It may have occurred to the reader that with the interpretation of sensory assimilation just suggested I am introducing into Plotinus' theory of perception what later philosophers have variously called "sense-impressions", "sensations", "sense-data", "sensa", "phenomenal entities", and so forth (for our purposes we may ignore the differences among these). I do not wish to deny that there is an affinity between the view I suggest we attribute to Plotinus and the modern views expressed in terms of these notions. The modern views typically suppose that in perception sensible qualities exist in the percipient in a special "non-material" way. This is an important feature that they have in common with the view I have in mind. Acknowledging this affinity I shall indeed adopt the terms "sensation" and "phenomenal colours" in my account of Plotinus' views. However, despite this affinity, there are certain features that typically, though not necessarily, go along with these modern notions that I want to disown as applying to sensory affections, as conceived by Plotinus.

First, at least some of the modern views suppose – this holds most conspicuously for the sense-data theories – that when we perceive, certain *entities*, sense-data, come into being and are the bearers of sensible qualities in an immaterial mode. Thus, if the percipient may be said to "have" the sensible qualities, it is because he has a certain item which in turn has the quality. Plotinus evidently did not reify sensory affections in this way. There is nothing in Plotinus which indicates that he entertained any such notion; indeed, as we shall see in Chapter VIII, his views would be antagonistic to it. Rather, according to the view I have been laying out, to have a sensory affection is to have sensible qualities. One might say the affection *is* the sensible qualities, rather than something which *has* them.

Secondly, the account I have given of assimilation in Plotinus is not meant to imply that colours are epistemically given entities, that being assimilated to something red by itself constitutes knowing what red is in any sense that presupposes the ability to recognize something as being of the sort red. For all I know, three-week old infants do not have this ability, but nevertheless there is no conclusive reason to deny that such infants undergo experiences of colours, that they feel differently when exposed to something blue than when exposed to something green. The ability to recognize something as red presupposes the mastery of the concept of red, and since we are supposing that the assimilation is what is left when we have stripped the visual experience of all conceptual content, it should follow that this ability is not included in the assimilation as such. As Sellars has shown, it is a characteristic of both traditional empiricism and twentieth-century sense-data theory to assume that sense-impressions, in addition to being instances of sensible qualities, are self-authenticating knowledge of sensible qualities in the strong sense that they are recognized as being qualities of the sort they are. Sellars has in my opinion convincingly argued that the claim that some one thing satisfies both these requirements leads to serious difficulties.[42]

I want to propose that we should not regard sensory affections in Plotinus as containing in themselves knowledge of their own content. This is not because I think Plotinus saw through the traps which ensnared traditional empiricism, but rather because he regarded the affections as entirely passive, to be contrasted with the active part played by the soul, and because he was not at all concerned, as the empiricists were, with grounding the bulk of our knowledge, not even knowledge of the sensible world, on sensory affections. This does not mean, however, that he rejected the idea that sensory affections put us in direct contact with the external world. As we shall see more clearly later on, he did in fact take them to perform some such role, but not in the way empiricists have imagined. At any rate, it is clear that if the sort of interpretation of sensory affection that I am attributing to Plotinus is to work, we must not take his sensory affections to be things which by their very nature constitute knowledge of what they are. For Plotinus maintains that we may be visually affected without noticing what we see. Consider the following passage:

When the perception of something is unimportant or is of no concern to oneself at all, and the sense-power is unintentionally moved by the difference in the things seen, sense alone is affected and the soul does not receive [the affection] inside, as the difference is of no concern to the soul either with respect to an application or to another sort of use. And when the soul's activity is completely directed towards other things, it does not retain the memory of such things when they have passed away, since it was not even aware of the perception of them when they were present.[43]

There are several things to notice about this passage. First, the case Plotinus is describing here is a case of mere sensory affection to which he denies the name of perception in III.6.1, 1–2. The activity (*energeia*) of the soul which here is said to be directed towards other things is the kind of activity with which perception is identified in III.6.1, 2. This claim is supported by a remark where Plotinus says that "it is not sufficient for there to be seeing or perception generally that a sense-organ is present, but the condition of the soul must be such that it inclines towards the sensibles" (IV.4.25, 1-3). Here, Plotinus is evidently thinking of cases like the one he describes in IV.4.8. This means that in the passage quoted from IV.4.8, Plotinus deviates from his normal doctrine insofar as in the last line the term "perception" applies to what he normally insists is mere affection.[44] Given that this is so and that the case Plotinus describes here is a case of sensory affection not constituting genuine perception, we can infer that sensory affections are not necessarily noticed. The case he describes is just like the familiar one of a person who is totally absorbed in his work and does not pay any attention to the traffic noises outside. On my interpretation of Plotinus' view, this would be a case of mere affection without perception, a case of mere sensing without perceiving. Am I saying, then, that by themselves sensory affections lie entirely outside the field of consciousness? And if so, how can I describe them as sensations, since, it might be claimed, sensation presupposes consciousness? The notion of the conscious is an extremely slippery one.[45] Contrary to the common belief motivated by a certain philosophical bias, it seems to me that consciousness is not something that is either clearly present or not, like an electrical light that is either fully on or off. If perceptual consciousness implies that we notice, under some description, the things that affect our senses, then sensing may be unconscious. On the other hand, it seems to me that in cases like the one Plotinus describes in IV.4.8 or in cases like that of the unnoticed traffic noise, it would not be exactly right to say that the phenomena in front of our eyes or the noises outside lie totally beyond our awareness. If it is hard to specify in what way they are objects of awareness, that perhaps just shows that the notions of awareness or consciousness are not particularly helpful in shedding light on these phenomena.[46]

One requirement that Plotinus' notion of affection must satisfy is that it has to do justice to the distinction between the affection, on the one hand, and the activities concerning affections and the judgements with which the perceptions are identified, on the other. The full treatment of the latter comes in later chapters, so that I will not now give an account of how the affections are related to these subsequent stages of the perceptual process. We

can affirm, however, that something which is merely an affection
in the sense we are presently considering will not count as a
complete perception. Especially if we take into account that
Plotinus understands perception as a kind of judgement about
states of affairs in the sensible world, it is clear that a mere
sensation is not a perception.

Let us now turn to the question whether the present hypothesis
about the nature of sensory affections fits Plotinus' statement that
the sense organs are the subjects of sensory affections. It might be
said that if, in the case of vision, the affections are colour
sensations, they cannot be affections of the eye because the colours
sensed are not located in the eyes, but rather in front of the eyes if
they admit of any location at all. In response to this, let me first
remark that I shall later argue that this very feature – that
phenomenal colours appear to be in the space in front of the eyes –
helps explain how Plotinus can maintain that the organs and their
affections are necessary to account for our seeing the qualities of
things out there where they are. But even if it is true that the
phenomenal colours are not locally present in the eyes (in the way
a physical change of the eyes would be), there is, I believe, a
non-trivial sense in which it can be said that such colours are
affections of the eyes. Look at it this way: let us agree that colour
sensations are the affections in the case of vision; obviously, in
some sense the percipient is the affected party, even if it is true that
the colours sensed appear, as it were, out there; for the sensed
colours are a state of the percipient: when he comes to sense blue
instead of green, it is the percipient who is changed, not the green
of the field or the blue of the sky. But we can be more specific: if it
is the percipient who senses the colours, we can ask whether it is
the percipient's body or the percipient's soul, and if the body,
whether it is the body as a whole or a particular part of it. Well,
first we may note that most parts of the body have nothing to do
with colour sensations, for instance the nose or the neck. On the
other hand, it is clear that colour sensations have a lot to do with
certain parts of the body, namely the eyes: damage to the eyes may
result in the loss of the capacity to sense colours, closing one's eyes
prevents this kind of sensation, and so forth. It seems to make
perfectly good sense to say that the eyes are the part of us that
senses colours.

Still, let us consider the possibility that the soul is the subject of
colour sensations. After all, one could admit most of what has
been said about the association between the eyes and colour
sensations and yet claim that the soul rather than the eyes is the

subject of them, even though it somehow senses colours through the eyes. We saw earlier that on Plotinus' view the soul by itself is incapable of perceiving sensible things, because it cannot undergo the necessary assimilation. The subject of the assimilation must be the organ. But could not the point then be turned into an argument against the present hypothesis about the nature of affection? Could one not say that since it is obviously the soul which senses colours and since on Plotinus' view it is the eye and not the soul which is the subject of affection, the affection, in the case of vision, cannot be colour sensation?

I believe that the naturalness that we may find in attributing colour sensations to the soul has two related sources. Firstly, I think that the objection just posed gains much of its plausibility by surreptitiously extending the sense of "colour sensations" so as to mean "seeing colours". In other words, the point is that obviously it is we, i.e., our souls, who see the colours in front of us, not the eyes as such. But what are colour sensations, anyway, if not seeing colours? Well, what is seeing colours? I grant that there is a sense of "seeing" according to which what we have called "colour sensations" is seeing colours. For instance, one need not deny that the infant introduced above sees the colour blue. Incidentally, this may explain why Plotinus, as it were despite himself, uses (in IV.4.8) "perception" and "seeing" of mere affections, to which his doctrine strictly speaking denies the name of perception and seeing. But there is another perfectly natural use of "seeing" according to which "seeing" implies "noticing", "attending to", or to use Ryle's term, "heeding". Thus, we can say that a person was so absorbed in his thoughts that he did not see the red traffic light. And this is perfectly compatible with the fact that the eyes of the person sensed the colours in the meaning I am giving to this expression. The difficulties that we find in conceiving of un-attended or unnoticed sensations are no doubt due to the fact that we fall victim to the idea, perhaps originating in Descartes and inculcated by the whole empiricist tradition, that sensations (sense-impressions), are, by their very nature, immediately known by the being who has them.

The second reason why we may feel naturally inclined to attribute sensations to the soul is that we tend to regard sensations as the paradigm of the mental: sensations are mental if anything is. And even if we usually prefer to talk about the mind and the mental rather than the soul and the psychic, we feel that at least outside religious contexts the soul and the mind are pretty much the same. I shall not venture to account for why we have come to regard sensations as the paradigm for the mental. But it seems that the view that sensations by themselves constitute self-authenticating knowledge of their own content is likely to have done much toward bringing this about.[47] However this may be, there is no good reason to suppose that Plotinus – or the ancients generally – felt inclined to regard sensations as purely mental. If one resists the temptation to regard sensations *per se* as epistemic, i.e., as an instance of knowing something to be so and so, then the main motive for regarding them as the same sort of thing as, for instance, the thought that $5 \times 7 = 35$ has disappeared.

Of course, according to Plotinus, sensations are not purely bodily phenomena either. They are psychosomatic in the sense that both body and soul are involved in sensation (sensory affections are, as we have seen, attributed to the animated body) and their ontological status is intermediate between the sensible (the physical) and the intelligible (iv.4.23, 25-6). Thus, when colour sensations are attributed to the eye, we must not understand the eye as merely a physical object, but as a live body of a special sort. And Plotinus evidently thinks that we, i.e. our higher souls, are related to the sense-organs in a special way which enables the higher soul to have access to the sensory affections of the organs, although it does not undergo them itself (cf. iv.5.1, 1-13).

It has already been claimed that the supposed intermediate status of sensory affections serves as evidence against the hypothesis that Plotinus regarded sensory affections as mere physical changes in the sense-organs. But admittedly the mere statement that affections are intermediate in this way is rather vague.[48] So, let us see if we can get clearer about what the statement amounts to. As it turns out, the most reasonable interpretation of it will provide independent support for the line of interpretation of sensory affection that I have suggested and will also enable us to make it more precise.

Firstly, let us reaffirm that in the case of vision the affections consist in the eyes' receiving the colours of the things seen or, to put it differently, the assimilation of the organ to the external sensible consists somehow in the eyes' becoming qualified by the colours of the thing. Plotinus says in iv.4.23, 24-5 that the affection is not the same as the agent (i.e., the colour in the external body), but as it were retains something of the agent while being itself intermediate between the sensible and the intelligible. As we noted earlier the assertion that the organ as it were retains something of the agent describes the assimilation referred to earlier in the chapter, i.e., it describes the fact that the organ becomes qualified in the same way as the object. This, taken together with the additional point, that the affection is not the same as the agent but intermediate between intelligible and sensible, surely seems to fit the suggestion that sensory affections in vision are colour sensations. The colours in our visual fields are plausible candidates for things which are intermediate in this way. But let us consider the matter still more closely.

Plotinus frequently says or indicates that the primary characteristic of bodies and sensibles generally is that they have an underlying mass (*onkos*) with the concomitant features of spatiality and extension.[49] The soul and the intelligible, generally, are without mass and its concomitant features: they are without extension and spatially distinct parts.[50] We can see exactly this idea at work in IV.4.23, 11-19, where Plotinus claims that the soul by itself, because of its intelligible nature, would not be able to grasp any sensible *qua* sensible even if it received its form: it would merely grasp an unextended intelligible form. We are further given to understand that sense-perception is an apprehension of the sensibles *qua* extended and spatially located.[51] And for this sort of grasp bodily organs are needed. Now, given Plotinus' general tendency to demarcate the sensible from the intelligible in terms of an underlying mass, spatiality and extension, and given the presence of this idea in IV.4.23 itself, it is reasonable to suppose that the intermediateness in question is an intermediateness with respect to these features. Thus, we should look for something which either possesses just some but not all of these features or possesses them in a qualified manner.

Now, the colours in a percipient's visual field are arguably intermediate in just this way. They appear to be extended and thus to have spatially different parts, and they seem to have spatial location. On the other hand, we do not conceive of such colours as having an underlying mass or bulk. Plotinus, in fact, explicitly makes the point that what comes through the eyes is merely the form, while the mass remains outside; "the magnitude comes along with it [the form], large not in mass but in form".[52] This, when put together with what he says about affection in IV.4.23, suggests that the eyes do not become assimilated with the mass of external bodies but merely with their colour. The upshot is that the colours that the eyes take on have a status intermediate between the sensible and the intelligible in that they have extensions and spatiality but lack underlying mass. This does indeed conform fairly well with our notion of phenomenal colour.

We should note that some other philosophers in Plotinus' era express views that have obvious affinities with the views on sensory affection I have here attributed to Plotinus.

We mentioned Galen's views in the previous chapter, and noted that in conscious opposition to the Stoics, the Epicureans and the Peripatetics, he holds that in vision the percipient must be affected out there where the object is, because otherwise we cannot give a satisfactory account of how we see the sizes of things. This shows at least that Plotinus was not the only antagonist of the view that sensory affections are impressions on the percipient's body.

Alexander regards sensory affection as affection of a special sort, different from normal physical affection and different from the affection of the diaphanous by the colours of things, which is itself extraordinary.[53] According to Alexander the eyes are affected "*qua* something ensouled and capable of representation (*phantasiousthai dynamenon*)".[54] And in one passage in *De anima* Alexander implies that the forms we receive in sense-perception are somehow intermediate between forms in matter and intelligible forms: "Even though in sense-perception we receive the forms without the matter and do not grasp them in the way matter receives form, nevertheless we perceive the object under its material conditions." He goes on to explain that this means that "when we see colour we apprehend along with it and in the same sensory act, extension and shape, motion and rest, and the like".[55] In what follows Alexander says that the intelligible forms differ from the sensible ones in that they are apprehended without these features. Alexander is evidently saying that the forms received in sense-perception are intermediate between the sensible and the intelligible in a manner similar to that proposed, on my interpretation, by Plotinus: such forms have spatial features but are without the underlying mass, or matter, and hence their presence to the eye is different from the presence of qualities in bodies.

Another aspect of Plotinus' sensory affections, their passivity, is brought out by Sextus. He says that the senses are by their nature non-rational, have no capacity beyond being impressed and are hence "wholly disqualified for discovering the truth. For that which is to grasp what is true in external sensible objects must not only be moved whitishly or sweetishly (*leukantikôs ê glykantikôs*), but to the representation of such a thing must also be brought 'this is white' and 'this is sweet'."[56] Now, there are of course various differences between Plotinus' views and those of Sextus. For instance, Plotinus would not agree that the senses are wholly non-rational. He thinks sensory affections are so, but that there is more to the senses than affections. However, like Plotinus, Sextus makes, as we see here, a distinction between sensory affection and judgement. Moreover, it is most likely that Sextus' conception of affection is the same as the one I have attributed to Plotinus: it is a purely passive sensory experience.[57] But Sextus of course does not commit himself to any views about the nature or ontological status of affections.

Finally, we should mention St Augustine's views. In *De Trinitate* XI.2 he argues for several distinctions between kinds of *species* or forms. There is (1) the form of the external body (*species corporis*); (2) the form generated in the senses (*species quae fit in sensu*); (3) the form in memory (*species quae fit in memoria*); (4) the form in the intuition of thought (*species quae fit in acie cogitantis*). Such a tendency toward the multiplication of the form is already at work in Plotinus as we shall see even more clearly in later chapters. But we may here remark that the nature of the *species quae fit in sensu* distinguished by Augustine is close to the nature of the form that our organs take on in Plotinus' theory. This *species* belongs to the ensouled body, and seems to be a phenomenal entity.[58]

This brief survey shows that it should come as no surprise that Plotinus holds views of the sort here attributed to him. Various aspects of these views are to be found in other philosophers.

V

The unity of the senses

Plotinus' views concerning the unity of the senses, and the inferences which he draws from them, constitute what is perhaps the most original aspect of his theory of perception. I want to claim that Plotinus' position on this issue is the result of a historical dialogue and represents the sort of statement that one might expect a dualist to make after the floor has been held for some time by the Stoics and Peripatetics. In order to set Plotinus' views in a proper context, we shall, before we turn to them, consider what some of his predecessors had to say about this subject.

1 The views of Plotinus' predecessors on the unity of the senses

In the *Theaetetus* at 184 D ff. Plato distinguishes the senses from one another by reference to the differences in their objects: sight has proper objects that cannot be perceived through any other sense, so does hearing, and so does each of the other senses. But above the special senses he posits a central faculty of perception. With this faculty "we apprehend the black and the white through the eyes, and objects of other kinds through the other senses" (184 D). Here, we need not go into the details of Plato's analysis of the function of this central faculty, interesting as they are in themselves.[1] It suffices to point out that Plato's introduction of a central faculty is prompted by observations about the unity of consciousness in perception: "It would be very strange," he says, "if there should be many senses sitting in us as in wooden horses, and all these things should not converge in some single nature" (184 D).

Plato is here making the point that there is a unique subject of perceptual experiences despite the multiplicity of sensory objects. This may seem to be an obvious and trivial point. But it is actually of no little significance. As we shall see, later Greek philosophers took this observation to be important and found it necessary to take it into account in their theories of perception. It is also worth remarking that Plato suggests that the central faculty of perception is a power of the soul whereas the organs are parts of the body (184 D-E).

We find the idea of the unity of the senses also in Aristotle, though expressed in quite different terms. In *De Anima* Aristotle asks: "Since we discern the white and the sweet and each of the sensibles in relation to each other, by what do we perceive that they are different?" (*De An.* 426b 13-15). He answers that evidently we must perceive this with some sense since these are sensible objects. Clearly this sense cannot be any of the special senses, because the difference between white and sweet cannot be the object of either vision or taste. But the sense which perceives this difference must be one. Aristotle argues for this by saying that not only does this sense say that white and sweet differ but that they differ *now*. The point is presumably that their difference is grasped in a single mental act, and thus evidently by the same sense.[2] But this presents a problem: the unity of the apprehension indicates that the sense is one and undivided, but "it is impossible that the same sense is moved at the same time with contrary movements in so far as it is indivisible and in indivisible time" (*De An.* 426b 30-3). Aristotle does not provide a clear answer to this problem. His final word on the subject in *De Anima* depends upon a rather obscure metaphor: that which judges (*to krinon*) is said to be both divisible and indivisible like what some call a point: "[It] is one and judges at one time in so far as it is indivisible, but in so far as it is divisible it simultaneously uses the same point twice. In so far then as it uses the boundary-point twice it judges two separate things in a way separately; in so far as it uses it as one it judges one thing."[3] We can agree with Hamlyn that the analogy of the point "is not perspicuous in its implications, to say the least".[4] This much is clear, however: Aristotle sees the disparity, and especially the possible oppositeness of sensory affections (as between black and white), as causing problems for the evident unity of con-

95

sciousness in perception. The underlying assumption is of course that sensory affections are related in the same way as the qualities that cause them: since black and white are opposite, the affections caused by them are changes in opposite directions. This leads him to ascribe to the judging faculty – which is the ultimate subject of perception, corresponding to the soul in the *Theaetetus* 184 – a special kind of simultaneous divisibility and indivisibility that the analogy of the point is intended to express. As we shall see, this point about the indivisibility of the subject of perception is taken up by Plotinus, who uses it to make metaphysical claims about the nature of the soul.

Now, a lot more could of course be said about this analogy and indeed about this whole issue in Aristotle. But Aristotle's views are not our primary concern and hence what has already been said must suffice. However I will give a more detailed treatment of Aristotelian doctrine when I take up the views of Alexander of Aphrodisias, whose account of this subject is both fuller and clearer than that of his master. And, as we shall see, Alexander is more relevant as an influence on Plotinus here than Aristotle. But before we turn to Alexander let us have a brief look at the Stoics.

The Stoics divide the soul into eight parts: The five senses, the reproductive faculty, the faculty of speech and the principal faculty (*to hegemonikon*).[5] The last mentioned faculty, said to be located in the heart, has a variety of functions. As its name indicates, it is the ruler of the organism: it is that which gives or refuses assent to representations (*phantasiai*) and as such it controls the behaviour of the organism.[6] But it is also the seat of representations and inclinations.[7] As the seat of representations the principal part of the soul is also the seat of perception; for, according to the Stoics, perception presupposes representation.[8] All accounts agree that the five senses are supposed to be outgrowths of hot pneuma from the principal part in the heart to the organs. There are indications, however, that Chrysippus took the principal part itself to be extended throughout the body.[9] This seems incompatible with a distinction between the five senses and the principal part, and with the specific location of the principal part in the heart. But Chrysippus' point is presumably that the five senses are extensions of a single substance, which has the heart as its centre, both physically and functionally. This is what emerges from his metaphor of the spider, reported by Calcidius: the principal part of the soul is said to be like a spider located at the centre of its web; by holding the ends of threads that go in all directions by its legs, it becomes aware of any movement anywhere in the web. Thus, the heart is the place where tensional motions, containing messages – the Stoics describe the special senses as "messengers" – about states of affairs in the external world converge.[10] It seems that there is no perception until the sensory affection has reached the principal part of the soul in the heart: reports tell that according to Zeno and Chrysippus the movement caused by an impingement from the outside must be transmitted from the affected part to the starting-point of the soul (the principal part) if the animal is to perceive.[11] Plotinus criticizes the Stoics' division of the soul into a principal part and subordinate parts, and we shall come back to this aspect of the Stoic doctrine in the context of Plotinus' views.

In the Stoic notion of the principal part we find a reaffirmation of the idea, which we have already found in Plato and Aristotle, that there is a single centre of the conscious life of an organism. But even our limited sources suggest that at least in some respects the Stoics carried the idea further than did Plato and Aristotle. For instance, this idea cannot be said to play a central role in the psychology of either Plato or Aristotle, whereas the Stoics put it into the foreground. The Stoics' principal part is not merely the centre of perceptual experience, but also the seat of desire and, in man, of rationality.[12] Thus the whole of what we call the conscious life of an organism is unified in the principal part.[13] It is true that there are indications that in Aristotle the general sense (*to prôton aisthêtikon*) performs some such function: at any rate this is the meeting-place of impressions from the senses, memories, desires and thoughts.[14] But the Stoics seem to have been much more systematic in their treatment of this subject and more explicitly concerned with the connectedness of the various functions that make up the conscious life.

The psychology of Alexander of Aphrodisias must be seen against a Stoic background. Alexander is of course primarily concerned with expounding and defending Aristotle's doctrines, and on the whole he is as faithful to his master as one could expect any disciple to be. Sometimes Alexander says things that are not clearly warranted by Aristotle's texts. But usually this is where Aristotle is either silent, unclear or ambiguous; thus, what Alexander presents is always a possible and usually a plausible interpretation of Aristotle. There are however certain new emphases in Alexander. We have already mentioned that Alexander makes much more of the idea of the unity of the subject in perceptual experience than Aristotle, though most of what Alexander says about the matter has Aristotelian antecedents. It is natural to suppose that the prominence of this subject in Alexander's *De Anima* is due to the Stoics. Stoic doctrines had infiltrated the philosophical forum at the time; even somebody like Alexander, who on the whole is an ardent antagonist of the Stoics, is bound to have views about subjects discussed by the Stoics and cannot escape the influence of their views.

Alexander distinguishes between the special senses and a general sense (*koinê aisthêsis*). Such a distinction is also made by Aristotle: what we called "the judging faculty" in the presentation of Aristotle's views above corresponds to Alexander's general sense. In the *Parva Naturalia* Aristotle uses the term *to prôton aisthêtikon* (the primary sense) to refer to this same power.[15] Alexander's term *koinê aisthêsis*, is also used by Aristotle in *De Anima* but to denote the sense by which we perceive the common sensibles (things that can be perceived by more than one sense) such as number and notion.[16] But in any case, Alexander uses Aristotle's term *koinê aisthêsis* to refer to what Aristotle calls the *to prôton aisthêtikon*. To avoid any confusion with the sense that perceives the common sensibles, I use the expression "general sense" for *koinê aisthêsis* in Alexander rather than the more literal "common sense".

Aristotle says in the *Parva Naturalia* that the general sense has a sense-organ of its own and that this organ is the heart.[17] As one would expect, Alexander holds the same view, but in addition he attempts to explain much more fully than does Aristotle the relation between the general sense and its organ, and between it and the individual senses. Since the questions that arise in connection with Alexander's discussion of this matter are directly relevant for the same issue in Plotinus, we shall look closely at what Alexander has to say.

Both Aristotle and Alexander introduce the general sense through considerations about the perception of differences between objects of the different special senses such as the white and the sweet. According to Alexander, each of the special senses perceives the differences among objects that belong to the genus over which it ranges. For instance, sight by itself discerns that colours differ from one another, hearing that sounds do, and so forth. But since there is obviously perception of the differences among sensibles falling under different genera, the general sense is introduced specifically to account for this (Bruns, 60-1). Thus one might think that the general sense is distinguished from the special senses primarily by virtue of ranging over the differences between different genera of sensibles while the former discern the differences within a single genus.

This position, however, involves some difficulties. It is surely not Alexander's intention to maintain that the function of the general sense is restricted to the perception of the differences between genera of sensibles *qua* genera, so that the difference between the general sense and the special senses amounts to one of generality. The general sense perceives not only that colours as a genus are different from gustative qualities as a genus, but also specifically that this white is different from that sweet. This seems to imply that the general sense itself is involved in the discernment of this particular white and presumably thereby in the discernment that this particular white is different from that particular black. And if so, it is no longer clear how labour is divided between the special senses and the general sense. Of course it could still be maintained that there are different genera of sensible qualities that are associated with different organs. But it seems that the original distinction between the general sense and the special senses in terms of the differences between the objects they discern cannot be maintained.

As we shall see, Alexander also ceases to talk about the special senses discerning their proper sensible objects, as he proceeds with his account of the general sense. We noted that Aristotle is led to his obscure account of the way in which the judging faculty is both divided and undivided by the consideration "that the same faculty cannot be moved in opposite directions, in so far as it is indivisible, and in indivisible time".[18] Alexander takes up this problem and discusses it at some length. He begins by affirming that the affections at issue are not such that the sense-organs become literally qualified in the same way as the object. If this were so, the problem would be insurmountable, he says.[19] It is not clear, however, what sort of non-literal qualification the sense-organs are supposed to undergo. He points to the colours reflected by mirrors as an analogous case, and there are other indications that he regarded the eyes as working like mirrors.[20] Nor is it clear what is the significance of this special nature of the affections, for in his final and definitive account of the problem (Bruns, 63, 5–64, 11), he continues to talk about the affections as movements in the sense-organs and he still understands these movements to be such that contrary ones cannot exist simultaneously in the same subject.

Alexander uses the analogy of a circle and its radii to explain his final position about the relation between the general sense and the special senses. The centre of a circle is both one and many: "it is many inasmuch as it is the terminal point for a number of different lines, but a unity in that all these lines blend themselves together within it."[21] This analogy of a circle and its radii replaces Aristotle's analogy of the point. It seems likely that the Stoics' doctrine of the relationship between the ruling part and the five special senses played a role in this shift of model (cf. Chrysippus' spider metaphor). Alexander continues with the details of his theory as follows, claiming that the general sense is simultaneously one and many in an analogous way:

> The general sense, by virtue of being the terminal point in the ultimate sense-organ for each of those sensory movements which originate in sensible objects . . . is a plurality, being the terminal point of many different movements. But, by virtue of being an incorporeal power, uniformly the same in the whole ultimate sense-organ and in each of its parts, it is an indivisible unity. Thus the sensory power is at once one and not one. (Bruns, 63, 12-20)

In virtue of being thus identical as a whole in each part of the ultimate sense-organ, the general sense can discern different affections at once. Discernment in perception, whether within a single genus of sensibles or between different genera, has here altogether become the function of the general sense. The function of the special senses and their organs is thus restricted to the reception of the affection from the outside and its transmission to the heart.

We noted earlier that the notion of a central power of perception which we find in Plato and Aristotle, and most conspicuously in Alexander, is an attempt to deal with the unity of consciousness in perception. It is true that none of these authors uses, in this context, a term that corresponds to our "consciousness". There can be no doubt, however, that the phenomenon they are dealing with is the same as what is now called "the unity of consciousness": witness Plato's remark in the *Theaetetus* about the warriors in the Trojan horse and the similar remarks of Aristotle and Alexander.[22] In Aristotle and Alexander the fact that the unity of perceptual consciousness is their central subject is to some extent obscured by their concern with the problem of simultaneous, opposite movements in the same subject, a problem which arises in this context because of their particular views about the nature of sensory affection. But this problem is really accidental to the issue of the unity of perceptual consciousness and the problem of reconciling this unity with the multiplicity involved in perception, as we shall see in dealing with Plotinus' views, to which we now finally turn.

2 Plotinus on the unity of perception

In the early treatise "On the Immortality of the Soul" (IV.7.[2] 6-7) Plotinus advances several arguments against Stoic materialism, according to which the soul is a kind of body. These arguments and what they reveal about Plotinus' position are in my opinion among his most interesting passages. This is so because they are the clearest expression of Plotinus' dualism with respect to soul and body. They are also interesting for their implications for Plotinus' position on the relation between perception and the faculty of representation. I shall in the remainder of this chapter comment on each of these aspects. In the concluding chapter there will be a further, more general, consideration of Plotinus' dualism and its significance.

In the course of his refutation of the Stoics we find the following passage:

That which is to perceive something must itself be one thing and everything must be apprehended by the same entity, even if many things arrive through many sense-organs or many qualities belong to the same thing, or if something complex is apprehended through one sense, for instance a face. For it is not one thing that perceives the nose, another that perceives the eyes, but the same perceives all the parts together. And if one feature is perceived through the eyes, another through hearing, there must be one thing to which both arrive.   (IV.7.6, 3-10)

Having set forth the circle analogy familiar from Alexander and affirmed that all percepts (aisthêmata) must arrive in something that is "truly one", Plotinus goes on to argue against the Stoics that that in which all perception converges cannot be anything extended.[23] He says:

if this were extended and the perceptions arrived at as it were each end of a line, then either they must be conjoined in one and the same point as before, say in the middle, or else each point would have a perception of its own, just as if I were perceiving one thing and you another. And if it is a question of a single percept, say a face, then either it is contracted into a unity (this appears in fact to be the case, for it is contracted already in the pupils) or how would we see the largest things through them? hence, still more when they reach the principal part [of the soul], they will become like partless objects of thought (hoion amerê noêmata) – and the principal part will be partless; or the percept is a magnitude and hence that which apprehends would be divided along with it so that each of its parts would apprehend a different part of the object and none of us would have apprehension (*antilêpsis*) of the sensible thing as a whole. (IV.7.6, 19-26)

In the next chapter, IV.7.7, Plotinus reaches the same conclusion from consideration of pain: he attacks the notion of transmission (*diadosis*) from the affected parts of the body to the ruling part of the soul, claiming that such theories have the absurd consequence that, instead of one, there would be an infinite number of different perceptions of the pain and that the ruling part would only perceive pain in the part next to it, not in the originally affected part.[24] He then concludes that since perception of pain cannot be explained in terms of transmission "nor can one body, being a mass, know when another body is affected, for every magnitude has one part different from another; one must suppose that which perceives to be of such a nature that it is everywhere identical with itself. But to accomplish this suits some other kind of being than body."[25]

Thus, Plotinus holds that no theory according to which the soul is a kind of body can satisfactorily account for the unity of perception. Plotinus and the Stoics agree that the soul (or a faculty of the soul) is that which perceives. But they disagree about what the soul is. The Stoics held that the soul is a kind of body, and Plotinus' strategy is to claim that the fact of the unity of the perceiving subject reveals that that in us which does the perceiving cannot be a body.[26] Hence, the soul cannot be a body. According to Plotinus the defining characteristic of a body is magnitude (*megethos*).[27] This is in agreement with Stoic doctrine according to which a body is "that which has three dimensions along with resistance".[28] The Stoics held that the principal part of the soul, located in the heart, is the central faculty of perception in which affections from all the sense-organs converge. Thus, the Stoics were in perfect agreement with Plotinus in holding that the senses are unified. The difference is that the unity the Stoics posit, that of a body, does not satisfy Plotinus. As we have seen, a body, understood as a spatial magnitude, is in Plotinus' view such that none of its parts is identical either with any other part or with the whole (cf. IV.2.1, 11-17). This means, I take it, that in a body each part is numerically distinct from every other part and also from the whole. Elsewhere he says that the same holds for bodily qualities such as colours and shapes: the quality inherent in a part of a body is numerically different from a quality in a different part of the same body (VI.4.1, 17-24). Thus, if that in which affections from all the senses converge is a body, different impressions must reach different parts, and if so, the kind of unity Plotinus takes to be evident in perception is not achieved: there is really, after all, not *one* entity in which everything converges. For a body has unity only in the sense of spatial continuity, which by itself implies division into non-identical parts (IV.2.1, 60; cf. IV.2.2, 11).

There are common features in all of Plotinus' attacks on Stoic physicalism. We can generalize his arguments as follows: (a) it holds for bodies generally that if a body performs distinct acts at the same time, these acts are to be ascribed to its distinct parts severally. To illustrate this, consider the human body: the body regulates the amount of water in itself and it pumps its own blood. And it performs individual such acts at the same time. These acts are ascribed to distinct parts of the body, i.e. to the kidneys and to the heart, respectively. Moreover, each individual act a body performs with one of its parts is ascribed only to the part involved, not to the other parts: even if the heart and the kidneys are parts of the same body, the fact that an individual pumping of the blood is ascribed to the heart does not make it ascribable to the kidneys. This seemingly trivial point is, I take it, what Plotinus has in mind in his obscure remarks noted above about the non-identity and independence of distinct parts of the same body. Thus, since seeing and hearing or perception of pain in the toe and in the finger are distinct acts that may be performed simultaneously by the soul, the foregoing should hold for these acts, if the soul is a body. But (b), it would clearly be absurd to hold that a given physical part of the soul perceives A and another part B. For in that case each of the parts should perceive its object on its own, just as the heart pumps the blood on its own or a given part of a body is blue all on its own. It is not the case here that one part does this and another part that, and all the acts are ascribed to the whole soul only by virtue of belonging to the parts severally. It is evident that numerically the same entity is the subject of seeing and hearing or the perceiving of pain in the various parts of the body. Individual acts of perception are not performed by parts of the soul to the exclusion of other parts. Thus, we must suppose that the soul is present as a whole in all the sensitive parts of the body. This very feature, presence as a whole in different parts, marks the soul off as an entity of an ontologically different order than bodies.

Now, this refutation is of course far from conclusive and various responses could be advanced on behalf of the Stoics.[29] For example, one might say that the assumption that individual acts of perception can be ascribed to individual parts is unjustified, that in fact the whole body of the soul is always involved in each act. Plotinus would have to modify his arguments if they were to apply to such a position.

As we have seen, Alexander also associates the pervasive presence of the common sense power in its organ with the incorporeality of the power, which, it seems, means for him that the power is a form of a certain type of body, not a body itself, for forms as such are incorporeal. He does not seem, however, to be tempted to take the step Plotinus was to take and cite this feature as evidence against physicalism: in none of the various arguments Alexander advances against Stoic physicalism in his little treatise on the subject does the unity of perception play a role.[30] It is an interesting question how Alexander would explain the pervasive undivided presence of the general power in its organ in terms of his Aristotelian hylomorphic theory of the soul. Plotinus maintains that the hylomorphic theory entails that the soul, as the substantial form of the body, is spatially extended and divisible along with the body: its relation to the body should be like that of the shape of a statue to the bronze (IV.7.85, 5-9).[31] But as we have seen, in Plotinus' view the soul cannot be divisible in this way and the hylomorphic theory suffers from the same fault as the Stoic physicalism, i.e. to render the soul divisible. This is not an occasion to discuss how fair an objection this is against the Peripatetic doctrine. It is indeed a vexing question to what extent the soul is analogous to bodily shape. But we may add, incidentally, that the question of the divisibility of the soul continued to be a difficult issue for Aristotelians. Aquinas denies that the soul is extended and quantitatively divisible at all.[32] Pomponazzi, on the other hand, holds that all faculties of the human soul are extended but denies, at first, that the intellect is divisible, which he however eventually concedes.[33]

Provided one regards it as a problem, as both Alexander and Plotinus clearly do, how to reconcile the evident unity of perception with the equally evident fact that perception is somehow at work in different parts of the body, Plotinus' position is more intuitive than Alexander's. Alexander supposes that the different parts of the central organ of perception are affected but that, since the power of perception is present as a whole throughout the central organ, the same thing, i.e. the power, is the subject of different perceptions. The reason why Alexander holds that the same power must be present throughout the central organ is, of course, that otherwise he would have to admit either that the same thing can simultaneously undergo contrary affection in the same part or else that there is no single subject of perception, neither of which is acceptable to him. Given, however, that one finds it necessary to posit a power endowed with the properties which Alexander attributes to the central organ, why restrict this to a central organ? The very point of positing a central organ of perception is to account for the unity of perception. That is what leads Alexander to suppose that affections are transmitted from the exterior sense-organs to the heart. But it is as if Alexander realizes that no doctrine about transmission of affections to a central organ as such quite succeeds in accounting for the unity of perception; for given that the central organ is an extended body the same problem which prompted the hypothesis of a central organ – reconciling the unity of the subject of perception with the multiplicity of sensory affections – arises with respect to the central organ itself. Hence the need for the omnipresence of the power of perception throughout the central organ. I do not think that Alexander's position is incoherent, but it is somewhat awkward inasmuch as it seems to involve a twofold explanation of the same phenomenon. Plotinus' view of the matter is much simpler. Basically all he does is to develop one of Alexander's two solutions so that a uniform account can be given in terms of it.

One question that naturally arises with respect to Plotinus' theory of the omnipresence of the perceptive soul, and the apparent lack of any doctrine concerning the transmission of affections to a central organ, is what role he assigns to the brain and to the nerves in perception. For Plotinus, following the *Timaeus* in locating the higher activities of the soul in the head, holds that the brain is in some sense the seat of perception. And in this context he mentions that the nerves have the brain as their starting-point (see IV.3.23). In this he is undoubtedly relying on the discoveries of Herophilus and Erasistratus perfected by Galen.[34] Would this not suggest that after all the brain is supposed to function as a central organ of perception in a similar way as the heart does for Aristotle, Alexander and the Stoics? A close look at the only passage where Plotinus discusses the role of the brain and the nerves shows, however, that this is not his view. After stating that the power of vision resides in the eyes, that of hearing in the ears, and so forth, he says:

Since the sense of touch has as instruments the first nerves, which also contain the power of movement for the organism, and thus this power distributes itself there, and since the nerves have their starting points in the brain, they have established the principle of perception and of impulse and in general of the whole organism in the brain, supposing that obviously the place where the organs have their starting-points must also be the location of that which employs these organs. But it would be better to say that the starting point of the activity of the power is there. For it had to be at the place from which a tool is to be moved that the corresponding power of the craftsman is, as we may say, fixed. Or rather, not the power – for the power is everywhere – but the starting-point of the activity of the power is where the starting-point of the tool is.[35]   (IV.3.23, 9-21)

This passage does not mention any sort of transmission of affection from the organs to the brain. If Plotinus had held some such view, one would surely expect him to have expressed it here. But instead we get a rather subtle account of the way in which the brain can be said to be the seat of perception, an account which manages to reconcile Plato and known scientific facts with Plotinus' own view, that the psychic powers are immune to localization.

An interesting passage in the same vein is IV.3.3, which concerns the unity of all souls. Plotinus there considers whether the relation between the Soul and the individual souls is a part–whole relation. He raises the question whether the Soul and the individual souls might be related in the same way as the soul of the whole animal and the soul that animates its parts. Plotinus' ultimate response to this question is not quite clear.[36] But at any rate he says that if these are analogous relations, the Soul would not be divided but would be "everywhere as a whole, everywhere in its entirety one and the same in many" (IV.3.3, 9-10). As a proof of this he points to the unity of perception, this time stated in terms of the unity of the power of judgement (*krisis*) (cf. III.6.1, 1-2). That which judges is one and the qualitative difference between the perceptions is not due to the power, but to the differences between the affections, which in turn must be explained by the differences in the constitution of the sense-organs (cf. IV.3.21-3). It follows from this that there is no qualitative difference between the individual powers of perception as such. Thus, there emerges the picture of a single, undifferentiated faculty of perception, which operates from the brain but is present as a whole in the various parts of the body. We shall now turn to the implications of this view for Plotinus' theory of perception as a whole.

3 The faculty of representation and the unity of
perception

The notion of the general sense employed by Aristotle and Alexander has disappeared in Plotinus.[37].The reason is, I think, to be found in the differences which have already been noted between Plotinus' views and those of Alexander. One, and perhaps the most important, function of the general sense is to serve as the focal point in which the special senses converge. Because for Plotinus perception as such is an undifferentiated power, present as a whole in various parts of the body, there is no need to posit a central sense above the special senses to perform this function. But this raises the question what becomes of the other functions assigned to the general sense by Aristotle and Alexander: the perception that we see, hear and so forth and the quasi-sensory apprehension of images (*phantasmata*) that in the *Parva Naturalia* are assigned to the general sense. I take it that perception of the so-called common sensibles is included in what Plotinus calls, simply, "perception" (cf. II.8.1).

Now, Plotinus posits a faculty which he calls *phantasia* or *to phantastikon*.[38] He holds that perceptions terminate in this faculty.[39] This has been taken to imply that there is no perceptual consciousness before percepts have reached the faculty of *phantasia* and that the unity of the senses is really the work of this faculty which, it is said, has replaced the Aristotelian common sense.[40] Now if *phantasia* and perception are two separate faculties this would present us with the following problem: if the unity of the senses is due to the fact that all the senses terminate in a single faculty which is different from each, and from sense-perception in general, then there is no unity of perception on the level of perception proper. This would of course contradict what we have just claimed. In what follows I will discuss the relation between perception and the faculty of *phantasia* and will try to clarify the problem just presented as well as the issue of what becomes of the other functions assigned by Alexander to the general sense.

There are at least two different notions of *phantasia* current among Plotinus' predecessors. The Stoics and the Hellenistic philosophers generally regarded *phantasiai* as intrinsic to perception, yet much wider in scope. Over-simplifying a bit we could say that *phantasiai* are appearances, where "appearances"is used in a wide sense including perceptions and any other sort of presentation.[41] Aristotle, on the other hand, employs the word *phantasia* primarily as the name of a faculty. It is difficult to find a single formula that captures everything that Aristotle says about this faculty. The most plausible candidate seems to me to be the one suggested by Malcolm Schofield when he remarks that "Aristotle seems to be concerned with a capacity for having . . . non-paradigmatic sensory experiences".[42] This includes various different sorts of experiences such as dreams, imaginations, interpretations of indistinct perceptions, memory-images and so on. This account has at least two important virtues: it fits the scope of Aristotle's examples, and it makes good sense of Aristotle's claim that the objects of *phantasia* are residua of sensory affections.[43] In any case, as Schofield points out, only the absence of *phantasia* in Aristotle's account of perception in *De Anima* strongly suggests that in his view *phantasia* is not involved in normal perceptions of external objects.[44]

Plotinus' notion of *phantasia* is much closer to that of Aristotle than to that of the Hellenistic philosophers, although there are passages where *phantasia* seems to cover all kinds of apprehension below the level of intellection.[45] But it is clear that what Plotinus usually refers to as *phantasia* is something much narrower, and the instances of the broader use can easily be explained as his slipping into a Stoic terminology. According to Plotinus *phantasia* (*to phantastikon*) is the faculty by which we have images or representations (*phantasmata, phantasiai, typoi*).[46] Both memory and reasoning involve such images, and hence the faculty of *phantasia* is at work in the operation of these other faculties.[47]

But even if the scope and function of *phantasia*, according to Plotinus, are thus similar to what we find in Aristotle, there is a notable difference between Plotinus' and Aristotle's views. As one would expect given Aristotle's statement that *phantasia* is concerned with residua of sensory affections, he maintains that *phantasia* is a psychic function that depends on the body (*De An.* 403a 8-10). Plotinus, on the other hand, holds that *phantasia* does not depend on the body for its operation although it is linked with the functions of sense-perception and bodily desires which do depend on the body.[48] This view is in accordance with Plotinus' views of the objects of *phantasia*. We have mentioned earlier that Plotinus maintains that perception results in the generation of extensionless "entities" in the soul that are variously described as "intelligible representations" (*typoi noêtoi*), "forms", or "images" (*phantasmata*). Their lack of extension is in turn linked with the unity of perception. For it is clear from Plotinus' argument against the Stoics in IV.7.6-7, which we considered in the previous section, that the non-extension of the percipient goes together with the non-extension of that which the percipient receives (cf. IV.7.8). As we shall see more clearly in what follows, the objects of *phantasia* are these unextended entities. I will henceforth translate *phantasia* in Plotinus as "representation". The most important function of *phantasia* is to be the "locus" of these unextended entities that are involved in memory and reasoning, and it is clear that these entities are in some sense representations of things.

Let us now turn to the relation between representation and perception. The most informative passage on this issue comes in IV.3.29 as a result of a long discussion of the question by what faculty we remember (IV.3.26-9). In chapter 26 Plotinus first states his usual doctrine that perception is a function that belongs to the composite of body and soul (IV.3.26, 1-8). He then goes on: "In this case, perception should certainly be called a common function, but memory would not thereby necessarily belong to the common entity, since the soul has already received the representation (*typos*) and preserved it or rejected it" (9-12). This is in accordance with what we have already noted: perception is the soul's reception of an (incorporeal) representation or form of the external object, and these forms are the subject matter of memory, reasoning and the other functions that involve the faculty of representation. At this stage Plotinus has not yet affirmed that memory belongs to the faculty of representation, and before he formulates his final position he discusses the question whether the memories of the operations of each psychic power belong to the power that performs the operations in question. He however soon abandons this suggestion and comes to the following conclusion:

But again, if it is going to be necessary for each [the power of memory and the power of perception] to be different, and a different thing will remember what perception has perceived, will that latter power also have to perceive what it is to remember? Now, there is no reason why the object of the remembering power's perception should not be an image (*phantasma*), and the memory and retention of it should belong to the faculty of representation (*to phantastikon*) which is different from that of perception. For it is in this that perception terminates, and what is seen is present to it when there is no longer perception (*aisthêsis*) of it. (IV.3.29, 19-26)

I believe that a close reading of this passage will enable us to clarify the question about the relationship between perception and representation. First, let us note that Plotinus unambiguously affirms that perception and representation have different objects: the objects of the perception of the faculty of representation are images, and the implication obviously is that these are different in kind from the objects of sense-perception itself. Ordinary sense-perception results in the formation of an image (also called impression, form). These images are apprehended by the faculty of representation and may later be recalled as memories or reasoned about and so forth. But this sort of apprehension is distinct from sense-perception, which has a different object – no doubt an external sensible object though this is not explicitly said here.

A passage from III.6.1 supports this account of the relation between perception and representation and contains some additional information. After identifying perceptions with judgements of the soul and denying that the judgements are affections, Plotinus continues:

> Nonetheless we had a problem at this point whether the judgement as such has nothing in it of what is judged. If it has an impression (*typos*) of it, then it has been affected. But it would, however, be possible to say about the so-called impressions that their character is quite different from what has been supposed, and is like that which is also found in acts of thought; these too are activities that are able to know without being affected in any way. (III.6.1, 6-12)

Although the faculty of representation is not mentioned here, this passage reveals important facts about the relation between perception and representation. We see that Plotinus does not deny that judgement leaves a *typos* in the soul. It seems to be implied that in fact it does. But he wants to emphasize that these *typoi* are not impressions, as the Stoics and Aristotle hold, but incorporeal representations, indeed, the same entities as the *typoi* and *phantasmata* that we find in IV.3.26 and 29. The present passage permits us therefore to fill out the account we have already given as follows: the judgement that constitutes the original sense-perception leaves an intelligible representation of what is perceived in the soul. These intelligible representations are the objects of the faculty of representation. In Chapters VI and VIII I shall have more to say about both Plotinus' notion of intelligible representations and his notion of judgement in perception. But the foregoing gives us at least the outline of the picture: representation is, so to speak, the perception of things that have been internalized by the soul, whereas sense-perception is the judgement of external objects that are internalized in or by this judgement, because the judgement leaves an intelligible representation of the external object judged.[49]

Now what stand are we to take on the question of whether

representation is the power that unifies the senses and on the meaning of the claim that perception terminates in the faculty of representation? As to the latter, let us note that Plotinus may have good reasons for holding that perceptions terminate in representation without thereby implying that this faculty is responsible for the unity of the senses. Given that representation is operative in memory and reasoning, there must lie some path from perception to the faculty of representation, since we can obviously remember and reason about what we have previously seen or heard, and Plotinus' statement need not signify anything more than this. As to the former, if Plotinus held that the unique subject of perception is really the faculty of representation, where this latter faculty is understood as something distinct from sense-perception, one would expect him to state his thesis of the unity of the perceptive subject explicitly in terms of representation. But he does not – which would suggest that we can maintain our original conclusion that the unity of the senses pertains to the faculty of perception itself.

However, the issue may be slightly more complicated. In the passage from iv.3.29 quoted above Plotinus says that the power responsible for memory must previously have perceived that which it is later to remember. The object of this previous "perception" is an image, and we suggested above that sense-perception itself consists in the formation of an image or a representation in the soul. But it is not clear how sharply Plotinus intends to distinguish between the act of judging, whereby the representation is formed, and the first apprehension of this image by the faculty of representation. The passage from iv.3.29 suggests that the act of sense-perception and the original apprehension of the image by the faculty of representation are simultaneous. For at what previous point could the remembering power have perceived what it is later to recall, if not when the thing was originally perceived? So perhaps Plotinus' actual position is that the perception of something, where "perception" is understood as "perceptual judgement", involves in itself the apprehension of the representation that constitutes the judgement. If this is so, there is no sharp distinction between sense-perception and representation:[50] sense-perception is directed towards the external, but it apprehends its object by means of a judgement that itself is simultaneously apprehended by the faculty of representation. Now, if this account is the correct one – and I think it is quite likely that it is, though I cannot offer decisive arguments – it is misleading to ask for a clear-cut answer to the question of whether

111

it is the faculty of perception or the faculty of representation that is responsible for the unity of the perceiving subject, for these two faculties meet in the act of perception itself. When Plotinus is concerned with the apprehension of the external, he usually talks simply about perception, though this may include the original reception of the image in the faculty of representation. When the focus is on apprehension of what has been perceived in the absence of the sensory affection representation alone is involved.

Plotinus nowhere explicitly discusses the question by which faculty we are aware that we perceive. He does say about intellection, however, that it is the same thing to think and to think that one thinks, i.e., thinking that one thinks is contained in the act of thinking itself, though a logical distinction can be made between the two (II.9.1, 34–46). Aristotle's concern with the question by which faculty we are aware that we see, hear and so forth, has, I think rightly, been taken to show his recognition of the phenomenon of consciousness.[51] Although Plotinus does not discuss this question, that does not mean that he was not concerned with the phenomenon of consciousness. In fact no previous Greek thinker was as much or as clearly concerned with it, even though Plotinus does not say much about consciousness in connection with sense-perception as such. I will not address the subject of consciousness in Plotinus in general, since this is a vast and difficult issue that demands separate treatment, but will confine myself to a few remarks. If we are engaged in a given activity or are in a given state, there may, but need not, be an awareness that we are engaged in the activity or are in the state in question. Plotinus takes as an example a reader who is absorbed in the act of reading, and points out that such a reader is not aware that he is reading. Such second-order awareness would only be a hindrance (I.4.10, 24–34).[52] Although Plotinus does not discuss a case of a pure sense activity in this connection, it seems that he would have to say the same about such cases: while we are seeing, for example, there is not necessarily a second-order awareness *that* we are seeing. Of course this does not mean that we are unconscious when we read or when we see. Plotinus' point is precisely that our consciousness is so wholly engaged in the content of what we read (or perceive) that there is no reflexive awareness that we are doing so. But it is quite clear, even from this same passage, that Plotinus allows for the possibility of such second-order awareness. Presumably it is a function of the faculty of representation, though this is not explicitly said (see I.4.10, 19–22).

VI

The objects of
perception

It is widely held that according to Plotinus perception never reaches to the external things themselves, that perception is always of something in the percipient rather than in the external world.[1] There are two main reasons for this view: (a) Despite Plotinus' whole-hearted expressions of realism about perception in IV.6.1 and elsewhere, it has seemed to his interpreters that his doctrine about the mediation of sensory affections precludes such realism. (b) In an important passage on perception, I.1.7, Plotinus says things that have been understood as an explicit denial of realism. Hence, some interpreters have seen this passage as Plotinus' recognition of a logical consequence of his own position. To this we may add another passage, V.5.1, which in my opinion causes equally severe difficulties for a realist.

It goes without saying that if these interpreters are right, Plotinus is guilty of a serious inconsistency.[2] Moreover, this inconsistency would neither be the hidden, implicit sort of inconsistency which is laid bare only after a scrutiny of the texts and their implications, nor would it be the sort of inconsistency that is likely to arise from an author's uncertainty or ambivalence about a subtle issue. Rather, we would be faced with a patent contradiction. This is, perhaps, a possible situation but not a very probable one. As a matter of principle one should adopt such an interpretation only if there is no alternative. I think that in fact the views of Zeller and Blumenthal are seriously misguided in ways which I will soon explain. My own position on the matter can be stated as follows: I think, firstly, that a fresh look at the two passages, 1.1.7 and v.5.1, which seem to affirm antirealism, will show that this affirmation is merely apparent. Thus, I hold that Plotinus is not badly inconsistent in maintaining a realist position. On the other hand, I do admit that it is a real question whether Plotinus' views about the mediacy of sensory affections *can* allow him to hold the realist position he clearly means to hold. However, in this he does not seem to be any worse off than anyone else who believes in direct realism.

In section 1 of this chapter I deal with 1.1.7 and v.5.1. In the course of that discussion I make some additional remarks about the relation between representation and perception that we discussed in the preceding chapter. In section 2 I deal with the notion of judgement, which is highly relevant to Plotinus' views on the objects of perception.

1 Charges of antirealism

In the first chapters of 1.1, "What is the Organism", Plotinus ponders the question of what is the subject of perception and the emotions. In chapter 7 he comes to the conclusion, which is in accordance with his teaching elsewhere (cf. iv.3.26, 1-12), that the compound (*synamphoteron*) or, which is the same thing, the organism (*zôion*) is the subject of sense-perception and the emotions generally.[3] He then continues:

But then how is it we who perceive? It is because we are not separated from the organism so described, even if other and worthier things are present for us in the whole essence of man, which is made up of many elements.[4] And the soul's power of perception need not be of sensibles, but rather it must be apprehensive of the representations produced by perception in the organism; for these are already intelligible entities. So external perception is the image of this perception of the soul, which is in its essence truer and is contemplation of forms alone, free from affection. From these forms, from which soul alone receives its leadership over the organism, come reasonings, and opinions and acts of intuitive intelligence.[5]

The crucial element in this passage is of course the statement "the soul's power of perception need not be of sensibles, but rather it must be apprehensive of representations produced by perception in the organism". Now, the only way to see this statement as an affirmation of the relevant species of antirealism is to understand the expression "soul's power of perception" as referring to sense-perception. Blumenthal, who interprets this statement in such a way, points out that the word *aisthêsis*, "perception", must be used in two senses in this passage, if the statement is to make sense: the perception attributed to the soul must be something other than perception from which the representations of which the soul is apprehensive arise. He goes on to claim that in the first case *aisthêsis* means sense-perception proper, whereas in the latter it means sensation.[6] Blumenthal is clearly right in holding that "perception" cannot refer to the same phenomenon in both cases, but, I shall argue, he is wrong in his diagnosis of its referents. He, and others who concur with him, may be tempted to take up such a view by the fact that Plotinus often says or implies that perception (evidently meaning sense-perception) is a function of the soul (cf. III.6.1,1-4). This fact, which I do not wish to dispute, does not however justify the assumption.

The assumption might, perhaps, be justified if the perception that Plotinus attributes to the compound (which Blumenthal takes to be sensation as opposed to perception) could not be the same as the perception of which he elsewhere speaks as belonging to the soul. But this is not so, as is evident from a passage in IV.3.26 that we discussed in connection with representation in Chapter V.[7] Plotinus says there that one could regard sense-perception as a function common to body and soul but that memory need not thereby belong to the compound, for the soul has already received the representation (9-12). And a few lines below he says about the compound that if one understands the organism to be the compound of body and soul in the sense that it is a third thing constituted by both, it is nevertheless absurd to say that the organism is neither soul nor body, for the constituents of the organism are not changed in forming the union which makes up the organism (18-22). This passage clearly shows that Plotinus sees nothing against referring to the soul in connection with functions that are to be attributed to the organism, for the organism is a compound of soul and body, and each of these components retains its identity and its separate functions, in the union. But Plotinus often discusses perception without explicitly introducing the organism as an object of reference and speaks simply about the body or the soul (or both) according to his concerns in a given context.[8] Thus, the attribution of perception to the organism is quite compatible with Plotinus' doctrine that indeed it is the soul which perceives (the *krisis*, which is the perception, is done by the soul), but with the instrumentality of the body. Whatever function is exercised with the instrumentality of the body is a function of the compound, the organism.

This understanding of the matter is confirmed even in the context of I.1, where, in chapter 9, Plotinus summarizes the preceding as follows: "So we have distinguished what belongs to the compound and what is proper to the soul in this way: what belongs to the compound is bodily or not without body, but that which does not require body for its activity is proper to the soul" (I.1.9, 15-18). This is evidently meant to apply to what is said in chapter 7. And given that, it becomes clear that what is meant by "the soul's power of perception" as opposed to that of the organism is a contrast between a kind of perception that belongs to the soul without the involvement of the body and a kind of perception in which the body is involved. And this implies in turn that by "the soul's power of perception" Plotinus cannot mean sense-perception; for as we have seen he elsewhere insists on the point that sense-perception is a function of the compound. Thus, his view is evidently that the soul's perception in I.1.7 is a sort of internal apprehension different from sense-perception; the latter is the sort of perception attributed to the compound.

A bit more needs to be said about Plotinus' use of the terms *aisthêsis* and *aisthanesthai*, "to perceive". In Plotinus these words are by no means restricted to sense-perception. He uses them to denote any sort of mental apprehension.[9] We find an interesting instance of such an extended use in IV.3.29, 20-1, where Plotinus says that the power responsible for memory must previously have perceived what it is to remember, and that the object of this perception is an image (*phantasma*).[10] In order to see that what Plotinus has in mind by "the soul's power of perception" in I.1.7 is the sort of apprehension that belongs to the faculty of representation, let us compare the latter passage with the passages on perception and memory in IV.3.26 and 29. The apprehension proper to the faculty of representation is apprehension without the involvement of the body, for the body is not directly involved in memory. And the most natural way to understand the contrast between the soul's perception and that of the organism in I.1.7 is to take the former to be a sort of apprehension in which the body is not directly involved. Plotinus refers to the objects apprehended by the power responsible for memory as *phantasmata* (IV.3.29, 23). But in the same discussion he also describes these objects as intelligible representations (IV.3.26, 25-32), which is exactly the description of the objects of the soul's perception given in I.1.7. Further, we may note that the perception attributed to the compound is said to be of the external, and that this is evidently intended as a contrast with the soul's perception, which therefore must be of something internal.

Consideration of other passages leads to the same conclusion. In v.3.2, 7-14 Plotinus says that the faculty of reason makes an evaluation (*epikrisis*) of the images or representations that derive from sense-perception by combination and division (cf. i.1.9, 10-13). This process, which clearly involves the apprehension of already internalized representations, is an example of the sort of internal perception mentioned in i.1.7.[11] This act of evaluation, which is evidently subsequent to the original sense-perception of the object, is implicitly contrasted with sense-perception understood as apprehension of the external (cf. v.3.2, 2-6).

Concerning i.1.7, then, we can summarize our conclusions as follows: There is no compelling reason to understand Plotinus as affirming antirealism in i.1.7. Both the internal evidence and Plotinus' statements elsewhere suggest a different interpretation. The soul's perception, as contrasted with that of the organism, is a power of apprehension that belongs to the soul without any involvement of the body. The objects of this power are internal intelligible entities that may result from sense-perception. More precisely – if my contentions in the previous chapter about the identity of perceptual judgements and the generation of intelligible representations are correct – sense-perception *is* the generation of such representations in the soul. This view is in fact supported by i.1.7, where Plotinus speaks of intelligible representations in the organism: these must be the judgements passed on the external object (cf. iv.4.23, 31-2). But, nonetheless, these representations, themselves objects of apprehension, are different from the external objects of sense-perception in that they are intelligible and internal.

The other passage in the *Enneads* that seems to affirm antirealism is the beginning of the famous and important treatise "That the Intelligibles are not Outside the Intellect, and on the Good" (v.5.[32]). Plotinus begins by affirming that the Intellect is free from error, that its knowledge neither involves guesswork nor ambivalence and that it is not founded on demonstration. In fact all the things it knows are self-evident to it (*autothen*) (v.5.1, 1-9). Then, he continues, arguing against some unnamed opponents:

But now, as to the knowledge that is admitted to be self-evident, whence is its clarity supposed to come to the Intellect and whence does it acquire the confidence that this is so [i.e. self-evident]? For even in the case of those objects of perception, that seem to have the greatest trustworthiness, one can have doubt whether they have their apparent reality not in the substrates, but in the affections, and Intellect or reason are needed as judges; and even if it is conceded that that which perception is to apprehend is in sensible substrates, it is nevertheless the case that what is known through perception is an image (*eidôlon*) of the thing, and perception does not grasp the thing itself. For it remains outside.[12]

For our concerns, the last three lines are the crucial part of the passage. Neither Zeller nor Blumenthal, both of whom want to maintain an antirealist interpretation of Plotinus on the basis of I.1.7, have comments on this passage. Clark, who advocates a realist interpretation, points out explicitly that this passage may present a difficulty for a realist view. He dismisses it, however, rather quickly, claiming that it is likely to be an *ad homines* argument against the Epicureans.[13] The latter interpretation derives from Bréhier, who thinks that Plotinus is concerned with Epicurean doctrines in this passage, and he takes the occurrence of the word *eidôlon* to be one sign of this.[14] Now, I think, for reasons that I will give shortly, that the word *eidôlon* is not being used in the Epicurean sense at all. And if so, we are left with Clark's problem.

There are two good reasons against interpreting the last three lines of v.5.1 as an *ad hominem* argument against the Epicureans. It is true that in the preceding lines Plotinus is evidently talking about the doctrines of some other philosophers. There is however no compelling reason to suppose that these are Epicurean doctrines: the expression "the greatest trustworthiness" (*pistis enargestatê*) is not a technical Epicurean expression, and there is nothing in these lines that suggests the Epicureans rather than other philosophers who hold that perception is a source of genuine knowledge. It seems to me that if one wants to speculate whose doctrines Plotinus has in mind, the Peripatetics or the Stoics would be a more plausible guess: one could for example understand Plotinus' remarks about demonstration and perception as a criticism of the Aristotelian model of scientific knowledge, according to which scientific knowledge is demonstrative and the principles of demonstration ultimately founded on sense-perception.[15] But even granting, for the sake of argument, that in lines 9-15 Plotinus has Epicurean doctrines in mind, it does not follow that the word *eidôlon* in line 18 is to be understood in the sense of the Epicureans. For, firstly, in the last statement of the passage above Plotinus appears to be stating his own views rather than reporting the views of others. Secondly, Plotinus himself frequently uses the word *eidôlon* in a semi-technical sense, which is only a distant relative of the sense which it has in the Epicurean theory of vision. In Plotinus *eidôlon* usually means "image" or "reflection" in the sense in which an ontologically posterior item is said to be an image of an ontologically prior one. Thus, standardly in Plotinus, *eidôlon* is used synonymously with *eikôn* and with *mimêma*.[16] This point holds not only as a general remark about Plotinus' use of *eidôlon*. Moreover, as we shall see, further consideration of v.5 shows that the sense of *eidôlon* in the passage we are considering must be this standard Plotinian sense.

In the beginning of the next chapter, v.5.2, Plotinus says, by way of summarizing his conclusions:

One must neither look for the intelligibles outside [the Intellect] nor suppose that the Intellect contains representations (*typoi*) of the things that are (*ta onta*), nor should we deprive the Intellect of truth and thereby make the intelligibles unknowable and nonexistent and moreover annihilate the Intellect itself. Rather, if one is to suppose that there is knowledge and truth and preserve being – and this means knowledge of the quiddity of each thing (*tou ti hekaston estin*) and not knowledge of its quality (*tou poion ti*), inasmuch as in that case we obtain an image (*eidôlon*) and trace (*ichnos*) and not the things themselves and we do not come together with them and mingle ourselves with them – we must attribute all this to the true Intellect.   (v.5.2, 1-9)

For our concerns the interesting feature of this passage is the contrast between the knowledge of the quiddity of each thing with knowledge of its quality, and the identification of the latter with knowing a mere *eidôlon* or image. For the context and the connection of this passage with the preceding v.5.1 make it virtually certain that *eidôlon* here is used in the same sense as in v.5.1, 18.[17] First, let us note that even though sense-perception is not mentioned in v.5.2, 1 ff., perception must be what Plotinus has in mind by "knowledge of the quality of each thing". For, as we pointed out, he is summarizing and generalizing the point of the preceding chapter, where intellection is contrasted with perception. Furthermore, that perception is of the quality of things as opposed to their quiddity or substance is in accordance with Plotinus' teaching elsewhere, as is the view that qualities or forms in matter are images of ontologically prior forms.[18] Let us now consider what implications this has for the interpretation of v.5.1, 15-19.

Considering the very end of the passage quoted above from v.5.1. by itself, "it is nevertheless the case that what is known through perception is an image of the thing and perception does not grasp the thing itself. For it remains outside", one might easily

119

think that the contrast between the image and the thing itself is the contrast between an external object "as it is in itself" and something in us of which we are immediately aware, a contrast familiar from modern philosophy. But Plotinus' text, even in v.5.1, speaks against such an interpretation. For he writes that "even if it is conceded that that which perception is to apprehend is in sensible substrates, it is nevertheless the case that what is known through perception is an image of the thing, and perception does not grasp the thing itself". Thus, the image spoken of here is clearly assumed to be a feature of the external objects themselves, and hence it seems that the contrast at issue is not a contrast between the external objects or objective features of the objects and features in or of the percipient. The latter contrast was at issue in the first part of the passage from v.5.1 quoted above. Here, Plotinus is making a new point.

Now v.5.2, 1 ff. requires that we understand the word "image" here as denoting the quality of the thing as opposed to its quiddity. And this in turn indicates that by "the thing itself" is meant the quiddity or substance of the thing. This is evidently compatible with regarding the image as an objective feature as the context seems to require rather than as a subjective one. Furthermore, it is perfectly in line with Plotinus' views to use the expression "the thing itself" to refer to the quiddity of each thing. For after all the sensible world as a whole is an image of the intelligible world which is the real thing itself.[19]

Nevertheless, it seems that here in v.5.1 "the thing itself" does not refer to an item on the level of the supreme Intellect. The statement that "the thing itself remains outside" suggests that the "thing itself" is here understood to be internal to the substrate in question. And this does not seem to fit items on the level of the Intellect. On the other hand, we know that Plotinus posits intermediate intelligibles which stand between the Intellect and the forms in matter. These intermediate intelligibles are the inherent *logoi* or *physis*, of which the perceptible qualities are inferior manifestations.[20] Moreover, he elsewhere speaks of such intermediate intelligibles in a way that shows how the expression "the thing itself" here in v.5.1 might naturally be taken to refer to the internal nature of the thing as opposed to its perceptible form. A passage from vi.3.15 is particularly revealing:

It was stated concerning the quality that it, mingled together with the other determinations of matter and quantity, makes up the complement of the sensible substance; and it looks as if this so-called substance turns out to be this mixture of many, not a quiddity but rather a quality, and that the rational formative principle (*logos*) of fire, for instance, rather signifies the quiddity, the figure which it produces, the quality. Thus, the formative principle of man is the quiddity, but what results from it in the bodily nature, an image (*eidôlon*) of the formative principle, is rather a quality. As a likeness on painting, colours and painting stuff, is called "Socrates" by virtue of there being a man, the visible Socrates, so also the sensible Socrates, colours and shapes of a different sort that are imitations (*mimêma*) of those in the formative principle, is Socrates by virtue of there being a formative principle. But this formative principle stands in the same relation [i.e. image–model relation] to the truest principle (*logos*) of man.   (VI.3.15, 24–38)

The relevance of this passage to our concerns is obvious: the formative principle is described as quiddity as opposed to quality, and the quality is identified with the perceptible features of things and described as an image (*eidôlon, mimêma*) of their formative principles, which by contrast are the real thing.

I will henceforth take it to be established that the contrast between the image and the thing itself in v.1.5 is a contrast between the superficial features of things grasped by perception and their internal nature and not a contrast between the subjective and the objective.

2 Perceptions as judgements

It has repeatedly been mentioned that according to Plotinus perceptions are judgements (*kriseis*).[21] Now let us consider the notion of *krisis* as such. Here we encounter the same sort of difficulty that we have so often run into before, namely that Plotinus does not really explain, either through examples or by other means, what he has in mind. Plotinus is by no means the first Greek thinker for whom *krisis* is a key notion in the context of perception. Virtually all the philosophers who are known to have influenced Plotinus' views on this subject used *krisis* or the corresponding verb, *krinein*, in connection with perception.[22] And when he makes a point of saying that perceptions are judgements as opposed to affections he seems to be echoing Alexander of Aphrodisias.[23]

Unfortunately for us who are trying to understand Plotinus, the term *krisis* had a very broad use, which makes Plotinus' failure to spell out the details of his theory particularly regrettable. The root meaning of the verb *krinein* is "to separate". But *krinein* came quite early to be used to denote various kinds of mental acts which

121

involve an element of separating or picking out: choosing, deciding, distinguishing and so forth. From this came the sense of "to
judge".[24] In the ancient literature on perception, however – and
this is particularly clear in the writings of Aristotle and Alexander
– *krinein* and *krisis* most often retain an association with the notion
of difference, reflecting the original sense of "picking out":[25] the
work of the senses is seen as that of picking out objects or features
of objects in the environment. This picking out is in turn possible
by virtue of there being differences in the environment that are
somehow "taken in" by the senses. Translators often try to
capture this aspect of *krisis* by rendering it as "discrimination" or
"discernment". I have used the latter term myself in the presenta-
tions of the views of Aristotle and Alexander above.

Appropriate as it sometimes is to render *krisis* as "discrimination" or "discernment", I think it would nevertheless be misleading to do so in translating the statement that perceptions are *kriseis*,
as it appears in Alexander and Plotinus. I believe that there the
broader term "judgement" is more appropriate. In order to see
this let us consider what Alexander has to say about *krisis* in his *De
Anima*. Alexander makes a distinction between practical (*praktikai*)
and judicative (*kritikai*) faculties of the soul.[26] The distinguishing
feature of the latter is that their acts contain truth or falsity (Bruns,
66, 9-10). Perceiving, imagining, assenting, opining, knowing
and intuiting are all listed as instances of *krisis*.[27] Alexander thus
uses *krisis* to cover all varieties of cognition. He makes it quite
clear that perceptions are supposed to be *kriseis* in the same sense as
these other mental acts listed. In modern parlance we might call
his judicative faculties "cognitive faculties", because his *kritikai
dynameis* seem to cover exactly the cognitive functions. But the
traditional term "judgement" and the adjective "judicative" are
quite in order as renderings of *krisis* and *kritikos*: "judgement" is a
wide term that can be taken to cover all the mental operations
listed by Alexander. Even if it is true that in the context of
perception "discrimination" or "discernment" often indicate
aspects of what is meant by *krisis* that "judgement" fails to show,
the former pair of terms tends to conceal the unity of the notion of
krisis that Alexander wants to emphasize.

So far we have mostly been talking about *krisis* in Alexander.
But the fact that Plotinus is clearly echoing Alexander in declaring
that perceptions are *kriseis*, strongly suggests that he wants to
make precisely the same point, i.e., that perceptions are judgements, something to which truth and falsity apply, rather than
specifically discriminatory powers. Internal evidence suggests the

same: Plotinus holds that no form of cognition is an affection.[28] By subsuming perception under the general heading of *krisis* as he does in III.6.1 Plotinus is putting it in a class with cognitive powers in general and thereby separating it from affections.

The statements "this is blue", "this is a man", "this is far away", "this is plausible", are all possible cases of judgement. But since the scope of judgement is much wider than that of perception, it does not follow that all these are possible cases of perception. If the preceding account of what Plotinus intends by saying that perceptions are *kriseis* is correct, the question arises what are the distinguishing features of those judgements that are perceptions. A possible answer to this question is that perception is limited to the judgements of the special sensibles and that other judgements, even those which concern whatever may be presently affecting the senses, say, "this is a man", are the work of reason. Albinus, for instance, holds such a view.[29] But there are no indications that Plotinus understands perception so narrowly, even though he holds that the special sensibles are somehow primary sense-objects (cf. II.8.1, 13). On the contrary: Plotinus clearly implies that the judgement that something is beautiful may be the work of perception (I.6.3). In V.3.3, 1-5 he says that the power of perception sees a man and gives its representation to the faculty of reason. The context indicates that "sees a man" is to be understood intentionally. In II.8.1, 45 vision is said to measure (*metrein*) the sizes of things. And in I.1.9, 11-12 Plotinus says it happens that "the perception of the common entity[30] sees falsely before reason passes an evaluation (*epikrinein*)". In the context Plotinus is trying – not very convincingly – to show that the soul is faultless when the body is not involved, and hence error must be due to its association with the body. I take it that the *epikrisis* involved here is subsequent to a prior *krisis* that is the perception of the common entity (cf. V.3.2, 8). Now, if error is thus to be found in the work of the faculty of perception, it is surely not likely that such error is only supposed to be in judgements of the proper sensibles, about which we are least liable to err according to the Aristotelian doctrine. When Plotinus speaks of evaluation of the perception of the common entity, it is more likely that he has in mind reconsideration of such perceptual judgements as "the oar is bent" or "the tower is round", which in turn presupposes that such judgements can count as perceptions. I conclude therefore, that for Plotinus sense-perception includes all judgements that can fill the blanks in "I see that —", "I hear that—", and so on, when the perception words in question are used to refer to the activity of the senses and not metaphorically.[31]

But granting that this is so, nothing has yet been said about what are the marks of perceptual judgements as such. It can be assumed that perception is necessarily of something presently acting on the senses. This is implied by the statement that perceptions are acts with respect to affections (III.6.1, 2). But such a characterization includes too much: I may judge of the book which is presently acting on my eyes that it cost £8.00, even though I do not *see* that it cost £8.00. Plotinus gives certain indications of the further requirements that perception must satisfy.

In Plotinus' view perception is immediate in a way that knowledge attained by the use of reasoning and memory is not.[32] He says that perception shows different things but does not give an account of them.[33] Adding these points to what has already been said, we can conclude that for Plotinus perceptual judgements are judgements that are immediately passed about objects presently acting on the senses, and that these judgements do not involve an account of why the objects are such as they are judged to be, but only affirm that such and such is there. This seems to rule out judgements such as "this book cost £8.00", as these are normally made.

It may seem that every judgement must be based on evidence and hence involve an inference or reasoning. If so, it looks as if Plotinus cannot maintain both that perception does not involve reasoning and that perceptions are judgements.[34] And even if it is admitted that some perceptions do not involve reasoning – perhaps those of the special sensibles – there may remain a feeling that others surely must, for instance the perception that something is far away. In answering this let us note that when Plotinus speaks of reasoning he often emphasizes that reasoning is a temporal process whereby the mind moves stepwise from premises to conclusion in an internal dialogue.[35] It is reasonable to suppose that when he denies that perception involves reasoning, he has in mind this sort of step by step process. And this is in fact in accordance with ordinary intuitions: those judgements that we call perceptions are direct apprehensions at least in the sense that they are not apparently inferential. Plotinus once uses the word "read" (*anagignôskein*) to describe the act of the sense of hearing (IV.6.2, 14). Generalizing from this metaphor, sense-perception can be viewed as immediate in the way that the trained reader's apprehension of clearly printed words is immediate: the trained reader can hardly be said to infer what words are printed on the page; he immediately knows.

VII

Perceptions as Acts and Forms in Perception

1 Perceptions as acts

The notion of act (*energeia*) is an Aristotelian borrowing, which Plotinus, like Aristotle, uses in various contexts. As a first approach to Plotinus' notion of *energeia* in connection with perception, it will be instructive to compare his views with those of Aristotle. But first, a remark about terminology: The term *energeia* in Aristotle has been translated variously as "act", "activity", "actuality", "actualization", and "realization". As will become clear, I think that so far as Plotinus is concerned, his notion of *energeia* is best captured by "act" or "activity", though "actualization" may sometimes be appropriate. But since we are concerned with finding what it means for him to say that something is *energeia*, and since a choice between the different English words listed above may prejudge the question at issue, I will use the Greek term to begin with.

Several commentators have remarked that Plotinus' description of perceptions as *energeiai* shows that he thinks of perception as something active, where "active" is contrasted with "passive" in the sense according to which things are said to be passive when they are "mere recipients" or do not contribute anything of their own. Now, I think that this interpretation of Plotinus is quite right and that the point is an important one. However, it seems to me that it is far from self-evident that this is what the term *energeia* suggests, especially if we consider its Aristotelian origin. According to Aristotle and, as we shall see, Plotinus as well, the notion of

126

energeia is correlated with that of *dynamis* (potency). But on Aristotle's view potencies may be either active or passive, or, to put it more precisely, according to Aristotle, for x to act on y, x must have a potency to act and y must have a corresponding potency to be acted on. When x acts on y, there is just one *energeia*, which is the actualization of x's potency to act *and* y's potency to be acted on (*Phys.* 202a 13 ff.).

Aristotle uses the dative forms of *dynamis* and *energeia* in a special technical way: the bronze is said to be potentially (*dynamei*) a statue before the sculptor gives it the shape, and actually (*energeiai*, dat.) a statue after it has received the shape. The same can be said of motion: the billiard ball may be either potentially or actually moving depending on whether its potency of being moved is being actualized or not. Thus, this technical use of the dative forms is systematically related to the non-technical use: X is actually F, if and only if the actualization of its potency of becoming F is occurrent. Aristotle maintains that everything which is potentially F becomes actually F by being acted on by something which is already actually F (*Met.* ix, 1049b 23-9). It seems to follow from this that all potencies corresponding to being potentially F are passive potencies.

Now, let us turn to Plotinus' general account of potency and *energeia* in the short treatise "On What Is Potentially and What Is Actually" (ii.5.[25]). The most striking difference between Plotinus' and Aristotle's views in this respect is that Plotinus denies that there is any such thing as a passive potency, i.e., a potency to be affected. Plotinus, perhaps influenced by the Stoic notion of *dynamis*, wants to restrict the term *dynamis* to "power to act" (ii.5.1). Thus, while he allows that there are such things as being potentially F, for instance, the bronze is potentially (*dynamei*) a statue, he denies that there are necessarily corresponding potencies (*dynameis*) in the things that are said to be potentially such-and-such (ii.5.1, 21-24). However, Plotinus seems to allow that things which have powers to act, *dynameis*, can be said to be *dynamei* when the powers are not acting (see ii.5.2, 17-23).

This would lead one to suppose that on Plotinus' view *energeia* is closely related to *poiein*, to act. And in fact this is what Plotinus' discussion of *poiein* and *paschein* in his commentary on the Aristotelian categories in vi.1.15-22 confirms. There we find him suggesting that the name of the category corresponding to *poiein* is *energeia* rather than *poiêsis* (vi.1.15, 10-11) and in his discussion in the subsequent chapters the terms *energeia* and the corresponding verb *energein* sometimes replace *poiein*. Towards the end of the discussion, however, Plotinus says that one should not take all *energeiai* to be *poiêseis* (VI.1.22, 27-8). As an example of *energeia* that is not a *poiêsis* he mentions thinking. The idea seems to be that only transitive actions are rightly called *poiêseis*. Earlier, however, in VI.1.19, 22 ff., Plotinus distinguishes between transitive and intransitive kinds of *poiein* so that there he seems to allow that intransitive acts are *poiêseis*, which is puzzling. But this is not a question of primary importance for us. The main point of concern is that, according to Plotinus, if something is an *energeia* of x, it is not an affection of x and vice versa. In VI.1.22, 1-10 he reaches the following conclusion about *poiein* and *paschein*:

Thus, a being is affected by virtue of having in itself a movement of alteration of whatever sort. To act (*poiein*) is either to have in oneself a free movement originating from oneself or a movement that is completed in another but originating from oneself. In both cases there is movement, but the difference that distinguishes action from affection is that action, insofar as it is action, remains unaffected, whereas what is affected is disposed in a different way than it was before, the substance (*ousia*) of the affected thing not gaining anything thereby, as it is some other thing which is affected in the generation of a substance.

It is clear that the mutual exclusivity of *poiein* and *paschein* also holds for *energein* versus *paschein*. For Plotinus either uses *energein* interchangeably with *poiein*, or restricts it to what he calls here "free movement originating from the thing", i.e. intransitive acts.

The foregoing considerations have important implications for our understanding of *energeia* in connection with perception. The fact that Plotinus borrows the term *energeia* from Aristotle as well as the fact that both philosophers use this term in their respective accounts of perception may give the impression that they must be making the same or a similar point. This is however not necessarily the case.

It has proved notoriously difficult to extract one consistent account of perception from Aristotle's discussion in *De Anima*, and much of the difficulty centres around the notions of affection, potency and act. Aristotle describes perception as a special form of affection. What makes it special, it seems, is the fact that the subject of perception is not changed as a result of the event (cf. *De An.* 416b 32-417b 16). We shall come back to this notion that the subject of perception is not changed, for in this Plotinus follows Aristotle. But for now let us just note that even if perception is an affection in this special sense, this is quite compatible with its being a passive potency in the sense indicated above, i.e. it may well be one of those potencies whose actualization is the result of the action of something else. In *De Anima* there are indeed indications that this is supposed to be the case. For Aristotle says that in perception the sense (or the sense-organ; Aristotle vacillates between the two), being potentially such as the object is actually, becomes so actually.[1] It seems that what Aristotle calls *energeia* in perception, the actualization of what is potentially perceiving, is just this transition whereby the sense is affected by the object, or perhaps the state that is the end-result of this affection (cf. *De An.*, 426a ff.).[2]

Now, however this may be according to Aristotle, it cannot be Plotinus' view that perception is a passive potency in any sense; and it is also clear that what he calls *energeia* in the context of perception is a subsequent event in the soul and not just the state brought about by the affection. The initial lines of III.6.1, where Plotinus says that "perceptions are not affections but *energeiai* concerning affections and judgements", show a clear contrast between the *energeia* and the affections in perception. It is also clear from this passage that the *energeia* is something subsequent to, and hence quite distinct from, the affections. This is also what our general account of *energeia* in Plotinus suggests: *energeiai* are for him correlated with active potencies, so that nothing which is merely the result of an external action on x could be an *energeia* of x. Now, we also find Plotinus referring to perception and the individual senses as potencies. In these places it is indeed said or implied that they are active ones.[3]

If the foregoing is correct, we can vindicate the claim that, according to Plotinus, perception is something active and that this is implied in describing perceptions as *energeiai*. Now, it is not at all easy to define the intuitive notion of being an active as opposed to a passive participant in some event or affair. I think that perhaps the best we can do is to ask of each of the participants whether its role in the event or affair is something which we would intuitively describe as doing something rather than having something done to one. This is of course less an analysis of what is meant by "being active" than a handy paraphrase of it. But suppose we content ourselves with relying on this as a kind of test. It then follows that in Plotinus' view the soul is active in perception, because the description of its role as an *energeia* implies that the soul is conceived of as doing something rather than having something done to it. Of course, just saying this does not explain why Plotinus thinks that the function of the soul in perception is intuitively a case of an action or doing something: so far we have only said that this is how he conceives of it, not why he does so. So let us raise the question: what is it about perception that makes it an act – hereafter we shall translate *energeia* by "act" – rather than an affection?

This is a question which Plotinus nowhere explicitly addresses. However, I think we can make some reasonable conjectures as to why Plotinus holds this view. Once sensory affections have been identified with mere non-epistemic sensations, it will appear that what is needed in addition, in order for there to be a complete perception, is not something which is appropriate to call an affection at all. This additional element is the judgement that we discussed in the preceding chapter. And given that the perceptions themselves are identified with the judgements, it is not at all surprising that Plotinus insists that perceptions are acts. For intuitively to judge of something is an act (and what judges is active); it is doing something rather than having something done to one. Perception is also said to tell or announce, and vision is said to measure the sizes and distances of things by the distinctness of their colours.[4] These operations, which, I take it, are all subsumed under the more general term *krisis*, suggest the same: to tell, announce and measure are all acts as opposed to undergoings.

The foregoing gives us some explanation of why Plotinus says that perceptions are acts and of what he means by this. The issue is however more complicated than the above account may suggest. For instance, we may agree to an intuitive distinction between acts and affections and may concur that perceptions are to be classified as acts, but still ask why nothing which is genuinely an act can involve an affection of the agent. It seems that the classification of something as an act implies only that the agent is not acted on by something else. Why could it not be affected by its own action? Now, one answer to this question might run along the following lines: it is simply a confusion of terms to call "affections" those occurrences in an agent that constitute the realization of its actions; by definition, only those occurrences that are the results of the act of another are affections. It seems to me that while this answer is in a sense correct, it is too dogmatic and not quite to the point. The important question is whether agents can be changed by acting. And while it is true that acts are realizations of potencies or powers and realizations of powers, so described, are not *ipso facto* genuine changes of the agent, it would need some argument to show that the powers are not changed by acting, that they do not become worn out, for instance.[5] As we shall see in a little while,

Plotinus is, quite rightly, not content with a dogmatic answer to this problem.

This issue is of considerable importance. We have mentioned in previous chapters that Plotinus wants to maintain the soul is unaffectable, and since perception is a *prima facie* case of the affection of the soul, he specifically maintains that the soul is not affected in perception. Now, it is evident that the characterization of perceptions as acts can be seen, and is to be seen, in the context of the doctrine about the soul's immunity to affection. However, unless the possibility we just brought up is disposed of, it has not been established that perception does not involve an affection of the soul itself.

A consideration of Stoic and other previous Greek theories of perception will help us see the weight of the present problem. For instance, the Stoic distinction between an external affection and an assent of the principal part of the soul parallels Plotinus' distinction between affections and judgements. I think it is fair to say that the Stoic assent is intuitively an act just as much as Plotinus' judgements.[6] However, the Stoics held that assent results in an alteration in the principal part of the soul.[7] Further, the whole idea of describing perception and memory on the model of sealings with a signet suggests that that which perceives or remembers is affected. Even if Plotinus wants to reject this analogy and argues forcefully against it, it seems that he cannot avoid employing its characteristic terminology, namely the terms *typos* and *typôsis*.[8] The upshot of this is that Plotinus cannot take it for granted that the agent in perception is unaffected even if the epistemic functions of the soul in perception are intuitively acts.

In III.6.1 Plotinus implies that the judgements which constitute perceptions leave intelligible representations in the soul, and that these representations are not alterations. In chapter 2 he continues along the same lines:

For just as sight, which has both a potential and an actual existence, remains essentially the same [when it is potentially and when it is actually], and its act (*energeia*) is not an alteration, but it simultaneously approaches what it has; in the same way the reasoning part is related to the Intellect and sees, and this is the power of thinking; there arises no stamp (*sphragis*) inside, but it has what it sees, though in another way it does not have it; it has it by knowing it, but it does not have it in [the sense] that something is put away in it from the seeing, like a shape in wax. (III.6.2, 33–42)

And a few lines later he adds:

For in general the acts of things without matter take place without any accompanying alteration, otherwise they would perish; it is much truer to say that they remain unaltered, and that being affected when acting belongs to things with matter. But if that which is immaterial is affected, it has no ground of permanence; just as in the case of sight what is affected is the eye, and opinions are like acts of vision. (III.6.2, 49-54)

There are several comments to be made on these passages. Firstly, it is worth pointing out that the quoted material, as well as the intermediate lines left out, constitute an argument aimed at showing that the soul is not altered by having opinions (*doxai*). This explains the reference to opinion in the last line. In the course of this argument Plotinus also argues that neither perception, thought nor memory are affected by acting, the point being that opinion is analogous to these. Secondly, it emerges in the last passage quoted that the reason why perception and other psychic activities are not accompanied by affections is that the agents, i.e. the psychic powers in question, are without matter, incorporeal. And this sheds some light on the difference between the Stoic notion of *typoi*, which Plotinus rejects, and his own: the kind of *typoi* which Plotinus evidently admits in III.6.1, and which are said not to be affections, are incorporeal; they are not to be thought of on the model of stamps on wax or some such material.

So far so good. But what is it about incorporeal things which makes them by their very nature unaffectable?[9] Firstly, let us consider what Plotinus has to say in the passage just quoted. He claims that if incorporeal things were to be affected, they would perish and that they would have "no ground of permanence" (*ouk echei hôi menei*). Now, this can be taken in at least two ways: (a) Plotinus might be saying that anyone who claims that incorporeal things such as the soul are affectable is thereby admitting that the soul may be perishable; this is a consequence which cannot be accepted, and hence the premise that leads to it must be rejected. (b) Plotinus may be understood as saying – and this is what the expression "has no ground of permanence" rather suggests – that incorporeal things differ from those that have matter in that any change or affection in the case of the former would be a destructive change whereas some degree of permanence, though not imperishability, is granted to things with matter by virtue of the permanence of the underlying matter. In other words, immaterial things have nothing that would endure a genuine change. In this case an implicit assumption of Plotinus' remark would be that since it *obviously* is the same thing which perceived, remembered etc. yesterday as perceives and remembers today, we must reject the hypothesis that the soul is affected at all.[10]

So it seems that Plotinus thinks that the unaffectability of the soul in perception is guaranteed by its incorporeality. This is however not all he has to say about the matter. In the former of the two passages quoted above he says that "the act [of vision] is not an alteration but it simultaneously approaches what it has" (III.6.2, 35-6). This statement is admittedly rather obscure. It seems to suggest, however, that the reason why an act of vision is not an alteration is that the power of vision already has what is contained in its act. This would make sense: if the act of vision is only an activation of something which is already present in the agent, it seems reasonable to say that it is not altered by activating it. The difficulty is to see how the power of vision can be said already to have what is contained in the act of vision. Plotinus holds the same doctrine about memory: to remember is only to activate something which is already there. But it is much easier to see in the case of memory why it would be suggested that memory is an activation of something that is already there. Both intuitively, and according to Plotinus' particular theory of memory, memory is the calling forth of something that already has entered the mind (cf. IV.6.3). But how can the same be said about perception? I suggest an answer to this question in the next section.

2 Forms in perception

"Forms in perception" is of course a subject that we have repeatedly brought up. Hence, I will to some extent be covering familiar ground. But I do this only in order to introduce some novel and important ideas. These, it will be seen, are based more on hints here and there in the text than on clear evidence. However, the value of these ideas lies in the fact that they enable us to see a certain unity in the account we have given of Plotinus' views and to suggest answers to certain important questions.

Let us first recall the essentials of what we know about forms in Plotinus. There are the Forms in the Intellect which are the archetypes of all other forms; and there are the forms in matter, also called qualities, which together with their underlying matter, make up sensibles (bodies). In between these two extremes there are other kinds of forms: we have seen that within sensible things there are *logoi* or forms which must be distinguished both from the

Forms on the level of Intellect and from forms in the sense of qualities – perceptible manifestations of the intermediate forms in the mirror of matter. Ensouled beings have forms in still another way. If the account given in Chapter IV and in section 3 of Chapter VI is correct, Plotinus holds that the *sense-organs* receive forms that are intermediate between forms in matter and intelligible forms. Moreover, the *soul* contains the forms of all things, and *we*, Plotinus says, "possess the forms in two ways, in our soul, in a manner of speaking unfolded and separated, in the Intellect, all together" (I.1.8, 6–8). A few comments on this are in order. As we noted in Chapter II, Plotinus holds that we, i.e. individual human souls, have a counterpart on the level of Intellect and that in a sense the true self exists on that level. As I.1.8 makes clear this is his reason for saying that we possess the Forms in the Intellect. The unfolded forms we possess in our souls, on the other hand, are the familiar entities that we have repeatedly come across in our account of perception: they are the entities that in I.1.7, III.6.1 and IV.3.26 are called (intelligible) representations (*typoi noêtoi*) and images (*phantasmata*) in IV.3.29 and V.3.2.[11] It is also this sort of form to which Plotinus is referring in IV.4.23, 32 when he says that the affection of the sense-organ becomes a form in the soul.[12]

It is clear that Plotinus conceives of all these different levels of forms as a hierarchy in which the levels, starting from qualities in matter, are characterized by increasing unity. One might think, however, that the forms that are internal to sensibles, and of which the perceptible qualities are manifestations, cannot be on a level with the other sorts of intermediate forms whose function is to account for certain kinds of cognition; hence it may seem that the different levels of forms that we have mentioned cannot be visualized on a single vertical line. But, interestingly, Plotinus does see the forms in nature and the forms in the soul as the same sort of thing. For the forms in the soul do not only function as elements in cognition, they are also the models on which the craftsman produces his work, and this is exactly analogous to the function of the forms in nature[13].

It was suggested above that one could make sense of Plotinus' statement in III.6.2, 35–6 that "the act [of vision] is not an alteration but simultaneously approaches what it has", by supposing that perception involves the activation of something already present in the soul.[14] Now, there are actually some remarks in the *Enneads* to the effect that perception depends on the previous presence of forms in the soul. Plotinus also says that we can perceive the harmony present in sensibles because the sensitive man fits it to the intelligible harmony.[15] And he goes on to say that the man on the level of Intellect has intellectual perception of the intelligible counterparts of sensible objects, and that owing to this fact the lower man has their concepts in the forms of images (*eiche tous logous en mimêsei*). Unfortunately Plotinus does not explain the significance of this possession of the concepts of things. But there are other passages suggesting that sense-perception depends on our possession of Forms. In i.6.3, 1–5 he says that we perceive beauty in bodies by fitting it to the Form of beauty inside of ourselves, thus using the latter to judge beauty as we use a straight-edge for judging straightness. The idea that forms function as standards of judgement is also to be found in v.3.4, where Plotinus says of discursive reason that it judges what it judges by means of standards that it contains in itself (cf. v.3.3, 8).

One might suppose that Plotinus subscribes to a doctrine like the wax-tablet hypothesis presented (and rejected) in the *Theaete-tus* 191 C ff. and that this is the reason why he thinks that perception depends on the prior possession of Forms: the Forms do the job of the pre-existent imprints on the wax-tablet.[16] As we have seen Plotinus talks about fitting what comes in through perception to the Forms we previously possess, and this may indeed suggest something like the wax-tablet account. But this can hardly be the complete account, for it seems to require that every perceptual judgement involves a jump all the way up to the Intellect itself. Plotinus cannot mean to maintain that. Hence, let us consider whether something more can be said about the function of the prior possession of Forms in perception.

The unfolded forms that we possess in our souls are something like what we nowadays call "concepts", "notions" or "mental representations". This emerges from the following passage in iv.3.30:

Perhaps, what is received in the faculty of representation is the verbal expression (*logos*) that accompanies the thought. For the thought is partless, and so long as it is not expressed externally it escapes us. But the verbal expression unfolds the thought, and acting from it towards the faculty of representation it reveals the thought as it were in a mirror and thus comes about its apprehension and also its preservation, memory. For this reason also, even though the soul is constantly moving towards intellection, our apprehension of it first takes place when it comes to the faculty of representation. For we are always engaged in intellection. But we are not always aware of it. This is so because that which receives the thoughts not only receives thoughts but also perceptions from the other side. (iv.3.30, 5–16)

Here the phrase "expressed externally" is not to be understood in the sense of "uttered words": the faculty of representation cannot produce actual sounds from thoughts in Intellect. Plotinus is talking about something like internal speech or unuttered propositions, perhaps accompanied by mental images. He elsewhere speaks of a threefold division of *logoi* into *logos* in the Intellect, *logos* in the soul and the uttered *logos*.[17] By *logoi* in the Intellect he clearly means the Forms, whereas the *logoi* in the soul are the unfolded forms that we have mentioned, and it is evidently this latter kind which he has in mind in IV.3.30. Even if there is an implication that the verbal expression has parts (as it is contrasted with the partlessness of the pure thought), this does not mean that it has spatial parts: the point is that the forms in the soul no longer have the unity characteristic of the Intellect. In the terms of I.1.8 they are not "all together" but "unfolded and separated". My best proposal as to why Plotinus holds that the forms in the soul are unfolded and separated in comparison with those in the Intellect, is that, in Plotinus' view, thinking on the level of the (embodied) soul is essentially propositional and that propositional thinking involves a loss of the intuitive grasp of the interconnections between notions that characterize thinking on the level of Intellect (cf. Plotinus' criticism of the Stoic notion of *lecta* in V.5.1, 38-43). The identification of the unfolded forms with mental language, or "the words in the soul" of which the uttered words are expressions, clearly supports the claim that the unfolded forms are concepts or something of much the same kind.

We have already seen that in perception there arise forms or intelligible representations in the soul, and that these forms or intelligible representations are examples of the so-called unfolded forms. The passage from IV.3.30, considered above, shows that such unfolded forms are latent in us. If perception is a matter of entertaining unfolded forms, this passage shows how we could regard that as merely the activation of something already present. This would of course not mean that we already know what we come to know by sense-perception: the sensory affections would determine which combinations of unfolded forms are activated. Given the identification of unfolded forms with the entertainment of concepts, perceiving a man turns out to be something like affirming internally "this is a man" or "there is a man over there".

Now, it must be admitted that Plotinus nowhere describes sense-perception in this way, and there is only one passage, VI.7.6, 1-11, that can be taken to suggest something like the account above. However, I think various considerations make it tempting to attribute to Plotinus a view along these lines. First let us consider VI.7.6, 1-11. In the preceding chapters Plotinus has discussed the question how it can be that the soul acquires an additional power, that of sense-perception, by descending into the body. The gist of his answer is that this is really not the right question to ask, because it is not really correct to say that a new power comes into being. Rather, sense-perception is as it were a lower form of intellection, obscure thought.[18] It is a power that depends on pure thought: thanks to our relation to the Intellect, the soul that uses the body has the notions of sense-objects in the form of images. It is clear from the context in VI.7.6 that such possession of the notions of things is specifically meant to explain something about sense-perception. Since the possession of notions is supposed to depend on the percipient's relation to the Intellect, Plotinus' point cannot just be that the external objects of sense are images of the Forms. He must be making the point that in perception we come to entertain these notions and that this capacity depends on our prior possession of their archetypes. Thus, when we perceive, we activate latent concepts that we already possess.[29]

It seems to me that our main conclusions concerning perception in Plotinus also lead us to expect a view of this kind. Sensory affections are in themselves non-epistemic. In Plotinus' view no form of cognition is merely a matter of being affected from the outside. So what is needed in addition to the affection in order for there to be a complete perception must be an act stemming from within the percipient. This act is described as a judgement. It is reasonable to suppose that judgements involve the use of concepts, and since the affections in themselves are non-conceptual, their interpretation must be accomplished through the use of concepts that come from within. In fact Plotinus says things along these lines with respect to the judgements of the discursive reason.[20] I see no reason why he would not say the same about perceptual judgements, especially since he says about perception, considered as a judicative power, that it judges with the aid of intellect (*meta nou*) (IV.9.3, 26-7).

A pitfall which anyone engaged in giving an account of perception must try to avoid consists in making perception too rational: everyone knows and admits that animals can perceive; if we account for perception in such a way that it involves the use of capacities that are exclusively human, we run the risk of denying perception to animals, which is evidently absurd. It may seem that if Plotinus held the position I have just attributed to him, he falls

137

right into this pit: to entertain concepts is an honour we normally do not grant to brutes. It might be said in response to this, that the capacity to have beliefs involves the capacity to use concepts or something quite close to that, and that some animals do seem to have beliefs: can anyone deny that a cat who has been chased by a dog and has climbed up a flagpole and stays there while a dog waits beneath, believes that a malicious dog is waiting beneath? Plotinus nowhere discusses explicitly what capacities he thinks the higher animals are endowed with, and I confess I do not know for sure how he would respond to the objection just brought up. But the following points seem to be in order. He seems to regard reason as a distinctively human faculty, whereas perception is granted to the animals. So the question is: is it conceivable that a being incapable of reasoning can entertain concepts? If "entertaining concepts" presupposes something like human linguistic capacity, the answer is clearly "no". But perhaps there is some weaker sense of this expression according to which this is conceivable. Plotinus does not have much to say about language or linguistic capacity. But he clearly wants to make a distinction between perception and the discursive reason. The latter faculty has the power of manipulating unfolded forms and unfolding new ones from the stock of Forms at the level of Intellect.[21] Perception, on the other hand, even if it is a judicative faculty, can only make immediate and non-inferential judgements with respect to present affections. This means that to perceive is the mere realization that something in the sensible world is the case or that something is present. If this involves the use of concepts it is nevertheless true that perception's use of concepts is quite limited in comparison with that of the discursive reason. I think it is quite likely that Plotinus would grant such limited use of concepts to brutes. Let us not forget that in Plotinus' view brutes too are dependent on the Intellect even if they are farther removed from it than man.

We have frequently come across the notion of an image in the context of perception and in the context of the Plotinian hierarchy: the unfolded forms we possess in our souls are images of the Forms. And the internal productive principles of things are also images of the Forms, whereas the perceptible qualities of bodies are described as images of the productive principles. And so on. I believe that one of the most important issues in the study of Plotinus' thought in general is the problem of explaining his notion of the model-image relation. One of the difficulties involved is to give an account of the similarity relation that must hold between model and image. It is beyond the scope of the present work to address this issue in full. However, I want to discuss briefly one part of it, namely the similarity involved between the forms we possess in our souls and the external sensible objects.

When Plotinus speaks of representations in the soul (or in the organism) in the context of perception, he evidently intends the term "representation" to be understood as representation of the sensible object. This suggests that the external object is a kind of model and the representation in the percipient its image. But there is a tendency in Plotinus to look at the matter the other way around: from an ontological point of view the way things are present in a percipient is prior to the way they are present to bodies as spatially extended qualities. This is particularly clear from the following passage.

How do bodies accord with that which precedes all bodies? On what principle does the architect, when he finds the house before him correspondent with his inner idea of a house, pronounce it beautiful? Is it not that the house before him, the stones apart, is the inner form dispersed in the mass of exterior matter, the indivisible exhibited in diversity? When sense-perception then, sees the form in bodies binding and mastering the shapeless nature opposed to it and shape being gloriously carried by other shapes, it gathers into one that which appears dispersed and brings it back and takes it in – now without parts – to the soul's interior, and presents it to that which is within as something in tune with it, and fitting it, and dear to it. (1.6.3, 5-15)

Thus, it is as if by perceiving things we rescue their forms from low-grade, spatial existence and reinstate them at the intelligible level. But whichever is to be regarded as the image – the extended sensible object or its counterpart in the soul of a percipient – Plotinus evidently believes that some sort of similarity relation holds between the two. The question is: in what way are the forms in our souls similar to the forms that are dispersed in matter? The representations are non-spatial and hence intelligible things, whereas the objects represented are dispersed in matter. It is not obvious how these could be similar. J. Fielder has argued, primarily on the basis of his own analysis of the passage just quoted, that what is common to model and image in general is a pattern of arrangement that can exist in more than one kind of thing.[22] Fielder refers to Wittgenstein's notion of logical form – that which is common to a thought, the proposition that expresses it and the state of affairs it describes – as something similar to the notion of "common pattern" that he attributes to Plotinus. I think this is a fruitful comparison. Model and image are often so vastly different that it is hard to see in what they could be similar at all unless the similarity in question is some kind of identity of pattern. Applying this suggestion to the present case, we would say that intelligible representations and external objects share a common pattern. The hypothesis set forth earlier in this section, that the representations at issue are some kind of mental language, seems to fit nicely with Fielder's use of the notion of logical form: Wittgenstein's main use of the notion of logical form is to account for what a proposition and what it represents must have in common.[23]

VIII

Conclusions

In the previous chapters we have considered various aspects of Plotinus' account of sense-perception. There are two topics that seem to me to stand out in this account in the sense that we have been led to them in many different contexts: Plotinus' direct realism and his soul–body dualism. In this final chapter I summarize and expand our main conclusions concerning these two central topics. As regards the former, the survey given here is also meant to show how the main conclusions from previous chapters can be interpreted as elements in a single, relatively coherent view.

1 Judgement, affection and the objects of perception

We have seen that Plotinus' doctrine is that the objects of perception are external objects and their qualities. It remains to be seen whether and, if so, how Plotinus reconciles this with his doctrine about the mediacy of sensory affections in perception. The problem can be stated as follows: perceptions are described as judgements; the judgements belong to the soul and they are to be sharply distinguished from sensory affections that belong to the animated body; the affections function as mediators between the soul and the external objects because the soul cannot directly assimilate sensibles; but if the affections are thus in between the external qualities and that which perceives, it may seem that the affections and not the external objects or qualities are what is

141

immediately apprehended. Or how would Plotinus respond to such a charge?

First, let us recall what we noted in Chapter iv, that Plotinus holds that the affections are necessary in order to account for how we apprehend things in space. The hypothesis that the affections are sensations allows us to make better sense of this than does any other hypothesis about the nature of sensory affections. It was argued, for instance, that the hypothesis that the affections are physical assimilations is evidently insufficient. On the other hand, the interpretation we adopted works because in having sensations we are presented with qualities in space. Alexander holds that sense-perception, even if it does not receive the sensible forms with matter, nevertheless perceives them as existing in matter.[1] As I interpret Plotinus, something like this is an underlying assumption of the view expressed in iv.4.23 that the affections are necessary to account for how we can grasp spatial features of things: the sense-organs assume the forms of things in their material conditions, though without their matter.

There is no doubt that Plotinus' realism is connected with his views on visual transmission. We saw in Chapter iii that in connection with visual transmission Plotinus accuses others of holding views entailing that we do not see the things themselves. His critical points in iv.5.1-4 lead one to expect a theory according to which vision is some sort of "contact at a distance". The suggestion that the affections in vision are the colours in the percipient's visual field meets this expectation. The forms that are present everywhere in the intermediate space between object and percipient are what brings about this contact. When such a form meets the eye, there arises a sensation in the eye. This sensation is in Plotinus' view a kind of contact at a distance: in a sense the sense-organ reaches out to the object (cf. vi.4.12, 3-9).

But even if it is granted that our view of the nature of the affections succeeds in this respect, it may seem that Plotinus is not yet entitled to say that we perceive the things themselves. For even if I am presented with a quality *as if* it is out there, it may seem that this quality is nevertheless an affection and not the very external quality itself. How is this puzzle to be solved? It is noteworthy that Plotinus seems to admit that in perception the soul is in direct contact only with the affections, while at the same time maintaining that through this contact the soul reaches the things themselves (iv.5.1, 6-13). Given my interpretation of sensory affection, this suggests that Plotinus conceived of the matter in such a way that having sensations amounts to being presented with the things themselves. Something like this is also suggested by passages where Plotinus describes the work of the sense-organs as participation in the objects perceived (IV.5.3, 18-21). Let us consider how this may be.

First, it is worth noting that even though Plotinus accuses others of holding theories which entail that we see only "shadows and images", and not the things themselves, his realism is not stated in opposition to a sceptical view that denies, or attempts to question, the possibility of perceiving the things themselves. The thinkers he charges with antirealism are not *conscious* antirealists. The moral to draw from this is that although we should expect Plotinus to hold a view that circumvents his criticisms of others' views, we should not necessarily expect an elaborate realism designed to answer all possible antirealist objections.

Plotinus thinks of knowledge as "having" what is known. This is why he says in IV.4.23, 6-8 that if the soul is to know sensibles it must first acquire them (see pp. 68-70 above). But obviously neither the soul nor the sense-organs can acquire the external sensible bodies quite literally: the mountain I see does not become internal to me or to my eyes as the food I consume becomes internal to my body. But I think Plotinus tries to come as close to literal possession as he can. This means that he thinks that what our sense-organs come to have in perception is really a quality of the external body, ontologically transformed so as to be accessible to our souls. What this comes to in vision, for example, is this: the colours of external things exist in our visual fields in a non-material, but still spatial, way.

Plotinus says of the view he criticizes in IV.6.1 that it entails us seeing shadows and traces of the things and not the things themselves which we obviously see. So what we see, according to his own view, should not be something that is appropriate to call a shadow or a trace of the thing. The following considerations may help us see why Plotinus thinks his own view is in this respect essentially different from the one he attacks.

According to the view he criticizes, that which the percipient comes to have in vision is an impression, which Plotinus evidently understands as a physical impression like a seal on wax. This impression is physically located in the percipient. According to the present interpretation of Plotinus' view, the affection, understood as the phenomenal colour, is not a physical property of the eye. It is something of the eye, but not in the eye. As Plotinus remarks in IV.6.1, 37-9, the impression must not be in that which sees, it must lie elsewhere (see p. 82 above). Somebody who holds that the affection in vision is a physical impression in the percipient and that this is what the percipient immediately apprehends, cannot conceivably suppose that he is immediately presented with the quality of the thing itself: the percipient is presented with a quality that exists materially in a different substrate, i.e. in the percipient's body. On the other hand, if my interpretation of Plotinus is right, the colours that our eyes take on are as such not materially the colours of anything in the percipient (it would be impossible for someone else to see them).

One way to think of sensations that is obviously incompatible with realism is to suppose that what happens in vision is something like the following: The percipient receives a sensation of a red roof, inspects it in *foro interno* and then reasons as follows: "Since I am having a sensation that is red and rooflike, there is presumably a red roof out there." Thus, the thing and its qualities are inferred from the qualities of the sensation, which is inspected as an item in its own right. Plotinus' view of the function of sensory affections in perception cannot be at all like this. If it were, he could not be the realist he claims to be. In iv.4.23 Plotinus implies that the soul uses the sense-organ and its affection to judge the quality of the external body, and that the form assumed by the organ is intermediate between the form in the external body and that in the soul. Given that we rule out an account of the sort just mentioned, we can think of the following way of interpreting this: in normal perception, when we have an affection of a certain sort, say, a phenomenal red in our visual field, the soul does not pass a judgement on the affection as such. Rather, the affection is that by means of *having* which we judge that an external body is red (or that it is a roof or that it is about 50 feet away). Suppose someone asks me to take down the book with the violet cover from the topmost shelf. If I am to be able to accomplish this, the colour of the book must enter my visual field, or in more Plotinian terms, my eyes must be assimilated to the colour of the book. Further, if my suggestions here and in Chapter iv are correct, this colour, as an affection of the eye, exists in a special way, a way that is different from its mode of existence as a quality of a body. But even if it is this affection of which we are immediately aware, it is not, in normal vision, an object of judgement in its own right. Thus, when the violet of the book enters my visual field, I judge without any inference: "Here is the violet book!" This I accomplish by means of having its colour non-materially in my visual field and by applying notions that I already possess in my soul. To see the book is to realize that a given colour in one's visual field demarcates a book. To see that the book is violet is to realize that the colour in one's visual field that demarcates the book is violet. What Plotinus has in mind by "judgement" in the context of perception must be something like this.

It is evidently Plotinus' view that if we are to be able to say we see the things themselves, we must suppose that what the eyes take on is really the colour of the thing (and not the colour of something in the intermediate air, nor merely a physical impression stemming from the thing). But given that what the eyes take on is the quality of the thing in a special mode of being, he does not see any reason to contrast this quality with the quality as it exists externally.

If the main conclusions reached so far are correct, Plotinus' theory of perception is not a representational theory. That is to say, Plotinus does not hold that the percipient receives "pictures" of external objects and judges of the objects by, as it were, inspecting the pictures. Although, as we have noted earlier, he occasionally speaks of "impressions" in describing what happens to the sense organs, it appears that these do not have a picture-like function in his theory. Plotinus also speaks of intelligible impressions in the soul in connection with perception, and we have referred to these as "representations". But this does not mean that his theory is representational in the sense just indicated, for these impressions are not the objects of perception.

2 Plotinus' dualism

As we have noted in previous chapters Plotinus' account of perception is in various ways connected with his views on the relationship between soul and body. Perhaps this is philosophically the most interesting aspect of his views. As is well known, many of Plotinus' predecessors discussed the nature of the soul and its relation to the body. Some, most notably the atomists, held that the soul is made of especially fine and light corporeal stuff. Others, Aristotle and his followers, thought that the soul is not to be identified with any specific physical stuff in the body, and that the relation between the soul and body is an instance of that between form and matter. Still others, most notably Plato, held that the soul is an entity of a different order than the body and separable from it. However, most ancient discussions of such matters appear to modern minds as having at best a loose connection with post-Cartesian discussions of the mind–body

145

problem. In Plato's dualism the notion of body with which the soul is contrasted has moral and, according to modern lights, psychological traits. The contrast depicted never comes close to being that between *res extensa* and *res cogitans* in the Cartesian sense. As for Aristotle's views, even if his account of the soul–body relation is now praised by some who wish to resist dualism, it is nonetheless clear that this account was not originally thought of as an alternative to the kind of dualism these contemporary philosophers reject. Aristotle never even dreamt of the latter kind of view.

What then does it take to have a Cartesian type of mind (soul)–body problem? I think that someone who uses introspection to make claims about the nature of the soul (or mind) and contrasts his findings with the nature of the body considered from an external and hence public point of view, is about to produce such a problem for himself – and for others too if others find his reasoning persuasive or challenging. If we are to speculate further as to why none of Plotinus' predecessors reasoned in such a manner, I think that at least a part of the explanation lies in Burnyeat's remark that "One's own body has not yet become for philosophy a part of the external world."[2] In so far as the ancients made an internal – external distinction, the line tended to be drawn between the organism and what is outside it. A related point is that the boundary between the soul and the living body was not very clearly drawn. The upshot is that it is by no means certain that everything we would today classify as introspective reports would have been regarded by the ancients as reports specifically about the soul.

With Plotinus, however, we can see a development towards a soul–body distinction closer to the one modern philosophers are familiar with, (which is not to say that all of Plotinus' psychology is familiar to the modern mind). But Plotinus presents such a picture of the human soul that there is an ontological gap between it and bodies, even between it and the human body. The distinguishing feature is extension. Bodies and all their properties are extensional phenomena: they have spatial location and are divisible into spatially different parts. The soul, by contrast, does not have these features. The result is that for the first time ontological remoteness between learner and learnt made it difficult to explain how the soul can learn about the physical world at all: sense perception – which, it is assumed, is that through which the soul learns about the external physical world – was seen to involve the crossing of an ontlogical gap.[3]

146

In Plotinus' arguments against materialism that we discussed in Chapter v we find the very remarkable line of thought that the soul has properties that are somehow such that nothing which is a mere body could have them. Magnitude or extension (*megethos*), which is characterized by divisibility *ad infinitum*, is the essential attribute of bodies. Plotinus also seems to suppose that any quality of a body must share in the defining characteristic of a body, i.e. it must have extension and be located in physical space and hence be spatially divisible.[4] Thus, for Plotinus extension is really more than an essential attribute of bodies in the sense of being an attribute a thing must have in order to be a body; he also holds that all other qualities of a body – colour, shape, texture, etc. – are extensional in the sense that they are divisible along with the extension. Using Descartes' terminology we might say extension is a principal attribute of bodies, i.e. one which all the others presuppose.[5] Hence, a position according to which the body has non-physical properties is ruled out from the beginning: if Plotinus can point to something which neither is nor presupposes extension – divisibility is the criterion – he will infer that that entity is neither a body nor a property of body.[6] As the soul appears to have properties which do not exhibit this feature, he concludes that the soul is not a body.

It should also be noted that Plotinus arrives at his antimaterialist conclusions by introspecting his own sensual experiences. He clearly believed that his statements about the unity of the subject of perception are based on the soul's knowledge of its own nature and activities. Thus it seems that Plotinus' views and in particular his attacks on materialism contain the seeds of many of the fundamental questions associated with the mind-body problem with which philosophers have been so occupied since Descartes. As we have seen, one consequence of Plotinus' general position on the nature of the soul is that it becomes somewhat mysterious how the soul can relate to the extended realm at all, be in it, know it and causally participate in it.[7] Plotinus himself was quite aware of difficulties that his position involved. And his claims against Stoic (and Stratonic) materialism could for instance easily and directly generate discussion of the relation between what goes on physically in the body and what goes on in the soul as viewed from the inside or a discussion of the possibility of explaining the apparently non-physical features of the soul in terms of the physical. But these seeds did not sprout, no doubt because there were no materialists around who would respond to Plotinus and carry the dialogue further.

Neither in the arguments against the Stoics we have considered nor elsewhere in Plotinus' writings is it suggested that either indubitability or privileged access or any such specific mode of apprehension is a crucial feature that serves to mark off the psychic from the corporeal. In this Plotinus differs from Descartes and a great many other modern and contemporary philosophers and even from St Augustine in so far as the latter anticipates the Cartesian cogito.[8] In short, the "cogito" and its implications are absent in Plotinus. But while this is significant, I do not think it warrants the inference that Plotinus' type of dualism is something quite different from the modern type. In fact there is really no one modern type of dualism. For instance, very few if any contemporary philosophers embrace Descartes' views on the mind-body relation as they stand. And if we consider the contemporary scene, what we find is not committed dualism so much as aggressive dissatisfaction with materialism. The arguments advanced by contemporary philosophers against materialism can usually, in one way or another, be referred back to Descartes. But only some of them rest upon the indubitability of the mental or kindred epistemological notions. In modern times there are for example philosophers who hold that lack of spatial location is a characteristic of such phenomena as thoughts and after-images, and consider this as a threat to reductive materialism or even to the identity theory, which claims that mental states are identical to some bodily states.[9] Albeit different, there are obvious affinities between this type of argument and Plotinus' antimaterialist arguments and, notably, neither is explicitly nor implicitly in terms of privileged access or indubitability.

The foregoing seems to entitle Plotinus to be called the father of the mind-body problem or, let us say, at least its grandfather – we may take this title as honorific or derogatory according to our individual tastes. Most of what Ryle denounces as "Descartes' myth" in the *Concept of Mind*, with the exception of a doctrine about the mechanistic working of the human body, fits Plotinus' views (and St Augustine's as well). This teaches us that even if the Cartesian notion of mind is perhaps not a basic human intuition, it is also not simply a single historical accident.

Abbreviations

AGP	*Archive für Geschichte der Philosophie*
Bruns	*Alexandri Aphrodisiensis Praeter Commentaria Scripta minora: De Anima cum Mantissa*, ed. I. Bruns. Supplementum Aristotelicum, vol. 2, part 1 (Berlin, 1887)
CQ	*Classical Quarterly*
DG	*Doxographi Graeci*, ed. H. Diels (Berlin, 1879, repr. 1958)
D. L.	Diogenes Laertius, *Vitae Philosophorum*
Ennéades	*Plotin: Ennéades*, ed. E. Bréhier (Paris, 1924–38)
H-S²	*Plotini Opera*, ed. P. Henry et H.-R. Schwyzer (Oxford, 1964–82)
HLGP	*Cambridge History of Later Greek and Early Medieval Philosophy*, ed. A. H. Armstrong (Cambridge, 1970)
Le Néoplatonisme	*Colloques Internationaux du Centre National de la Recherche Scientifique. Le Néoplatonisme* (Paris, 1971)
Les sources de Plotin	*Fondation Hardt. Entretiens sur l'Antiquité Classique*, vol. 5. *Les sources de Plotin* (Geneva, 1960)
SVF	*Stoicorum Veterum Fragmenta*, ed. J. von Arnim, 4 vols. (Leipzig, 1903–24)

Notes

Introduction

1 The treatises are: "How Distant Objects Appear Small" (II.8.[35]); "On the Difficulties about Soul III, or On Sight" (IV.5.[29]); and "On Sense-Perception and Memory" (IV.6.[41]).

2 The following provide the main studies of perception in Plotinus: G. H. Clark, "Plotinus' Theory of Sensation", *The Philosophical Review* 51 (1942), 357-82; J. H. Dubbink, *Studia Plotiniana. Onderzoek naar eeninge grond gedachten van het stelsel van Plotinus* (Purmerend, 1943); H. J. Blumenthal, *Plotinus' Psychology* (The Hague, 1971) and "Plotinus' Adaptation of Aristotle's Psychology" in R. Baine Harris (ed.), *The Significance of Neo-platonism* (Norfolk, Virginia, 1976), 41-58; M. F. Wagner, *Concepts and Causes: the Structure of Plotinus' Universe* (Ph.D. diss., Ohio State University 1979). Clark's article is a valuable attempt to reconstruct Plotinus' theory of perception. Dubbink's primary interest, so far as perception is concerned, is Plotinus' use of perceptual, especially visual, metaphors. He also gives lists of the occurrences of some common cognition terms and classifies their meanings. The reader of this work will note several occasions where I take issue with Blumenthal's views. This does not alter the fact that I am much indebted to his valuable poineering works on the psychology of Plotinus. In his work Wagner is concerned with many large issues in Plotinus and in philosophy in general. On a number of important issues, especially as regards the conceptual nature of perception, my conclusions about Plotinus' theory of perception are similar to views expressed by him.

3 Among the classics must be counted the following: R. Arnou, *Le désir de dieu dans la philosophie de Plotin* (Paris, 1921); E. Bréhier, *La philosophie de Plotin* (Paris, 1929); W. R. Inge, *The Philosophy of Plotinus,* 2 vols. (London, 1929); P. O. Kristeller, *Der Begriff der Seele in der Ethik des Plotin* (Tübingen, 1929); A. H. Armstrong, *The Architecture of the Intelligible Universe in the Philosophy of Plotinus* (Cambridge, 1940).

4 *Vita Plotini* 8, 1-2.

5 Ibid., 8, 8-12.

6 For an account of Plotinus' method and composition see Brisson et al. *La vie de Plotin* (Paris, 1982), 229 ff. and 329 ff.

7 See Blumenthal, *Plotinus' Psychology*, 68-9.

8 Porphyry testifies to the importance of Aristotelian and Stoic views to Plotinus: "His [Plotinus'] writings, however, are full of concealed Stoic and Peripatetic doctrines; Aristotle's *Metaphysics*, in particular, is concentrated in them" (*Vita Plotini* 14, 5-8). A recent penetrating philosophically oriented study of Plotinus' use and criticisms of Aristotle's metaphysics and category theory is offered by S. K. Strange in *Plotinus' Treatise "On the Genera of Being": An Historical and philosophical Study* (Ph. D. diss. The University of Texas at Austin, 1981).

9 The Platonist Albinus (2nd cent. AD) adopts various Peripatetic notions and doctrines in his survey of Platonic philosophy, the *Didaskalikos* (ed.C. F. Hermann in *Platonis Dialogi*,vol. 3 [Berlin, 1884]). This tendency was however presumably older, perhaps originating in Antiochus of Ascalon, who according to Cicero did not see a doctrinal difference between the Peripatos and the Old Academy, cf. Cic. *Acad. Post.* I, 17-18.

10 J. M. Rist, *Plotinus: The Road to Reality* (Cambridge, 1977), 169.

11 Rist offers an intelligent discussion of Plotinus' attitude towards his sources in *The Road to Reality*, chap. 13, "The Originality of Plotinus". See also R. Harder, "Quelle oder Tradition", in *Les sources de Plotin*, 325-32.

12 III.6.1, 1-3; III.6.2, 53-4; IV.4.23, 20-32; IV.3.26, 5-6.

13 III.6.18, 24-8; I.1.2, 26-7; I.6.3, 9-15; IV.3.3, 18-22; IV.4.23, 1-4; 20-2; V.8.2, 25-6.

14 IV.2.1-2; IV.7.6-7; VI.4.1.

15 IV.3.29, 24-6; V.3.2, 7-9; IV.4.8, 16-18.

16 III.6.1, 1-7; cf. also IV.3.3, 23-5; IV.3.26, 8-9; IV.4.23, 36-43; IV.6.2, 17; VI.4.6, 8-19.

17 III.6.1, 1-2; cf. also IV.6.2, 1-6; VI.1.20, 26-32.

18 IV.5.2, 50-3; IV.5.3, 10-13; IV.6.1, 14-40; also IV.4.23, 15-19; IV.5.1, 1-13.

1 Plotinus' metaphysics

1 A good account of unity in Neoplatonism is to be found in R. T. Wallis, The Neoplatonists (London, 1972), chap. 1.

2 See e.g. V.5.4, 28-37 and VI.2.11, 5-11.

3 In *Metaphysics* 1003b 22-34 Aristotle says that being and unity imply each other and that there are as many species of being as there are of unity, cf. ibid. 1053b 24-1054a 19. Merlan suggests that Aristotle's identification of unity with being permits the substitution of "unity" for "being" in Aristotle's definition of metaphysics as the study of being *qua* being and that Aristotle's *Metaphysics* is to be interpreted as Academic in character (P. Merlan, *From Platonism to Neoplatonism*, 3rd edn rev. [The Hague, 1968], 162-4). Whether or not we accept Merlan's views as an accurate interpretation of Aristotle, there is no doubt (as Merlan also claims) that Plotinus and other Neoplatonists took Aristotle's *Metaphysics* as the work of a Platonist, even if a somewhat aberrant one.

4 In general Plotinus maintains that unity and being go hand in hand and that a certain degree of being corresponds to a certain degree of unity (see e.g. VI.6.13 and IV.9.1). An exception is the One itself, which is beyond being. That a certain degree of being corresponds to a certain degree of unity in sensible things is however denied at VI.2.11, 14-16.

5 The Stoics systematically distinguished between different levels of unity in bodies (SVF 2, 366-8). Plotinus' views on the degrees of unity have to some extent been influenced by these Stoic distinctions, cf. especially VI.9.1, 10-14. Graeser is however probably right in warning against overestimating Stoic influence in this and similar passages (see A. Graeser, *Plotinus and the Stoics* [Leiden, 1972], 72-4).

6 I say "as if", because I do not want to imply that living bodies have literally been designed or planned by anyone. That is not really the Neoplatonists' view: planning and designing are temporal processes, but the principles responsible for the teleology in the sensible world are atemporal (see VI.7.2, 21-58 and 3, 1-9).

7 The view that the sensible world is an organism is prominent in Plato and the Stoics, see e. g. *Pol.* 269 D–270A; *Phil.* 30 A; *Tim.* 30 B, 34 A–37 C; *SVF* 2, 633-45. Plotinus' primary source for this view is of course the *Timaeus*, but his version of it is flavoured with Stoicism.

8 *Phaed.* 74 D, 100 C; *Symp.* 210 E6–211 D. The view that each Form is a supreme instance of that of which it is a Form (the so called "Self-Predication Thesis") has played an important role in recent discussion of the so called Third Man Arguments in *Parm.* 132 A–B and 132 D–133 A. Plotinus nowhere discusses these arguments explicitly, although he must have been aware of them. Recently S. K. Strange has argued that Plotinus has answers to these arguments that consist in denying that a predicate applies synonymously to the Form and its participants and that the similarity between the Form and its participants is reciprocal: the participants are similar to the Form but not *vice versa*, cf. *Plotinus' Treatise "On the Genera of Being"*, 77-83).

9 Plotinus also calls the One the Good, because he identifies the Form of the Good in the *Republic* with the One. Such an identification gained support from reports of Plato's lecture on the Good. There is no doubt that the legend of Plato's unwritten doctrines had much influence on Plotinus' interpretation of Plato. For the influence of the unwritten doctrines and the Old Academy in general on the Neoplatonic notion of the One, see Armstrong, *The Intelligible Universe* chaps. 1 and 2; H. J. Krämer, *Der Ursprung der Geistmetaphysik* (Amsterdam, 1964), chap. 3; Merlan, *From Platonism to Neoplatonism* and *HLGP*, Part I, chap. 2.

10 It took scholars a long time to discover that the main source of Plotinus' One is the first "hypothesis" of Plato's *Parmenides*, obvious though the matter is once pointed out. The honour of the discovery falls on E. R. Dodds ("The *Parmenides* of Plato and the Origin of the Neoplatonic 'One'", *CQ* 22 [1928], 129-42) and É. Bréhier, who points out the importance of the first two hypotheses of the *Parmenides* for Plotinus' first two hypostases in his introductions to several of the treatises of the 5th and the 6th *Enneads*. Bréhier appears to have arrived at his conclusions independently of Dodds' article: *Ennéades* 5 was published in 1931, Dodds' article in 1928; but Bréhier's interpretation is already hinted at in his *Ennéades* 2 (note to II.4.5, p. 59), which appeared in 1924. As both Dodds and Bréhier realize, not only is the first hypothesis of the *Parmenides* the main source of Plotinus' first hypostasis, the three Plotinian hypostases are based on the *Parmenides*, counting *Parmenides* 155 E-157 B as a seperate hypothesis. Later Neoplatonists extended this sort of reading of the *Parmenides* still further, so that the remaining hypotheses were identified with the lower strata in the Neoplatonic hierarchy (see e. g. Proclus, *In Parm.*, ed. V. Cousin [Paris, 1864], 1089-90). Thus the

Parmenides came to be seen as one of the most important Platonic dialogues, presenting the skeleton of Plato's metaphysics.

11 A particularly clear presentation of the One and its relation to what comes after it is given in v.3.15.

12 This is Plotinus' way of expression in v.3.12, 50-1: εἰ γὰρ τί ἕν, οὐκ ἂν αὐτοέν τὸ γὰρ "αὐτὸ" πρὸ τοῦ "τί" (if [the One] were one something, it would not be one in itself: for "in itself" comes before "something").

13 v.4.1, 8-9, vi.9.5, 30ff., cf. *Parm.* 141 E

14 "We neither grasp it by knowledge nor by intellectual intuition as the other intelligibles... This is why he [Plato] says it can neither be spoken of nor written about" (vi.9.4,1-3, 11-12). See also v.4.1, 9; v.5.6, 12; and v.5.13, 11 ff. The view that the One is unknowable and ineffable relies of course on *Parm.* 142 A.

15 For the Platonic and other sources of Plotinus' notion of matter see Merlan in *HLGP*, 26-7. Plotinus' views on matter are most thoroughly presented in II.4. and III.6.6-19.

16 See M. I. Santa Cruz de Prunes, *La genèse du monde sensible dans la philosophie de Plotin*, Bibliothèque de l'École des Hautes Études, vol. 81 (Paris, 1981), 129-30

17 IV.2.1, 15-17; 64-5; VI.2.4, 18-21.

18 See e.g. I.8.8, 13-16; II.4.5, 18-20; II.6.3, 14-20; III.6.9, 18-19; 12, 25-7; 13, 31-2; v.9.3, 36-7; vi.3.15, 24-36.

19 The Platonists could perhaps find Platonic authority for the adoption of Aristotelian immanent forms along with the transcendent ones in such passages as *Timaeus* 51 A. There is no certainty as to who introduced immanent forms into the Platonic tradition (cf. J. Dillon, *The Middle Platonists* [London, 1977], 135-7, 274). But in any event the notion of immanent forms is present in such pre-Plotinian Platonists as Albinus (see *Didaskalikos*, 155 [Hermann]).

20 The realm of Forms is described as "life that is present in its entirety at once, complete and indivisible in all respects; this life is the eternity that we are seeking" (III.7.3, 37-8). For Plotinus' views on time and eternity see W. Beierwaltes' commentary on III.7: *Plotin, Über Ewigkeit und Zeit (Enneade III, 7)* (Frankfurt am Main, 1967). For Neoplatonic views on time and eternity see R. Sorabji, *Time, Creation and the Continuum* (London, 1983).

21 vi.7.2, 11-12 and 19, 17-19. The formula comes from Aristotle's *An. Post.* 90a 14-18, cf. *Met.* 1044b 10-15. Aristotle's point is that the cause of an eclipse is identical with its essence. According to Plotinus this holds for everything in the realm of Forms.

22 See A. H. Armstrong, "The Background of the Doctrine 'That the Intelligibles are not Outside the Intellect'", *Les sources de Plotin*, 391-425, and Dillon, *The Middle Platonists*, 95, 158-9, 254-6.

23 Armstrong, "Background"; see Bruns, 81-91 and 106-13. It should be mentioned here that the authenticity of the treatises constituting the so-called *De Anima* II (the "Mantissa") of Bruns' edition of Alexander's psychological writings has been questioned: see P. Moraux, *Alexandre d'Aphrodise: Exégète de la noétique d'Aristote* (Paris, 1942), 24-8. Moraux, however, later accepted the *Mantissa* as authentic: see his "Le *De Anima* dans la tradition grecque. Quelques aspects de l'interprétation du traité, de Théophraste à Thémistius", in *Aristotle on Mind and the Senses*, ed. G. E. R. Lloyd and G. E. L. Owen (Cambridge, 1979), 281-324. R.B. Todd, *Alexander of Aphrodisias on Stoic Physics*, Philosophia Antiqua 28 (Leiden, 1976) 18-19. Cf. also B. C. Bazán,

"L'authenticité du 'De Intellectu' attribué à Alexandre d' Aphrodise", *Revue Philosophique de Louvain* 71 (1973), 468-87; F. M. Schroeder, "The Potential or Material Intellect and the Authorship of the *De Intellectu*: A Reply to B. C. Bazán", *Symbolae Osloenses* 57 (1982), 115-25; P. Thillet, introduction to the Budé edition of Alexander's *De Fato* (Paris, 1984), 63-5. Moraux, Todd and Thillet, however, all suppose that the *Mantissa* treatises stem from Alexander's circle. In this work they are referred to as Alexander's.

24 P. Merlan has pointed out (*HLGP*, 19) that there is one isolated passage in Plato, *Laws* 894 A, that speaks of a process resembling emanation. There is, however, no evidence that Plotinus made special use of this passage.

25 IV.9.5, 9-12; v.1.5, 11-13; v.9.6, 10-24.

26 See J. Fielder, "Plotinus' Copy Theory", *Apeiron* 11 (1977), 1-11 and in "Immateriality and Metaphysics", *Proceedings of the American Catholic Philosophical Association* 52 (1978), 96-102.

II Plotinus' views on the soul and man

1 I call this Plotinus' "orthodox view" because it emerges from his most detailed account of the subject in IV.3.1-8. Here Plotinus treats the World-Soul as different from Soul. He however often conflates the two (see e.g. II.3.17, 15-16, where *hê psychê tou pantos* [the soul of the whole] comes immediately after *nous*). For a detailed discussion see Blumenthal, "Soul, World-Soul and Individual Soul in Plotinus" in *Le néoplatonisme*, 55-63.

2 See Blumenthal, "*Nous* and Soul in Plotinus: Some Problems of Demarcation" in *Plotino e il Neoplatonismo in Oriente e in Occidente* (Rome, 1974), 203-19.

3 IV.3.4, 21-3; IV.8.2; IV.8.4, 4-6.

4 II.9.7,15-18; IV.3.4, 27 ff.

5 See D. O'Meara, "Plotinus on how Soul Acts on Body", in D. O'Meara (ed.), *Platonic Investigations* (Washington DC, 1985), 247-61.

6 In v.9.6, 20-4 Plotinus asserts the identity of nature and formative principles. The notion of a formative principle is Stoic in origin (cf. *SVF* 2, 580; 717; 1074), but, as is his custom with his borrowings, Plotinus modifies it so that it fits into his scheme. See R. E. Witt, "The Plotinian Logos and its Stoic Basis", *CQ* 25 (1931), 103-11.

7 IV.3.[27] 1-8; IV.9.[8] and VI.4.[22]. For IV.3.1-8 see W. Helleman-Elgersma, *Soul-Sisters: A Commentary on Enneads IV 3 (27), 1-8 of Plotinus* (Amsterdam, 1980).

8 See IV.9.1, 15 and Blumenthal, "Soul, World-Soul and Individual Soul in Plotinus", 55. It seems to me that Plotinus does not have a strict identity in mind. But it is true that it remains to show exactly what sense of identity is involved; it cannot be said that Plotinus' own attempts are altogether satisfactory.

9 The Stoics regarded individual souls as parts of the World-Soul, cf. *SVF* 1, 495 and D.I. VII, 156 (*SVF* 2, 774).

10 See VI.4-5 and Bréhier's introduction to these treatises (*Ennéades* 6, part 1, 161-75) and also F. M. Schroeder, "The Platonic Parmenides and Imitation in Plotinus", *Dionysius* 2 (1978), 51-73. In VI.4-5 Plotinus attacks Plato's problem of participation as presented in the first part of the *Parmenides*.

11 See v.7: "Are there Forms of Individuals?". Plotinus comes to the conclusion that there are such Forms. But in v.9.12 he has been taken to deny that there are Forms of individuals. A. H. Armstrong has convincingly argued that the

seemingly inconsistent passages can be reconciled ("Form, Individual and Person in Plotinus", *Dionysius* 1 [1977], 49-68). See also J. M. Rist, "Forms of Individuals in Plotinus", *CQ* ns 13 (1963), 223-31; H. J. Blumenthal, "Did Plotinus Believe in Ideas of Individuals?", *Phronesis* 11 [1966], 61-80; P. S. Mamo, "Forms of Individuals in the *Enneads*", *Phronesis* 14 (1969), 77-96; J. M. Rist, "Ideas of Individuals in Plotinus: A Reply to Dr. Blumenthal", *Revue Internationale de Philosophie* 24 (1970), 296-303; J. Igal, "Observaciones al Texto de Plotino", *Emerita* 41 (1973), 92-8.

12 See p. 17

13 i.1.8, 15-23; ii.9.13, 30-1; v.3.9, 28-36.

14 ii.1.5,18-24; ii.2.2, 4-5; iv.3.7, 25-31; iv.3.27, 1-3; iv.4.32, 4-13; 37, 11-15; 43, 9-11; vi.6.15, 12-13.

15 διὰ τι οὖν οὐ καὶ παρὰ τῆς ἡμετέρας ψυχῆς τὸ θρεπτικόν; ὅτι τὸ τρεφόμενον μέρος τοῦ ὅλου, ὃ καὶ παθητικῶς αἰσθητικόν, ἡ δὲ αἴσθησις ἡ κρίνουσα μετὰ νοῦ ἑκάστου.

16 See pp. 31-2

17 iv.3.26, 9-12; iv.3.27.

18 See for instance iv.3.4, where Plotinus claims that all psychic faculties are potentially in any given faculty, and I.1.11, 8-15, where he says that beasts are sometimes animated by sinful human souls, sometimes by the World-Soul.

19 This use of *hêmeis* is frequent in the *Enneads*: see J. H. Sleeman and G. Pollet, *Lexicon Plotinianum* (Leiden, 1980) s. v. *hêmeis*. That Plotinus is concerned with a special use of the word is brought out very clearly in i.1.7, 16-24 and 10, 4-7. For details of Plotinus' views on the self see J. P. O'Daly, *Plotinus' Philosophy of the Self* (Shannon, 1973).

20 In ii.3.9, in a discussion of the influence of the stars on terrestrial phenomena, Plotinus argues that although we receive our life and our temperament from the heaven (i.e. from the World-Soul), the true self, (*hoper esmen kat' alêtheian hêmeis*) is not to be accounted for in this way, and he goes on to introduce "the other soul", i.e. the individual soul, to account for this true self. Cf. also iii.1.4 and iii.1.8.

21 In *Alcibiades* i, 129 A-130 E, which Plotinus takes to be an authentic Platonic dialogue, the self is identified with "the soul that uses the body". This passage is of considerable importance for philosophy of man, see pp. 31-2. See also *Phd.* 64 E ff. and 115 C-116 A, where it is implied that the self is the soul. Another forerunner of Plotinus' notion of the self is Plato's notion of the inner man, *ho entos anthrôpos* (*Rep.* 589 A, cf. Plotinus, v.1.10, 10 and v.3.7, 26-7). Aristotle remarks that each man is identical with his rational faculty (*to dianoêtikon*), (*Eth. Nic.* 1166a 16-17, cf. 1168b 35 and 1178a 1-8). We hear an echo of this in i.1.7,16-17, iv.7.1, 22 and elsewhere. O'Daly in *Plotinus' Philosophy of the Self* gives a survey of pre-Plotinian views of the self with a special focus on the significance of the Delphic commandment "Know Thyself" for the philosophers.

22 See Bruns, 88-92 and 106-13.

23 A. N. M. Rich gives a survey of Plotinus' views on the soul–body relationship in "Body and Soul in the Philosophy of Plotinus", *Journal of the History of Philosophy* 1 (1963), 1-15.

24 This emerges from 130 B 11-12, where it is said that the compound could not rule the body without the co-operation of the soul. This would be senseless if the soul here was the same thing as that which, together with the body, constitutes the compound.

25 In *De An.* 403a 4 ff. Aristotle discusses the question whether all the so-called

affections of the soul are common to the soul and the body or whether there are some that belong to the soul alone. Cf. also 431a 16-17.

26 There is a fine survey of Plotinus' use of Aristotle's psychology by Blumenthal, "Plotinus' Adaptation of Aristotle's Psychology". He however does not pay due attention to Plotinus' use of Aristotle's notion of an organism.

27 See P. T. Geach, "Immortality", in *God and the Soul* (London, 1969), 17-29.

28 This, however, was presumably not Descartes' own position, which was closer to that of Plotinus: see M. D. Wilson, "Cartesian Dualism" in M. Hooker (ed.), *Descartes: Critical and Interpretive Essays* (Baltimore and London, 1978), 197-211.

29 See St Thomas Aquinas, *Supplementum Summae Theologiae* III, 70, 3; *Summa Contra Gentiles* IV, 90 and 93.

30 See Plotinus' criticisms of Aristotelian views on the soul in IV.7.8^5; cf. *De An.* 421b 6-8.

31 See IV.2.1, 34-53 and VI.4.1, 17-24; cf. IV.3.2, 12-19. Bréhier mistranslates an important phrase in the first passage: *kan to megethos de hen êi* (IV.2.1, 50) is rendered as "la qualité étendue est une seule qualité". But the meaning is "also in the case of a single magnitude". In his "Neoplatonic Logic and Aristotelian Logic I" (*Phronesis* I [1955], 58-72) A. C. Lloyd claims on the basis of IV.2.1 and IV.3.2 that in Plotinus' view the particular quality behaves like a universal. Lloyd says: "White in two bowls of milk is the same complete white, just as it is the same complete white throughout each bowl, because it is a quality (*poion*) and not a quantity (*poson*), and therefore has no parts. This seems to recognize the inapplicability of numerical difference" (p. 62). In fact, however, at IV.2.1, 47-53 Plotinus asserts the individuality of the particular quality, and in VI.4.1, 23-4 he says explicitly that the white in one part of a body is numerically different from the white of another part, even if they are identical in form.

32 For an account of Plotinus' sources see Blumenthal, "Plotinus' *Ennead* IV.3.20-1 and its Sources: Alexander, Aristotle and Others", *AGP* 50 (1968).

33 See ibid, 260-1. The example derives from Aristotle, *De An.* 413a 9, and is often brought up by Alexander (cf. Bruns, 14-15; 20-1 and 79).

34 Plotinus has interesting views on the nature of light: see especially IV.5.6-7. In his view light is neither a body nor a feature of a body; the light which comes from bodies is "the external activity of a luminous body" (IV.5.7, 33-4). Although he does not seem to regard light as a psychic phenomenon, because of its non-bodily nature it is a suitable example to illustrate many psychic and intelligible phenomena.

35 Plotinus does not hold firm to the analogy of air in light, for at IV.4.29, 1-2 he says that the body is like a heated object, not like an illuminated one.

36 IV.2.2; IV.3.3, 9-10; IV.4.19, 12-15; IV.7.7, 25-7 etc. I discuss this doctrine in detail in Chapter V, section 2 and VIII, section 2.

37 See especially III.6.1-5.

38 The doctrine that the soul cannot be affected by the body was subsequently taken up by St Augustine (cf. *De Musica* VI, 5.8).

39 *De An.* 406a 1-3; 408b 1-31.

40 *De An.* 431b 27.

41 See *Gen. Corr.* 324b 19-24.

42 In *De An.* 408b 18-24, however, Aristotle seems to imply that there is no more reason for sight to be destroyed through corruption of the body than there is for intellect. He is arguing that the deterioration of intellectual

capacities in old age is due to deterioration of the body, not of the intellect itself. He says that what happens is similar to what happens to sight: it is the organ which deteriorates but if an old person acquired a new eye of an appropriate kind, he would see like a young man. The conclusion of the passage is that intellect is not affected by what happens to the body, and the implication seems to be that sight is likewise unaffected.

III The relation between the eye and the object of vision

1 See J.I. Beare, *Greek Theories of Elementary Cognition from Alcmaeon to Aristotle* (Oxford, 1906). Beare gives a clear and thorough account of the views of the early Greek thinkers up to and including Aristotle on visual transmission. No comparable work covering the post-Aristotelian period exists. But valuable general information is to be found in D.E. Hahm, 'Early Hellenistic Theories of Vision and the Perception of Color' in P.K. Machamer and R. Turnbull (eds.), *Studies in Perception* (Columbus, Ohio, 1978), and R. Siegel, *Galen on Sense-Perception* (Basel, New York, 1970).
2 See Bruns, 127-50; Galen, *De Plac., Hipp. et Plat.* VII. 4-8; Plotinus, IV.5.1-4.
3 See *Ennéades* 4, 57-8 and note to IV.5.1, 156; *DG*, 403-4.
4 *Ennéades* 4, 57.
5 The technical use of the term *to metaxy* comes from Aristotle, who uses it in exactly the same way as Plotinus, cf. *De An.* 419a 20; 421b 9; 434b 28; 435b 16.
6 Alexander of Aphrodisias makes a similar critical remark in *In de Sensu, Comment. in Arist. Gr.* 3, 31, 25.
7 A. Graeser, *Plotinus and the Stoics*, 46-7; cf. Armstrong's note to IV.5.1 in *Plotinus* 4, 283.
8 See Bruns, 130, 15 (*SVF* 2, 864); Aetius, *Plac.* IV.15.3 (*DG*, 406; *SVF* 2, 866).
9 For the Stoic theory of visual transmission see *SVF* 2, 863-71. Good accounts of the Stoic views on visual transmission are offered by S. Sambursky in *Physics of the Stoics* (New York, 1959), 22-9, and by D. E. Hahm in "Early Hellenistic Theories of Vision".
10 See Theophrastus, "Fragmentum de sensibus" 51-5, (*DG*, 513-15).
11 εἰ μηδενὸς ὄντος μεταξὺ ἔστιν ὁρᾶν οἷον ἀέρος ἢ ἄλλου τινὸς τοῦ λεγομένου διαφανοῦς σώματος, νῦν σκεπτέον.
12 Plotinus' use of the word *diadosis* in chap. 3, 2 shows that he is thinking of a progressive affection, cf. his criticism of *diadosis* as an explanation of internal perception in IV.2.2 and IV.7.7. For Aristotle's views see esp. *Sens.* 446b 28-447a 12. Aristotle holds that transmission of light occurs by means of an instantaneous alteration and not by locomotion. Alexander follows Aristotle at least in expression and speaks of affection (*paschein*), movement (*kinêsis*) and alteration (*alloiousthai*) of the diaphanous medium (Bruns, 42, 50; 141, 26; 142, 28). But in the treatise "How Vision Occurs According to Aristotle" he qualifies the statement that the diaphanous is affected and denies that it is altered (Bruns, p.143, 4-30).
13 Aetius, *Plac.* IV.13.7-8 (*DG*, 403-4): "Strato says that colours are carried from the bodies, giving the same colour to the intermediate air Aristagoras [says] that shapes somehow make an impression on the air with themselves." The text has "Aristagoras", not "Aristarchus", but it is likely that Aristarchus is meant: see Diels' note in *DG*, 853. In the commentary to IV.5.2, 1 Theiler points out that Strato's views as reported by Aetius fit the doctrine described by Plotinus, cf. the H-S *index fontium*.

14 Again, if Plotinus had Alexander's version of the Aristotelian view in mind, this point would be inappropriate, for Alexander makes it quite clear that the affection of the medium is not ordinary bodily affection, cf. note 12 above.

15 See Cicero, *Acad. Pr.* II. 121 (frag. 32 Wehrli); cf. also frag. 114.

16 οὐ γὰρ μόνον ἡ ἁφὴ ὅτι ἐγγύς τι λέγει καὶ ἅπτεται, ἀλλὰ τὰς τοῦ ἁπτοῦ πάσχουσα ἀπαγγέλλει διαφοράς.

17 See Calcidius, *In Tim* . 236-43 and D. E. Hahm, "Early Hellenistic Theories of Vision", 61 ff.

18 See Galen, *De Plac. Hipp. et Plat.* VII.7.20 (*SVF* 2, 865); Aetius, *Plac.* IV.15.3 (*DG*, 406; *SVF* 2, 865); Bruns, 130, 14 (*SVF* 2, 864). The staff analogy was later taken up by St Augustine (cf. *De Quantitate Animae* 23.43).

19 See D.L. VII, 157: "They [the Stoics] hold that we see when the light between the visual organ and the object is stretched (*enteinomenon*) in the form of a cone".

20 K. Reinhardt, *Kosmos und Sympathie: Neue Untersuchungen Über Posidonios* (Munich, 1926), 187-92.

21 "Plotinus' Theory of Sensation", 365-6.

22 Clark (366, note 17) refers to IV.5.7, 23-5 and V.5.7, 27 as passages where Plotinus asserts the existence of visual rays. But neither of these passages actually asserts this: In IV.5.7, 23-5 Plotinus is alluding to the fact that the eyes of certain animals (e.g. of cats and sheep) shine in the dark; in V.5.7, 27 he is talking about the eye's internal light, and mentions as evidence of its existence that in the darkness of night this light may spring forward. It is not clear what phenomenon Plotinus is thinking of. It might be the "luminous" eyes of some animals as in IV.5.7 or it might be some kind of phenomenal brightness. In any case there is no evidence supporting the view that Plotinus thinks this light must proceed to the objects of vision.

23 "Plotinus' Theory of Sensation", 367.

24 Ibid., 367.

25 *De Plac. Hipp. et Plat.* VII.5.31-3; 7.16-19.

26 IV.5.4, 40-6. ἔδει τὴν ἀντίληψιν βίαιον καὶ ἀντερείδοντος εἶναι καὶ τεταμένου τοῦ φωτός, καὶ τὸ αἰσθητόν, τὸ χρῶμα, ἢ χρῶμα, ἀντιτυποῦν καὶ αὐτὸ εἶναι· οὕτω γὰρ διὰ μέσου αἱ ἁφαί. εἶτα καὶ πρότερον ἐγγὺς γέγονε μηδενὸς μεταξὺ ὄντος τότε· οὕτω γὰρ ὕστερον τὸ διὰ μέσου ἅπτεσθαι ποιεῖ τὴν γνῶσιν, οἷον τῇ μνήμῃ καὶ ἔτι μᾶλλον συλλογισμῷ· νῦν δὲ οὐχ οὕτως.

27 In *De Plac. Hipp. et Plat.* VII.7,20 Galen makes a similar remark against the Stoics' staff analogy, but his expression is no clearer.

28 See Graeser, *Plotinus and the Stoics*, 68-72. Graeser rightly points out that Plotinus' adoption of *sympatheia* is not a matter of a simple borrowing: the Stoic concept of *sympatheia* is itself developed on the basis of Plato and could easily be fitted to Plotinus' views. *Sympatheia* was also adopted by the Peripatetic school, though at least Alexander rejected the Stoic account of it (cf. Todd, *Alexander of Aphrodisias on Stoic Physics*, 216-17; D.L. v, 32). Thus, by Plotinus' time *sympatheia* had presumably become a household word in all the schools.

29 See Sambursky, *Physics of the Stoics*, 29-33.

30 See Sextus Empiricus, *Adv. Math.* IX, 78 (*SVF* 2, 1013); Alexander, *De Mixt.*, 135; 142-4 (Todd) (*SVF* 2, 441; 475); Cic., *Nat. D.* II, 19; Cleomedes, *De Motu Circulari Corporum Caelestium*, 8 (Ziegler) (*SVF* 2, 446). A clear account of the connection between *sympatheia* and the fundamental principles of Stoic physics is given by Sambursky in *Physics of the Stoics*, 9 and 41-2. After

Reinhardt's *Kosmos und Sympathie* there was a tendency to associate *sympatheia* primarily with the name of Posidonius. But as pointed out by M. Pohlenz already in 1926 in a review of Reinhardt's book (*Göttingensche Gelehrte Anzeigen* [1926], 277), cited by Todd, *Alexander on Stoic Physics*, 188), *sympatheia* was employed as a cosmological principle by Chrysippus himself, cf. *Plotinus and the Stoics*, 68-9 and 68 note 7.

31 See e.g. Sextus, *Adv. Math.* IX, 79; Cic., *Div.* II, 34 and *Nat. D.* II, 19.

32 There are however records connecting Posidonius' views on vision with the related notion of the *symphuia* of the pneuma: cf. Aetius, *Plac.* IV.13.3 (*DG*, 403) and Cleomedes, *De motu circ.*, 8 (Ziegler). In light of this it is possible that Plotinus has Posidonius and his followers in mind where he speaks of "those who say that vision takes place by means of *sympatheia*". But in any event Plotinus' views on *sympatheia* must have differed from those of Posidonius, since Plotinus disposes entirely of the notion of pneuma.

33 See e. g. IV.4.26, 14-16; IV.4.32, 1-17; IV.4.40; IV.9.3, 1-6.

34 II.3.12, 30-2; IV.3.8, 1-3. According to some MSS there is a reference to *sympatheia* between soul and body in VI.4.3, 20.

35 IV.5.8 is a notoriously difficult chapter. Bréhier's reconstruction, on which I am relying here, seems to be the best one can make of it. See his introduction to IV.3-5, *Ennéades* 4, 63.

36 I.6.9, 31; II.4.5, 10; IV.5.7, 24; V.5.7, 22-30; VI.7.1, 2.

37 II.4.5, 10-11; V.3.8, 20; V.5.7, 30.

38 IV.5.2, 46-8. εἰ οὖν τοῖς σώμασι διίσταται τοῖς τοιούτοις μηδὲν παθών, τί κωλύει καὶ ἄνευ διαστάσεως συγχωρεῖν παριέναι τοῖς εἰς ὄψιν εἴδεσιν;

39 IV.5.3, 32-8. νῦν δὲ πᾶν τε ὁρᾶται, καὶ ὅσοι ἐν τῷ ἀέρι κατά γε τὸ καταντικρὺ ἔκ τε πλαγίων ἐπὶ πολὺ ὁρῶσιν ἐγγύς τε καὶ κατόπιν οὐκ ἐπιπροσθούμενοι ὥστε ἕκαστον μόριον τοῦ ἀέρος ὅλον οἷον τὸ πρόσωπον τὸ ὁρώμενον ἔχειν.

40 IV.5.3, 36-8. οὐ κατὰ σώματος πάθημα, ἀλλὰ κατὰ μείξους καὶ ψυχικὰς καὶ ζῴου ἑνὸς συμπαθοῦς ἀνάγκας.

41 See p.68

42 The terms Plotinus uses for forms in the context of sense-perception are discussed in Chapter IV, note 24

43 II.8.1, 37-8.

44 See IV.4.29, 19-20 and VI.3.17, 16-27. We may remark, incidentally, concerning the latter passage that Plotinus rejects the Aristotelian notion of colors as points on a scale with white and black as extremes. He argues in effect as G. E. Moore was to do that colours are indefinable: colours are phenomena we can apprehend and distinguish by perception, but we cannot account for their intrinsic differences (cf. VI.3.17, 16-20, 19).

45 II.4.9, 7-12; II.6.1, 20-3; IV.4.29, 33-40; IV.7.4, 30-4; V.9.12, 9-11.

46 Aristotle also gives two accounts of colour that differ in an analogous way, see J. I. Beare, *Greek Theories of Elementary Cognition*, 60.

47 Plotinus was not alone in holding that colours are a kind of light and in positing as it were a double propagation of light: Alexander in the treatise "How Vision Occurs According to Aristotle" says that as light is the actualization of the potentially diaphanous matter, colors, being a second light, give by their presence a second actualization to the actually diaphanous. (ὡς οὖν ἡ τῶν φωτίζειν πεφυκότων παρουσία ποιεῖ διαφανὲς δυνάμει κατ' ἐνέργειαν διαφανές, ὅτως πάλιν τὸ κατ' ἐνέργειαν διαφανὲς τὸ χρῶμα τῶν ὁρωμένων ὡς δεύτερόν τι φῶς τῇ παρουσίᾳ αὐτῶν λαμβάνει δευτέραν τινὰ ταύτην ἐνέργειαν δεχόμενον [Bruns, 142, 10-13]). And Calcidius speaks of a

threefold *ratio* of vision, consisting of the internal light, which passes through the eyes, the external light, and a light "which flows from the bodies of visible forms, a colour or a glow" (*In Tim.* 245).

48 vi.4.12, 5-7. ὀφθαλμοὶ πολλοὶ πρὸς τὸ αὐτὸ εἶδον καὶ πάντες ἐπλήσθησαν τῆς θέας καίτοι ἐναφωρισμένου τοῦ θεάματος κειμένου.

49 See p. 50.

50 vi.4.12, 10-12. καὶ τὸ τῆς ὄψεως δέ, εἰ παθὼν ὁ ἀὴρ τὴν μορφὴν ἔχει, ἔχει οὐ μεμερισμένην· οὐ γὰρ ἂν ὄψις τεθῇ, ἔχει ἐκεῖ τὴν μορφήν. Here in vi.4, which is number 22 on Porphyry's chronological list and hence written before iv.5, which is number 29 (*Life of Plotinus* 4), Plotinus does not commit himself as to whether or not the air is affected by the visual forms. But already here it is clearly implied that the transmission is not by means of progressive affection of the air.

51 Bruns, 42-3, cf. 62 and 143. It is possible that Alexander had arrived at the idea that the affection produced by a large object is present as a whole at every point of the intermediate space (cf. Bruns, 146, 21-8). The relevant passage is however most obscure.

52 Such is Taylor's understanding of the *Timaeus* 45 B – C: see A. E. Taylor, *Commentary on Plato's Timaeus* (Oxford, 1928), 278.

53 *De Plac. Hipp. et Plat.* vii. 7, 9-10, cf. Plotinus iv.6.1, 14-17.

54 See *De Plac. Hipp. et Plat.* vii. 5, 5-10; 7, 19. For accounts of Galen's views on sense-perception see H. Cherniss, "Galen and Posidonius' Theory of Vision", *The American Journal of Philology*, 54 (1933), 156-61, R. Siegel, *Galen on Sense-Perception* and P. de Lacy's commentary on *Plac. Hipp. et Plat.* vii in vol. 3 of *Galen. On the Doctrines of Hippocrates and Plato* (Berlin, 1984).

55 Plotinus' criticisms of *diadosis* seem to fit Strato's views as well as Stoic doctrines, cf. Strato fr. 111 (Wehrli). As Blumenthal notes Plotinus may well be aiming at both: see *Plotinus' Psychology*, 73 note 16.

56 See iv.7.3, 2-5, where *sympathês* and *sympatheia* replace *homopatheia*, and iv.9.2, 20 and 32.

iv Sensory affection

1 P. O. Kristeller claims that there is a difference between Plotinus' use of the singular, *pathos*, and the plural, *pathê*. The former, he says, denotes "das blosse körperliche Betroffensein", the latter is "durchgehend für die unvernünftigen Empfindungen gebraucht" (*Der Begriff der Seele in der Ethik des Plotin*, 30). Actually, however, there is no such difference between the singular and the plural, although it is true that *ta pathê* often means specifically "the emotions" (see for instance iii.6.1, 1 and 5, where the plural and the singular must have the same sense).

2 iii.6.1, 2; iv.3.3, 22-3.

3 The words *pathos* and *pathêma* are derived from *pathein*, the aorist of *paschein*.

4 Aristotle, *Cat.* 2a 4-5; 11b 1-8. For *to poioun* and *to paschon* in Stoicism, see D.L. vii, 139 (*SVF* 2, 300); Sextus, *Adv. Math.* ix, 11 (*SVF* 2, 301); Alexander, *De Mixt.*, 139 (Todd) (*SVF* 2, 310). Plato in *Gorgias* 476 A – E seems to have been the first to discuss *poiein* and *paschein* systematically as correlatives.

5 For the development of ancient views on causation see M. Frede, "The Original Notion of Cause", in M. Schofield, M. Burnyeat and J. Barnes (eds.), *Doubt and Dogmatism* (Oxford, 1980), 217-49.

6 In the theory of perception presented in the *Theaetetus* 155 E – 160 E Plato

explicitly describes the objects of perception and the percipient in terms of *poiein* and *paschein*. See also e. g. Aristotle, *De An.* 424b 4-19; Aetius, *Plac.* IV.12.1 (*DG*, 401; *SVF* 2, 54); Sextus, *Adv. Math.* VII, 162 (*SVF* 2, 63).

7 In *De An.* 424a 1 Aristotle says that perceiving is a species of being affected, but previously (417b 29-418a 6), he has made clear that it is a special form of being affected, which applies to the move from potency to act.

8 Compare the views of, say, Philoponus in *In De An., Comment. in Arist. Gr.* 15, 303, 3-6; F. Brentano in *Die Psychologie des Aristoteles* (Mainz, 1867), 79-81; W. D. Ross in *Aristotle* (London, 1923), chap. 5; T. Slakey in "Aristotle on Sense-Perception", *The Philosophical Review* 70 (1961), 470-84; R. Sorabji in "Body and Soul in Aristotle", *Philosophy* 49 (1974), 63-89; and E. Hartman in *Substance, Body and Soul: Aristotelian Investigations* (Princeton, 1977), chap. 5.

9 See F. H. Sandbach's article, "Phantasia Katalêptikê" in A. A. Long (ed.), *Problems in Stoicism* (London, 1971). Sandbach convincingly argues that, according to the Stoic view, a *phantasia* is at once a physical impression on the principal part of the soul and an "interpretation" of that impression. Thus, *phantasiai* are in themselves meaningful entities, and hence belong to the same realm as propositions and thoughts.

10 III.6.1, 1-3; 2, 53-4; IV.3.3, 22-3; IV.3.26, 5-6; IV.4.23, 19-32; VI.4.6, 10-11; cf. also I.1.3, 4-7; IV.5.4, 29; IV.6.2, 16-18.

11 IV.3.26, 5-9. τοῦ μὲν σώματος πάσχοντος καὶ ὑπηρετοῦντος, τῆς δὲ ψυχῆς παραδεχομένης τὴν τύπωσιν τὴν τοῦ σώματος, ἢ τὴν διὰ τοῦ σώματος, ἢ τὴν κρίσιν, ἢ ἐποιήσατο ἐκ τοῦ παθήματος τοῦ σώματος.

12 *Vita Plotini* 5, 20.

13 τὰς αἰσθήσεις οὐ πάθη λέγοντες εἶναι, ἐνεργείας δὲ περὶ παθήματα καὶ κρίσεις, τῶν μὲν παθῶν περὶ ἄλλο γινομένων, οἷον τὸ σῶμα φέρε τὸ τοιόνδε, τῆς δέ κρίσεως περὶ τὴν ψυχήν.

14 δεῖ δὴ θέσθαι, ὡς τὸ αἰσθάνεσθαι τῶν αἰσθητῶν ἐστι τῇ ψυχῇ ἢ τῷ ζώῳ ἀντίληψις τὴν προσοῦσαν τοῖς σώμασι ποιότητα συνιείσης καὶ τὰ εἴδη αὐτῶν ἀποματτομένης.

15 ἢ τοίνυν μόνη ἐφ' ἑαυτῆς ἀντιλήψεται, ἢ μετ' ἄλλου. μόνη μὲν οὖν καὶ ἐφ' ἑαυτῆς πῶς; ἐφ' ἑαυτῆς γὰρ τῶν ἐν αὐτῇ, καὶ μόνον νόησις εἰ δὲ καὶ ἄλλων, δεῖ πρότερον καὶ ταῦτα ἐσχηκέναι ἤτοι ὁμοιωθεῖσαν ἢ τῷ ὁμοιοθέντι συνοῦσαν.

16 ἀλλὰ μόνη, κἂν εἰ οἷόν τε τῷ αἰσθητῷ ἐπιβάλλειν, τελευτήσει εἰς νοητοῦ σύνεσιν, ἐκφυγόντος τοῦ αἰσθητοῦ αὐτήν, οὐκ ἐχούσης ὅτῳ αὐτοῦ λάβοιτο. ἐπεὶ καὶ τὸ ὁρατὸν ὅταν ψυχὴ πόρρωθεν ὁρᾷ, κἂν ὅτι μάλιστα εἶδος εἰς αὐτὴν ἥκῃ, ἀρχόμενον τὸ πρὸς αὐτὴν οἷον λήγει εἰς τὸ ὑποκείμενον χρῶμα καί σχῆμα, ὅσον ἐστὶν ἐκεῖ ὁρώσης.

17 It is possible that the meaning is that the organ is sympathetic and similarly affected and made of one matter with the soul, not with the external object. This understanding even suits the grammar of the sentence better. However, I cannot make any sense of the statement that the soul and the organ are made of "one matter", whereas in light of IV.5 this and the reference to *sympatheia* make good sense, if we suppose that these terms describe the organ's relation to the object of vision.

18 οὐ τοίνυν δεῖ μόνα ταῦτα εἶναι, τὸ ἔξω καὶ τὴν ψυχήν· ἐπεὶ οὐδ' ἂν πάθοι· ἀλλὰ δεῖ τὸ πεισόμενον τρίτον εἶναι, τοῦτο δέ ἐστι τὸ τὴν μορφὴν δεξόμενον. συμπαθὲς ἄρα καὶ ὁμοιοπαθὲς δεῖ εἶναι καὶ ὕλης μιᾶς καὶ τὸ μὲν παθεῖν, τὸ δὲ γνῶναι, καὶ τοιοῦτον γενέσθαι τὸ πάθος, οἷον σῴζειν μέν τι τοῦ πεποιηκότος, μὴ μέντοι ταὐτὸν εἶναι, ἀλλὰ ἄτε μεταξὺ τοῦ

πεποιηκότος καὶ ψυχῆς ὄν, τὸ πάθος ἔχειν μεταξὺ αἰσθητοῦ καὶ νοητοῦ κείμενον μέσον ἀνάλογον, συνάπτον πως τὰ ἄκρα ἀλλήλοις, δεκτικὸν ἅμα καὶ ἀπαγγελτικὸν ὑπάρχον, ἐπιτήδειον ὁμοιωθῆναι ἑκατέρῳ. ὄργανον γὰρ ὂν γνώσεώς τινος οὔτε ταὐτὸν δεῖ τῷ γινώσκοντι εἶναι οὔτε τῷ γνωσθησομένῳ, ἐπιτήδειον δὲ ἑκατέρῳ ὁμοιωθῆναι, τῷ μὲν ἔξω διὰ τοῦ παθεῖν, τῷ δὲ εἴσω διὰ τοῦ τὸ πάθος αὐτοῦ εἶδος γενέσθαι.

19 Such an analogy is implicit in Plotinus' term for sense-organ, *organon*, itself: the original meaning of *organon* is tool. It came to be applied to the sense-organs because these were seen as tools used by the soul, cf. *Theaet.* 185 c.

20 καὶ τὰ τεχνητὰ δὲ τῶν ὀργάνων ἴδοι τις ἄν μεταξὺ τῶν κρινόντων καὶ τῶν κρινομένων γινόμενα καὶ ἀπαγγέλλοντα τῷ κρίνοντι τὴν τῶν ὑποκειμένων ἰδιότητα· ὁ γὰρ κανὼν τῷ εὐθεῖ τῷ ἐν τῇ ψυχῇ καὶ τῷ ἐν τῷ ξύλῳ συναψάμενος ἐν τῷ μεταξὺ τεθεὶς τὸ κρίνειν τῷ τεχνίτῃ τὸ τεχνητὸν ἔδωκεν.

21 See e.g. Sextus, *Adv. Math.* VII, 366-8.

22 In I.6.3, 9-15 and III.6.18, 21-8 the soul is said to receive the forms of the objects of perception; in IV.4.23, 21 the organ is said to receive the form, cf. VI.4.12, 2.

23 See I.1.8, 7-8 and Chapter VII section 2.

24 Although Plotinus' word for form here is not *eidos* but *morphê*, in the context of sensible forms the latter word is often used in the same sense as *eidos*. Cf. e.g. VI.4.12, 11 (quoted on pp. 56), where *morphê* is used to denote what in IV.5.2, 48 and 49, and in II.8.1 *passim* is called *eidos*. In connection with perception the terms *eidôlon* and *typos* are also used in similar contexts as *eidos* and *morphê*, cf. I.1.7, 12; III.6.1, 8-11; IV.3.26, 24-32; IV.6.1, 38; V.5.1, 18. For a discussion of the term *eidôlon* see Chapter VI, section 1.

25 Plotinus employs the notion of special sensibles in the sense that he supposes that colours are special objects of vision, sounds of hearing and so forth (cf. II.4.12, 29-32; II.8.1, 12-23). But he does not use the Aristotelian technical expression *koina aisthêta*, nor does he contrast special sensibles with common sensibles. In II.8.1, 12 ff. he describes sizes of things as something which is accidentally (*kata symbebêkos*) seen, and contrasts this with colours as primary objects of vision. As Bréhier notes in a footnote to this passage in *Ennéades* 2 this notion of something accidentally visible is different from Aristotle's notion of the accidentally perceived in *De An.* 425a21ff. Plotinus supposes that we see how large things are by the distinctness of their colours (II.8.1, 29-51).

26 Such a theory is argued for by D. M. Armstrong in *Perception and the Physical World* (London and New York, 1961) and *A Materialist Theory of the Mind* (London and New York, 1968) and by G. Pitcher in *A Theory of Perception* (Princeton, 1971).

27 Thus, Blumenthal writes: "Instead of being stamped the soul receives a kind of translation of the impression by which the body is affected: today we should think in terms of electrical impulses travelling along the nerves. It is these impressions in the body and its organs that the soul perceives" (*Plotinus' Psychology*, 71-2, cf. "Plotinus' Adaptation of Aristotle's Psychology", 47). Blumenthal thus holds that Plotinus' sensory affections are physical impressions and that these impressions are the immediate objects of perception. But even if it is supposed that sensory affections are physical changes in the sense-organs, it does not necessarily follow that these changes are what is perceived. Blumenthal however takes it to be so, presumably

because he thinks this is asserted by Plotinus himself in I.1.7. I argue later, in Chapter VI section 1, that this passage should not be so interpreted.

28 Armstrong's translation of III.6.1, 1-2 thus contains unnecessary interpretation where he gives "activities and judgements concerned with affections" for *energeias de peri pathêmata kai kriseis*. In VI.4.6, 8-9 Plotinus indeed speaks of affections as objects of *kriseis*, but there the context suggests that he has in mind *kriseis* of pains and pleasures which *are* affections of the body (cf. IV.4.19).

29 IV.5.5, 28-31. ἀλλὰ περὶ μὲν τούτου ἠπορήσθω ὁμοίου ἤδη καὶ ἐνταῦθα τοῦ ζητήματος γενομένου, ὅπερ ἐλέγετο ἐπὶ τῆς ὄψεως εἶναι, συναισθήσεώς τινος ὡς ἐν ξῴῳ καὶ τοῦ κατὰ τὴν ἀκοὴν πάθους ὄντος.

30 See I.1.11, 11; IV.3.26, 45; IV.4.2, 31; IV.4.8, 20; V.3.13, 21. Discussions of Plotinus' views on consciousness are to be found in H.-R. Schwyzer, "'Bewusst' und 'Unbewusst' bei Plotin", *Les sources de Plotin*, 343-90; A. C. Lloyd, "Nosce Teipsum and Conscientia", *AGP* 44 (1964), 188-200; E. W. Warren, "Consciousness in Plotinus", *Phronesis* 9 (1964), 83-97; A. Graeser, "Plotinus on συναίσθησις", *Plotinus and the Stoics*, chap. 7, 126-37; A. Smith, "Unconsciousness and Quasiconsciousness in Plotinus", *Phronesis* 23 (1978), 292-301.

31 Cf. III.4.4, 10; IV.4.24, 21-5; V.3.2, 4-5.

32 For the pre-Plotinian use of *synaisthêsis* see Schwyzer, "'Bewusst' und 'Unbewusst'", 357-63 and Graeser, *Plotinus and the Stoics*, 126-9.

33 III.6.1, 3-4; cf. IV.4.18-19, 28; VI.4.6, 11.

34 See I.1.5, 1-3 and I.1.7, 1-6, where the compound is said to consist of the qualified body and an image of soul. For the distinction between the compound and the qualified body see the commentary on these passages in *Plotins Schriften* 1 b and Blumenthal, *Plotinus' Psychology*, 61-2.

35 For the identification of Aristotle as Plotinus' target see Bréhier's introduction to IV.6., *Ennéades* 4, 169-71.

36 Bruns, 72, 5-12.

37 There are certain textual difficulties here that however do not seriously affect the sense. I follow the H-S^2 text.

38 See Chapter V, section 3.

39 There is one passage, IV.6.3, 16-21, where Plotinus might be understood as saying that the sensible object is a creation of the perceiving soul (cf. C. Boyer, *L'idée de vérité dans la philosophie de Saint Augustin* [Paris, 1941], 171). But in fact Plotinus is here talking about the memory of sensibles, not the perception of them.

40 See note 27 above and Chapter VI, section 1.

41 As G. Pitcher has noted, a distinction is to be made between a stringent and a liberal conception of seeing. When "to see" is used stringently, the statement "the hunter sees the pheasant" implies that the hunter recognizes what he sees as a pheasant. When used liberally, there is no such implication. On the liberal conception it is, however, implied that what the hunter sees is *in fact* the pheasant (cf. G. Pitcher, *A Theory of Perception*, 78-82). But in first person reports of occurrent vision, "to see" is always used stringently except perhaps in some very peculiar situations. Thus, "I am seeing the sky" normally implies "I believe that what I am seeing is the sky". (The last instance of "seeing" is an example of the liberal but non-stringent use; it is in the first person of course, but it is not a part of a person's report of *what* he is occurrently seeing.)

42 See W. Sellars, *Science, Perception and Reality* (London and New York, 1963),

69-70, 129-34 and 156-61, and *Philosophical Perspectives* (Springfield, Illinois, 1967), 211.

43 IV.4.8, 9-16. ὅταν γὰρ μηδὲν διαφέρῃ, ἢ μὴ πρὸς αὐτὸν ἢ ὅλως ἡ αἴσθησις ἀπροαιρέτως τῇ διαφορᾷ τῶν ὁρωμένων κινηθεῖσα, τοῦτο αὐτὴ ἔπαθε μόνη τῆς ψυχῆς οὐ δεξαμένης εἰς τὸ εἴσω, ἅτε μήτε πρὸς χρείαν μήτε πρὸς ἄλλην ὠφέλειαν αὐτῆς τῆς διαφορᾶς μέλον. ὅταν δὲ ἡ ἐνέργεια αὐτὴ πρὸς ἄλλοις ᾖ καὶ παντελῶς, οὐκ ἂν ἀνάσχοιτο τῶν τοιούτων παρελθόντων τὴν μνήμην, ὅπου μηδὲ παρόντων γινώσκει τὴν αἴσθησιν.

44 That by *aisthêsis* in IV.4.8,16 Plotinus means sensory affection is supported by the following considerations: In lines 10-11 it is said that *hê aisthêsis* is moved and it alone affected. It is clear that it is to this affection that Plotinus is referring in line 16. Now, on any interpretation this passage contains a deviation from Plotinus' normal account, which claims one must distinguish between the affection and the perception, and that the power of perception itself is not moved or in general affected by the external objects. The simplest way to fit this passage to the normal doctrine is to understand *aisthêsis* in line 10 to be the ensouled sense-organ rather than the power of perception as such, and to understand the *aisthêsis* that is said to escape the soul in line 16 to be the sensory affection.

45 See G. Ryle, *The Concept of Mind* (3rd edn, Harmondsworth, 1973), 150-6.

46 In any case Plotinus is not alone in holding that there are unnoticed sensations: see D. W. Hamlyn, *Sensation and Perception: A History of the Philosophy of Perception* (New York, 1961), 124-31.

47 Discussions relevant to this topic are to be found in W. Sellars, *Science, Perception and Reality*, chaps. 2, 3, and 5, and R. Rorty, *Philosophy and the Mirror of Nature* (Princeton, 1979), chaps 1 and 3.

48 Clark in "Plotinus' Theory of Sensation" suggests that the supposed intermediate status of the sense-organs and their affections is an *ad hoc* dogma introduced to bridge the wide gap between the soul and sensibles.

49 II.4.11, 1-3; II.9.17, 1-10; IV.2.1, 15-17; IV.7.1, 17-18; V.1.5, 10-13; V.9.9, 14-15.

50 IV.6.3, 70; IV.7.8; IV.7.12, 16; VI.1.26, 28-32; VI.4.1, 11-34; VI.4.12, 40-50.

51 VI.4.13, 2-3; VI.9.3, 27-32.

52 VI.8.2, 27-8; cf. III.6.18, 24-8.

53 See Chapter III, note 12 on p. 157.

54 Bruns, 145, 9-10.

55 Bruns, 83, 13-22.

56 *Adv. Math.* VII, 344, cf. 293.

57 Sextus' expressions "to be moved whitishly" and "to be moved sweetishly" presumably derive from the Cyrenaics (cf. *Adv. Math.* VII, 191). In "Idealism and Greek Philosophy: What Descartes Saw and Berkeley Missed" (*The Philosophical Review* 91 [1982]) M. F. Burnyeat says, commenting on the epistemology of the Cyrenaics: "it looks to be anachronistic to think we must be able to 'split' the Cyrenaic notion of experience into separate mental (subjective) and physical (objective) components" (28). Even if Burnyeat is right in this, it may well be the case that the Cyrenaics and Sextus were referring to precisely the phenomenon that we describe as "sensation", when they talked about "being whitened" or "being moved whitishly": certainly it seems to be possible to refer to sensations without being committed to the view that sensations are something mental as opposed to something physical.

58 See *Trin.* XI. 2, 4 and E. Ostenfeld, "Augustin om perception" in *Museum*

Tusculanum 40-43: *Studier i antik og middelalderlig filosofi og idéhistorie* (Copenhagen, 1980), 447-63.

v The unity of the senses

1 For detailed discussions of *Theaetetus* 184 ff. see e.g. J. M. Cooper, "Plato on Sense-Perception and Knowledge: *Theaetetus* 184-186", *Phronesis* 15 (1970), 123-46, and M. F. Burnyeat, "Plato on the Grammar of Perceiving", *CQ* 26 (1976), 31-51.
2 This is Alexander's understanding, cf. Bruns, 61.
3 Aristotle, *De An.* 427a 10-14. In "Sensation and Consciousness in Aristotle's Psychology" (*AGP* 48 [1966], 43-81) C. H. Kahn argues that the *Parva Naturalia* contains considerable advancement over *De Anima* in the treatment of the unity of the subject of perception. As Kahn interprets the relevant passages in the *Parva Naturalia*, Aristotle's views look very much like those of Alexander of Aphrodisias, which are discussed here below.
4 D. W. Hamlyn, *Aristotle's De Anima*: Books II and III, translation and commentary (Oxford, 1968), 128.
5 See Aetius, *Plac.* IV.4.4 (*DG*, 390; *SVF* 2, 827); cf. *SVF* 2, 828-33.
6 See Aetius, *Plac.* IV.21 (*DG*, 410-11; *SVF* 2, 836); Seneca, *Epist.* 113, 18 (*SVF* 3, 169).
7 See D.L. VII, 159 (*SVF* 2, 837); *SVF* 2, 826.
8 See Cic., *Acad. Pr.* II, 108 (*SVF* 2, cf. also ibid., 73; 74; 850 and 854).
9 See Seneca, *Epist.* 113, 23 (*SVF* 2, 836).
10 Calcidius, *In Tim.* 220 (*SVF* 2, 879).
11 *SVF* 2, 882, cf. ibid., 881 and 854.
12 A passage that clearly reveals the unity of the subject of perception and thought in Stoicism is found in Sextus, *Adv. Math.* VII, 307 (*SVF* 2, 849): "[The Stoics say that] the same thing is both reason and sense, but not in the same respect, it being in one respect reason, in another respect sense", cf. 359-60. Cf. also *SVF* 2, 826.
13 See E. Bréhier, *Chrysippe et l'ancien Stoïcisme* (rev. edn, Paris, 1951), 164-68.
14 This unifying function of the general faculty of sense is much more evident in the *Parva Naturalia* than in *De Anima*. See Kahn, "Sensation and Consciousness".
15 See e. g. *Mem.* 450a 14 and 451a 16; *Som.* 454a 23. Aristotle also uses the terms *koinê dynamis* and *to aisthêtikon pantôn* to refer to this same power, cf. *Som.* 455a 12 and *Sens.* 449a 17.
16 *De An.* 425a 27, cf. 431b 5. As to the possibility that Aristotle uses *koinê aisthêsis* in Alexander's sense in *Mem.* 450a 10 and *P.A.* 686a 31, see Kahn, "Sensation and Consciousness", note 36, p. 60.
17 *Som.* 456a 4 ff.; *Iuv.* 469a 13.
18 *De An.* 426b 30-2.
19 See Bruns, 61-2 and 83-4.
20 See Bruns, 62, 13-15 and 146, 25-6.
21 Bruns, 63, 11-12.
22 *De An.* 426b 17-21; Bruns, 60, 27-61, 3.
23 On Plotinus' use of Alexander and Aristotle in the development of his position on the unity of perception, see P. Henry, "Une comparaison chez Aristote, Alexandre et Plotin", *Les sources de Plotin*, 429-44.
24 There is a fuller and slightly different version of this argument in IV.2.2. Cf. also IV.4.19.

25 ιν.7.7, 24-8. μηδὲ σώματος, ὄγκου ὄντος, ἄλλου παθόντος ἄλλου γνῶσιν
εἶναι – παντὸς γὰρ μεγέθους τὸ μὲν ἄλλο, τὸ δὲ ἄλλο ἐστι – δεῖ τοιοῦτον
τίθεσθαι τὸ αἰσθανόμενον, οἷον πανταχοῦ αὐτὸ ἑαυτῷ τὸ αὐτὸ εἶναι.
τοῦτο δὲ ἄλλῳ τινὶ τῶν ὄντων ἢ σώματι ποιεῖν προσήκει.

26 For the Stoic view that the soul is a special kind of body see *SVF* 2, 773-800.

27 ιι.4.12, 1-3; ιιι.6.12, 53-7;16, 29-32; ιν.7.1, 17-18.

28 τὸ τριχῇ διαστατὸν μετὰ ἀντιτυπίας. *SVF* 2, 315; 381; cf. 357; 358.

29 Plotinus makes the Stoic account appear unduly crude. Our limited sources
give us reason to suppose that, within the bounds of their professed
materialism, the Stoics had quite sophisticated doctrines about the mechanism
of the soul, which among other things aimed at explaining the
interconnectedness of the functions of the soul. In particular, Plotinus fails to
take into account that according to the Stoic view states of the soul are
tensional states and that in a body in tension a change in part affects the state
of the whole.

30 "That the soul is incorporeal", Bruns, 113-18.

31 In *De Anima* 412b 6-8 Aristotle says: "Hence we should not ask whether the
soul and body are one, any more than whether the wax and the shape are one,
or in general whether the matter of each thing and that of which it is the
matter are one"; cf. Bruns, 11, 5-13. This and other similar remarks can be
taken to suggest that there is no essential difference between the ways in
which the shape is the form of the wax and the soul the form of the body. The
difference involved is just one of complexity (cf. Alexander, *loc. cit.*). In a
discussion of the theory according to which the soul is the actuality of the
body in ιν.7.8⁵, 5-9 Plotinus says: "If [the soul] is now compared with that
which it is likened to, the form of the statue in its relation to the bronze, then,
if the body is divided, the soul will be divided along with it; and if one cuts off
a part of the body there must be a part of the soul cut off with it."

32 *Summa Theologiae* ι. 76. 4.

33 See J. H. Randall's introduction to Pomponazzi's "De Immortalitate
Animae" in E. Cassirer, P. O. Kristeller and J. H. Randall (eds.), *The
Renaissance Philosophy of Man*, (Chicago and London, 1948), 276. Randall cites
Apologia Petri Pomponatii Mantuani (Bologna, 1519), ι, chap. 3, and *De
nutritione et augmentatione* in the Pomponazzi collection *Tractatus acutissimi,
utillimi et mere Peripatetici* (Venice, 1525) ι, chap. 11.

34 For this discovery and the reactions of philosophers to it, see F. Solmsen,
"Greek Philosophy and the Discovery of the Nerves", *Museum Helveticum*
17-18 (1961), 150-67 and 169-97.

35 Lines 15-21 (beginning from "But it would be better . ... "): βέλτιον δὲ
λέγειν τὴν ἀρχὴν τῆς ἐνεργείας τῆς δυνάμεως ἐκεῖ – ὅθεν γὰρ ἔμελλε
κινεῖσθαι τὸ ὄργανον, ἐκεῖ ἔδει οἷον ἐναπερείδεσθαι τὴν δύναμιν τοῦ
τεχνίτου ἐκείνην τὴν τῷ ὀργάνῳ πρόσφορον, μᾶλλον δὲ οὐ τὴν δύναμιν –
πανταχοῦ γὰρ ἡ δύναμις – ἐκεῖ δὲ τῆς ἐνεργείας ἀρχή, οὗ ἡ ἀρχὴ τοῦ
ὀργάνου.

36 See W. Helleman-Elgersma, *Soul-Sisters*, 294-301.

37 Plotinus once uses the term *hê koinê aisthêsis* (ι.1.9, 13). I take it, however, that
he is not referring to the Aristotelian general sense. Rather *hê koinê aisthêsis*
here means "the perception of the common entity" i.e. of the compound of
soul and body, cf. *aisthêsis hê en tôi koinôi* in ι.1. 8, 18-19 and *ta koina* in ι.1.9,
16. This is the understanding of Plotinus' translators, Harder and Armstrong
(see note to ι.1.9, 11 in *Plotins Schriften* 5b). But Bréhier gives "sens commun"

and such is also Blumenthal's understanding (cf. *Plotinus' Psychology*, 42, 79 and 106).

38 The most extensive passages dealing with *phantasia* are in iv.3.29-31.

39 iv.3.29, 25; iv.3.30; iv.4.8.

40 See E. W. Warren, "Consciousness in Plotinus", 87-8 and note 12, p. 88.

41 This use of *phantasia*, as the noun corresponding to *phainesthai*, "to appear", is to be found in Plato's *Theaet.* 152 c and is there associated with Protagoras (cf. *Soph.* 264 A-B). For a discussion of the formation of the word *phantasia* see M. Schofield, "Aristotle on the Imagination", in G. E. R. Lloyd and G. E. L. Owen (eds.), *Aristotle on Mind and the Senses* (Cambridge, 1978), 115 ff.

42 "Aristotle on the Imagination", 101.

43 See *Mem.* 449b 31 ff.; *De An.* 428b 10 ff.

44 Ibid., 114-15.

45 See for instance iv.4.13, 11 ff. where *phantasia* is described as the activity between nature (*physis*) and intellection (*noēsis*) without any mention of perception. Normally this place is assigned to perception or to perception and opinion, cf. i.1.8, 18-24; v.3.9, 28-36; iv.7.1-6.

46 In this context we should mention Blumenthal's view that Plotinus posits two faculties of *phantasia*, one that operates between sense-perception and reason, the other subsensitive. In this, Blumenthal suggests, Plotinus is following hints from Aristotle (see "Plotinus' Adaptation of Aristotle's Psychology", 51-5; cf. *Plotinus' Psychology*, 89-95). Now, it is undeniable that Plotinus thinks that the faculty of *phantasia* is somehow twofold (cf. iv.3.30 ff.). However, even though I do not clearly understand this whole issue myself, I am sure that Blumenthal's account of this duality is unsatisfactory in at least two respects: (a) neither of the two faculties of *phantasia* mentioned in iv.3.30 ff. is subsensitive; (b) the passages Blumenthal explicitly refers to as evidence of a subsensitive faculty of *phantasia*, in iv.4.20, 17 and vi.8.3, are not evidence of anything of the sort. I do not think these passages speak of a faculty of *phantasia* at all, but only of *phantasia* in the sense of "image". In iv.4.20, 17 the power that apprehends such an image is called simply perception (*aisthēsis*). The issue in these passages is apprehension of desires and affections originating in the body and the object of such an apprehension is referred to as *phantasia*, "image".

47 i.4.10, 19-21; iv.3.29-31; v.3.2-3.

48 See Chapter ii, section 3.

49 i.1.7, 12-13 and iv.4.23, 32.

50 H. von Kleist notes the close ties between *aisthēsis* and *phantasia* where he says that in normal perception "münden die Wahrnehmungen unmittelbar in das *phantastikon*" (*Plotinische Studien* [Heidelberg, 1883], note 1, 82-3).

51 See e.g. Kahn, "Sensation and Consciousness", 78-81; D. W. Hamlyn, *Aristotle's De Anima*, 121 and W. F. R. Hardie, "Concepts of Consciousness in Aristotle", *Mind* 85 (1976), 388-411.

52 Detailed discussions of this passage are to be found in E. Warren, "Consciousness in Plotinus" and in A. Smith, "Unconsciousness and Quasiconsciousness in Plotinus".

vi *The objects of perception*

1 See E. Zeller, *Die Philosophie der Griechen in ihrer Geschichtlichen Entwicklung* (4th edn, Leipzig, 1903), vol. 3, part 2, 637-8; C. Boyer, *L'idée de verité dans la philosophie de Saint Augustin*, 171; Blumenthal, *Plotinus' Psychology*, 71-2 and

"Plotinus' Adaptation of Aristotle's Psychology", 47; cf. S. Strange, *Plotinus' Treatise on the Genera of Being*, 151-2.

2 A change of mind is not a likely explanation of the apparent inconsistency: v.5 is number 32 on Porphyry's chronological list, i.1 number 53, but iv.6, which most expressly affirms realism, is number 41.

3 By *zôiou pathê* in i.1.7, 6 Plotinus has in mind the emotions: pleasures and pains, fears and assurances, desires and aversions, and the like, cf. i.1.1, 1 ff. These are said not to occur without perception (i.1.1, 12-13).

4 Professor Blumenthal has pointed out to me that *timiôtera* must mean "worthier than the organism", not "of more value than we are" as Armstrong's translation has it.

5 i.1.7, 6-16. ἀλλὰ πῶς ἡμεῖς αἰσθανόμεθα; ἤ, ὅτι οὐκ ἀπηλλάγημεν τοῦ τοιούτου ζῴου, καὶ εἰ ἄλλα ἡμῖν τιμιώτερα εἰς τὴν ὅλην ἀνθρώπου οὐσίαν ἐκ πολλῶν οὖσαν πάρεστι. τὴν δὲ τῆς ψυχῆς τοῦ αἰσθάνεσθαι δύναμιν οὐ τῶν αἰσθητῶν εἶναι δεῖ, τῶν δὲ ἀπὸ τῆς αἰσθήσεως ἐγγιγνομένων τῷ ζῴῳ τύπων ἀντιληπτικὴν εἶναι μᾶλλον· νοητὰ γὰρ ἤδη ταῦτα· ὡς τὴν αἴσθησιν τὴν ἔξω εἴδωλον εἶναι ταύτης, ἐκείνην δὲ ἀληθεστέραν τῇ οὐσίᾳ οὖσαν εἰδῶν μόνων ἀπαθῶς εἶναι θεωρίαν. ἀπὸ δὴ τούτων τῶν εἰδῶν, ἀφ' ὧν ψυχὴ ἤδη παραδέχεται μόνη τὴν τοῦ ζῴου ἡγεμονίαν, διάνοιαι δὴ καὶ δόξαι καὶ νοήσεις.

6 See Blumenthal, *Plotinus' Psychology*, 71-2 and "Plotinus' Adaptation of Aristotle's Psychology", 47.

7 See pp. 109-10.

8 See e.g. iv.4.19, 11-12; iv.4.23, 16; iv.6.1, 18.

9 See *Lexicon Plotinianum* s. vv. *aisthêsis* b and *aisthanesthai* a1. In "Plotinus' Theory of Sensation" Clark argues as I do here that "the soul's power of perception" in i.1.7 does not refer to sense-perception, but rather to intellection or other non-sensory apprehension of the soul. Clark points out that given Plotinus' system it would be appropriate to describe sense-perception as an image of intellection, and he suggests that this is how one should understand the statement in i.1.7, 13-14, that the perception of the external is an image (*eidôlon*) of that of the soul. He could have given further support to this claim by pointing out that in iv.7.5, 20-1 perceptions through the senses are described as images (*eikones*) of more perfect perceptions. The latter are evidently thoughts on the level of Intellect. There are however certain difficulties in identifying the soul's perception in i.1.7 with pure intellection of Forms. For the objects of the soul's perception here are representations and forms produced by perception. This suggests the forms involved in reasoning and memory rather than the Forms, which are not derived from sense-perception at all. However this may be, I am in agreement with Clark in taking "the soul's power of perception" to refer to apprehension above sense-perception, in which the body is not involved at all.

10 Cf. pp. 109.

11 See also v.3.3, 1-12

12 v.5.1, 9-19. Lines 12-19: ἐπεὶ καὶ τὰ ἐπὶ τῆς αἰσθήσεως, ἃ δὴ δοκεῖ πίστιν ἔχειν ἐναργεστάτην, ἀπιστεῖται, μή ποτε οὐκ ἐν τοῖς ὑποκειμένοις, ἀλλ' ἐν τοῖς πάθεσιν ἔχει τὴν δοκοῦσαν ὑπόστασιν καὶ νοῦ δεῖ ἢ διανοίας τῶν κρινούντων· ἐπεὶ καὶ συγκεχωρημένου ἐν τοῖς ὑποκειμένοις εἶναι αἰσθητοῖς, ὧν ἀντίληψιν ἡ αἴσθησις ποιήσεται, τό τε γινωσκόμενον δι' αἰσθήσεως τοῦ πράγματος εἴδωλόν ἐστι καὶ οὐκ αὐτὸ τὸ πρᾶγμα ἡ αἴσθησις λαμβάνει.

13 "Plotinus' Theory of Sensation", 361
14 See Bréhier's introduction to v.5, Enneades 5, 83-4
15 See *An. Post.* 99b 34-100b 4
16 I.1.7, 12; I.7.12, 5; II.4.5, 18-19; III.6.7, 28; III.6.9, 18; VI.3.13, 3; VI.8.18, 35. The list can be lengthened considerably: see *Lexicon Plotinianum s.v. eidôlon.* Plotinus' use of *eidôlon* is doubtless originally derived from the use of the term in such Platonic passages as *Rep.* 443 C and 516 A, and *Epist.* VII, 342 B.
17 The word *eidôlon* also occurs in v.5.1, 55 and 56, where Plotinus claims that if the Intellect knows the intelligibles without having them, it would "only receive images". Crudely put, Plotinus' problem is whether the Intellect has copies of the Forms or the originals themselves. If the Intellect has mere copies, the objects of the Intellect's thought will be what they are by participation in the original Forms, and not by virtue of themselves. And if so, the objects of the Intellect's thought are in this respect like those of sense-perception, which grasps mere inferior images of the true beings, expressed in a foreign material. By *eidôlon* in v.5.1, 55-6 is meant such an image of that which is what it is by virtue of itself. In v.5.1, 46-9 Plotinus says that the Intellect could not have a representation (*typos*) or outline (*morphê*) of the intelligibles. For the intelligibles would then be "like pictures in gold or some other such material made by a sculptor or a painter. But if so, the contemplation of the Intellect would be sense-perception" (v.5.2, 47-50). On my interpretation of v.5.1-2 the point of this statement is that the forms grasped in sense-perception are images of ontologically prior forms in a way analogous to the way artifacts are images of *logoi* and forms in the craftsman's soul (for this last mentioned idea see I.6.3; v.8.1, 23-40 and especially v.9.5, 36-48). Thus, the phenomena perceived through the senses are caused by something ontologically prior, as artifacts are caused by ontologically prior patterns in the craftsman's soul. Hence, if the Intellect has the intelligibles as "pictures in gold" it would have mere images.
18 For the view that sense-perception has qualities as its objects see pp. 68-72. That the forms in matter, i.e. qualities, are images of ontologically prior entities (and ultimately images of the Forms) is explicitly said in II.4.5, 18-19; III.6.7, 28; 13, 31-2; v.9.3, 36-7; 5, 18; 13, 4-5 and VI.3.15, 35-6.
19 It is true that the word for thing here, *pragma*, often refers to the sensible object. In IV.6.1, 31, for instance, *auta ta pragmata* clearly refers to the external sensible objects as opposed to something in a percipient (cf. above). But Plotinus also often uses *pragma* to refer to the intelligibles; cf. v.4.2, 47-8; v.9.5, 30-1; VI.5.3, 30 and VI.7.2, 10-11.
20 See p. 17 and p. 24.
21 III.6.1, 2; IV.3.3, 23; IV.3.26, 8; IV.4.22, 30-3; IV.4.23, 37-43; IV.6.2,17; IV.9.3.26-7; VI.4.6, 14. In IV.3.23, 31 Plotinus describes the faculty of perception as *kritikê.*
22 See e.g. Plato, *Theaet.* 186b; Aristotle, *De An.* 418a – 427a *passim*; and Alexander, Bruns, 60-73 *passim.*
23 Bruns, 78, 13 and 84, 5-6.
24 See H. G. Liddell, R. Scott and H. S. Jones, *A Greek-English Lexicon* (9th. edn, Oxford, 1940), s. v. *krinô.*
25 See Aristotle, *De An.* 426b 10-21; Bruns, 60-4, *passim.* T. Ebert in "Aristotle on What is Done in Perceiving" (*Zeitschrift für Philosophische Forschung* 37 [1981], 181-98) gives the gist of the early history of *krinein* and its cognates. He claims that in Aristotle *krinein* always means "to discriminate" rather than "to judge". Although Ebert makes an excellent case for this view, I am still

not convinced: at any rate if "to discriminate" is to be understood in such a way that it would be improper to say that one discriminates truly or falsely (cf. Ebert, op. cit., 184), it seems unlikely that it means specifically "to discriminate", for Aristotle seems to associate *krisis* specifically with those operations and faculties in virtue of which we are right or wrong (cf. *De An.* 428a 3-5).

26 Bruns, 73; cf. Aristotle, *De An.* 432a 15 ff.

27 Bruns, 78, 13-18; cf. Aristotle, *De An.* 428a 1-5.

28 III.6.1, 10-11; IV.6.2 and VI.1.20, 26-32.

29 In his dogmatic style Albinus says that primary perception judges primary sensibles such as whiteness (*leukotês*) and secondary perception secondary sensibles such as the white thing (*to leukon*); but the aggregate (*to athroisma*), of which fire and honey are given as examples, is judged by opinionative reason (*doxastikos logos*) though not without perception (*Didaskalikos*, 156 [Hermann]).

30 For the translation of *hê koinê aisthêsis* as "the common entity" in this passage see note 37 to Chapter V.

31 It may be asked whether such common reports of perception as "I see a man" do not constitute counter examples to the thesis that perceptions are judgements: "a man" does not express a judgement. I do not know what Plotinus' answer to this would be, but let us firstly note that it surely can be argued that perceiving *that* [proposition] is more basic than perceiving [object or event], that expressions of the latter type are in fact shorthand for, or analysable as, expressions of the former type. Thus, for instance, one might suggest that "Jones sees a house" can be analysed as "Jones sees that there is a house over there" or "Jones sees that x is a house". Secondly, it is worth noting that just as the verb "to perceive", the Greek verb *krinein* can be followed by a noun as well as by a proposition. I think, however, that this does not alter the fact that in Plotinus' view perceptions, considered as *kriseis*, are propositional: they are something to which "true" and "false" applies, and these apply only to propositions. It has been suggested that *kriseis*, though conceptual acts, are not propositional acts but classificatory, i.e. acts of recognizing (cf. M. F. Wagner, *Concepts and Causes*, chap. 1, note 10). But even if it is true that perceptual *kriseis* are often acts of recognizing or classifying, it does not follow that they are not propositional. At any rate it seems to me that "Jones recognizes (or classifies) x as F" entails "Jones believes that x is F"; hence, since the latter involves the entertaining of a proposition, the former does so as well.

32 See IV.5.4, 38-46 and pp. 45-6.

33 VI.3.18, 7-11. Perception cannot account for the difference between pale-green and yellow, because "giving accounts (*logon didonai*) is not its function, but only to point out different things (*mênuseis diaphorous poiêsasthai*)".

34 A lucid discussion of inference in perception is given by G. Harman in *Thought* (Princeton, 1973), chap. 11. Harman argues that perception involves unconscious inferences.

35 IV.3, 18; IV.4, 6, 10-16; V.3, 17, 21-8; VI.7, 1, 21-42.

VII Perceptions as acts and forms in perception

1 *De An.* 418a 3; 423b 27-424a 2.

2 There appears to be an inconsistency between Aristotle's statements that the

percipient becomes such as the object is actually, and the statement made in connection with the doctrine that the actuality of the object and of the sense is one in *De An.* 426a 15 ff., that actual sound requires an actual hearer, and similarly for the other senses. For the former statements imply that the object is actually sounding independently of whether the sound is being heard, whereas the latter excludes this (see E. Hartman, *Substnace, Body and Soul*, 193-6). But however this is to be resolved, if at all, it is clear that according to the unity-of-actuality doctrine the event which is the common actuality of the object and the percipient originates in the object, and that what happens in the percipient is an affection (cf. *De An.* 426a 5).

3 iv.3.23, 1-21; iv.6.2, 1-3.

4 ii.8.1, 45; iv.4.19, 13-29; iv.6.2, 1.

5 Aristotle in *De An.* 408b 18 ff. seems to imply that the powers of soul do not become worn out.

6 According to the Stoics assent (*synkatathêsis*) is "attributable to us" (*eph' hemin*) (cf. Cic. *Acad. Pr.* ii, 37 [*SVF* 2, 115]; Sextus, *Adv. Math.* viii, 397 [*SVF* 2, 91]), and hence it must stem from the agent.

7 The Stoics describe *phantasiai* in general as impressions (*typôseis*) in the soul (Zeno) or as alterations (*heteroiôseis*) of the soul (Chrysippus) (cf. Sextus, *Adv. Math.* vii, 227 [*SVF* 2, 56]). It is a corollary of Stoic physicalism that cognitive states are physical states of the principal part of the soul (*Adv. Math.* vii, 38 [*SVF* 2, 132]). This implies that the principal part is altered by assent.

8 Chrysippus also rejected it, although Plotinus shows no awareness of this fact. See preceding note.

9 Aristotle too says that those active powers whose forms are not embodied in matter, are unaffected by acting (*Gen. Corr.* 324b 5 ff.).

10 A point about the identity of the soul through time seems to be implicit in an obscure passage at iv.3.26, 39-46. The soul is there contrasted with those things that are in a state of flux.

11 See Chapter v, section 3 and Chapter vi, section 1.

12 See pp. 71-2.

13 i.6.3; v.8.1-2; v.9.5.

14 See p. 131 above.

15 vi.7.6, 7-11; cf. iii.6.18, 24-9.

16 In v.3.2, 11-13 Plotinus speaks in connection with the function of discursive reason about fitting new representations to old ones. This calls to mind *Theaetetus* 191 c ff.

17 i.2.3, 27-31; v.1.3, 7-9.

18 vi.7.5, 22-3; vi.7.7, 29-31.

19 The role of prior possession of concepts in Plotinus' theory of perception is noted by M. F. Wagner in *Concepts and Causes: The Structure of Plotinus' Universe*. See especially chap. 1, section 1 and chap. 4, section 2.

20 v.3.3, 6-9; v.3.4, 13-19.

21 See especially v.3.2-4 and Blumenthal's helpful account of discursive reason in *Plotinus' Psychology*, chap. 8.

22 See J. Fielder, "Plotinus' Copy Theory", 1-11.

23 See L. Wittgenstein, *Tractatus Logico-Philosophicus*, 2.18; 4.12.

viii Conclusions

1 Bruns, 83, 15-17.

2 "Idealism and Greek Philosophy: What Descartes Saw and Berkeley Missed", 30.

3 This view of the soul and the ensuing difficulty about explaining knowledge of the external extended world is clearly brought out in iv.4.23.

4 iv.2.1, 34-40; vi.4.1, 20-1.

5 See *The Principles of Philosophy*, part. 1, 53 (*The Philosophical Works of Descartes*, translated by G. R. T. Ross and E. S. Haldane [Cambridge, 1931], vol. 1, 240; *Œuvres de Descartes* ed. by C. Adam and P. Tannery [Paris, 1905], vol. 7, 25.)

6 Descartes, thinking in a similar manner, did not quite understand the doubt some of his objectors expressed as to whether he had excluded the possibility that his soul is a property of his body: he thought that since he had identified two distinct attributes, each of which constitutes a complete thing, it would be quite silly, self-contradictory in fact, to maintain that nonetheless they might belong to the same substance. See "Notes against a Programme" (Haldane and Ross, vol. 1, 434-8; Adam and Tannery, vol. 8, 347-52) and "Reply against Objections iv" (Haldane and Ross, vol. 2, 99-100; Adam and Tannery, vol. 7, 222-5).

7 Plotinus wants to deny that the corporeal can act on the soul at all (see especially iii.6), but action of soul on body is unproblematic for him, because in Plotinian metaphysics the whole sensible world is informed and regulated by the World-Soul. Thus such action in humans is really just an instance of a general pattern. See further D. O'Meara, "Plotinus on How Soul Acts on Body".

8 In "Nosce teipsum and Conscientia" (*AGP* 44 [1964], 188-200) A. C. Lloyd discusses St Augustine's notion of self-awareness and its precursors in Greek philosophy. He tentatively traces the cogito argument back to the debate between Stoics and sceptics in Hellenistic times. St Augustine's notion of a substantial self, as the object of self-knowledge, Lloyd traces to the Neoplatonists' notion of the Intellect's self-knowledge, and suggests that his doctrine about the soul's knowledge of itself in *De Trinitate* x emerges from combining these two notions.

9 See e. g. J. Shaffer, "Could Mental Events Be Brain Processes?", *Journal of Philosophy* 58 (1961), 815-16.

Bibliography

Useful Editions, Commentaries and Translations of the *Enneads*

Ennéades. Texte établi et traduit par Émile Bréhier. 6 vols. in 7. Paris, 1924–38

Enneadi. Prima versione integra e commentario critico di Vincenzo Cilento. 3 vols. in 4. Bari, 1947–49

Plotinus. English translation of the *Enneads* by S. Mackenna. 3rd edn, rev. by B.S. Page. London, 1962

Plotins Schriften. Übersetzt von R. Harder. Neubearbeitung mit griechischem Lesetext und Anmerkungen von R. Beutler und W. Theiler. 6 vols. in 12. Hamburg, 1956–71

Plotini Opera. Ediderunt P. Henry et H.-R. Schwyzer. 3 vols. Paris, Brussels and Leiden, 1951–73. (*Editio maior*)

Plotini Opera. Ediderunt P. Henry et H.-R. Schwyzer. 3 vols. Oxford, 1964–82. (*Editio minor*).

Plotinus . Text with an English translation by A. H. Armstrong. Vols. 1–5 (to be completed in 7). Loeb Classical Library. Cambridge, Massachusetts and London, 1966–

Modern Authors Cited in the Text

Armstrong, A. H. *The Architecture of the Intelligible Universe in the Philosophy of Plotinus*. Cambridge, 1940

"The Background of the Doctrine 'That the Intelligibles are not Outside the Intellect'". In *Les sources de Plotin*. Geneva, 1960

"Form, Individual and Person in Plotinus". *Dionysius* 1 (1977), 49–68

(ed.) *Cambridge History of Later Greek and Early Medieval Philosophy*. Cambridge, 1970

Armstrong, D. M. *Perception and the Physical World*. London and New York, 1961

A Materialist Theory of the Mind. London and New York, 1968

Bazán, B. C. "L'authenticité du 'De Intellectu' attribué à Alexandre d'Aphrodise", *Revue Philosophique de Louvain* 71 (1973), 468–87

173

Bibliography

Beare, J. I. *Greek Theories of Elementary Cognition from Alcmaeon to Aristotle.* Oxford, 1906

Beierwaltes, W. *Plotin über Ewigkeit und Zeit.* Frankfurt am Main, 1967

Blumenthal, H. J. "Did Plotinus Believe in Ideas of Individuals?", *Phronesis* 11 [1966], 61–80

"Plotinus' *Ennead* IV.3.20-1 and its Sources: Alexander, Aristotle and Others", *AGP* 50 (1968)

"Plotinus' Adaptation of Aristotle's Psychology", in R. Baine Harris (ed.), *The Significance of Neoplatonism*, pp.41-57. Norfolk, Virginia, 1976

Plotinus' Psychology. The Hague, 1971

"Soul, World-Soul and Individual Soul in Plotinus", in *Le Néoplatonisme. Colloques internationaux du Centre de la Recherche Scientifique*, 55-63. Paris, 1971

"Nous and Soul in Plotinus: Some Problems of Demarcation", in *Plotino e il Neoplatonismo in Oriente e in Occidente*, 203-19. Rome, 1974

Boyer, C. *L'idée de vérité dans la philosophie de Saint Augustin.* Paris, 1941

Bréhier, É. *La philosophie de Plotin.* Paris, 1928

Chrysippe et l'ancien Stoïcisme. Rev. edn, Paris, 1951

Brentano, F. *Die Psychologie des Aristoteles.* Mainz, 1867

Brisson, L. et al. *Porphyre. La vie de Plotin I. Travaux préliminaires, et index grec complet.* Paris, 1982

Burnyeat, M. F. "Idealism and Greek Philosophy: What Descartes Saw and Berkeley Missed", *The Philosophical Review* 91 (1982), 3-41

"Plato on the Grammar of Perceiving", *CQ* 26 (1976), 31-51

Charrue, J.-M. *Plotin: Lecteur de Platon.* Paris, 1978

Cherniss, H. "Galen and Posidonius' Theory of Vision", *The American Journal of Philology* 54 (1933), 154-61

Clark, G. H. "Plotinus' Theory of Sensation", *The Philosophical Review* 51 (1942), 357-82

Cooper, J. "Plato on Sense-Perception and Knowledge: *Theaetetus* 184-186", *Phronesis* 15 (1970), 123-46

Dillon, J. *The Middle Platonists.* London, 1977

Dodds, E. R. "The *Parmenides* of Plato and the Origin of the Neoplatonic 'One'", *CQ* 22 (1928), 129-42

Dubbink, J. H. *Studia Plotiniana. Onderzoek naar eeninge grondgedachten van het stelsel van Plotinus.* Purmerend, 1943

Ebert, T. "Aristotle on What is Done in Perceiving", *Zeitschrift für Philosophische Forschung* 37 (1981), 181-98

Fielder, J. "Plotinus'" Copy Theory:, *Apeiron* 11 (1970), 1-11

"Immateriality and Metaphysics", *Proceedings of the American Catholic Philosophical Association* 52 (1978), 96-102

Frede, M. "The Original Notion of Cause", in J. Barnes, M. Burnyeat and M. Schofield (eds.), *Doubt and Dogmatism.* Oxford, 1980

Geach, P. T. "Immortality", in *God and the Soul*, London, 1969

Graeser, A. *Plotinus and the Stoics: A Preliminary Study.* Leiden, 1972

Hahm, D. E. "Early Hellenistic Theories of Vision and the Perception of Color", in P.K. Machamer and R. Turnbull (eds.), *Studies in Perception.* Columbus, Ohio, 1978

Hamlyn, D. W. *Sensation and Perception: A History of the Philosophy of Perception.* New York, 1961

Aristotle's De Anima: Books II and III. Translated with introduction and notes by D. W. Hamlyn. Oxford, 1968

Bibliography

Harder, R. "Quelle oder Tradition?", in *Les sources de Plotin*. Geneva, 1960

Hardie, W. F. R. "Concepts of Consciousness in Aristotle", *Mind* 85 (1976), 388-411

Harman, G. *Thought*. Princeton, 1973

Hartman, E. *Substance, Body and Soul: Aristotelian Investigations*. Princeton, 1977

Henry, P. "Une comparaison chez Aristote, Alexandre et Plotin", in *Les sources de Plotin*. Geneva, 1960

    "The Place of Plotinus in the History of Thought". Introduction to MacKenna's translation of the *Enneads*. 3rd. edn, London, 1962

Igal, J. "Observanciones al Texto de Plotino". *Emerita* 41, (1973), 92-8

Inge, W. R. *The Philosophy of Plotinus*. 2 vols. London, 1929

Kahn, C. H. "Sensation and Consciousness in Aristotle's Psychology", AGP 48 (1966), 43-81

Kleist, H. von, *Plotinische Studien: Studien zur IV. Enneade*. Heidelberg, 1883.

Krämer, H. J. *Der Ursprung der Geistmetaphysik*. Amsterdam, 1964

Kristeller, P. O. *Der Begriff der Seele in der Ethik des Plotin*. Tübingen, 1929

Lacy, P. de, *Galen. On the Doctrines of Hippocrates and Plato*. Edition, translation and commentary by P. de Lacy. Part. 3. Corpus Medicorum Graecorum V 4, 1,2. Berlin, 1984

Lindberg, D. C. *Theories of Vision from Al-Kindi to Kepler*. Chicago and London, 1976

Lloyd, A. C. "Neoplatonic Logic and Aristotelian Logic I", *Phronesis* 1 (1955), 58-72

    "Nosce Teipsum and Conscientia", *AGP* 44 (1964), 188-200

Mamo, P.S. "Forms of Individuals in the *Enneads*", *Phronesis* 14 (1969), 77-96

Matthews, G. "Consciousness and Life", *Philosophy* 52 (1977), 13-26

Merlan, P. *From Platonism to Neoplatonism*. 3rd edn rev. The Hague, 1968

    "Greek Philosophy from Plato to Plotinus". Part 1 of *HLGP*. Cambridge, 1970

Moraux, P. *Alexandre d'Aphrodise: Exégète de la noétique d'Aristote*. Paris, 1942

    "Le *De Anima* dans la tradition grecque. Quelques aspects de l'interprétation du traité, de Théophraste à Thémistius", in G. E. R. Lloyd and G. E. L. Owen (eds.), *Aristotle on Mind and the Senses*, 281-324. Cambridge, 1979

O'Daly, J. P. *Plotinus' Philosophy of the Self*. Shannon, 1973

O'Meara, D. "Plotinus on how Soul Acts on Body", in D. O'Meara (ed.), *Platonic Investigations*. Washington D.C., 1985

Ostenfeld, E. "Augustin om perception", in *Museum Tusculanum* 40-43: *Studier i antik og middelalderlig filosofi og idéhistorie*. Copenhagen, 1980

Pitcher, G. *A Theory of Perception*. Princeton, 1971

Reinhardt, K. *Kosmos und Sympathie: Neue Untersuchungen über Posidonios*. Munich, 1926

Rich, N.M. "Body and Soul in the Philosophy of Plotinus", *Journal of the History of Philosophy* 1 (1963), 1-15.

Rist, J.M. "Forms of Individuals in Plotinus", *CQ* n.s. 13 (1963, 223-31

    "Ideas of Individuals in Plotinus: A Reply to Dr. Blumenthal", *Revue Internationale de Philosophie* 24 (1970), 296-303

    Plotinus: The Road to Reality. Cambridge, 1976

Rorty, R. *Philosophy and the Mirror of Nature*. Princeton, 1979

Ross, W. D. *Aristotle*. London, 1923

Ryle, G. *The Concept of Mind*. 3rd edn. Harmondsworth, 1973

Samburski, S. *Physics of the Stoics*. New York, 1959

Bibliography

Santa Cruz de Prunes, M. I. *La genèse du monde sensible dans la philosophie de Plotin*. Bibliothèque de l'École des Hautes Études, vol. 81. Paris, 1981

Sandbach, F. H. "Phantasia Kataléptiké", in A. A. Long (ed.), *Problems in Stoicism*. London, 1971

Schofield, M. "Aristotle on the Imagination", in G. E. R. Lloyd and G. E. L. Owen (eds.), *Aristotle on Mind and the Senses*. Cambridge, 1979

Schroeder, F. M.: "The Potential or Material Intellect and the Authorship of the *De Intellectu*: A Reply to B. C. Bazán", *Symbolae Osloenses* 57 (1982), 115-25

Schwyzer, H.-R. "'Bewusst' und 'unbewusst' bei Plotin", in *Les sources de Plotin*. Geneva, 1960

Sellars, W. *Science, Perception and Reality*. London and New York, 1963
Philosophical Perspectives. Springfield, Illinois, 1967

Shaffer, J. "Could Mental Events Be Brain Processes?", *Journal of Philosophy* 58 (1961), 815-16

Siegel, R. E. *Galen on Sense Perception: His Doctrines, Observations and Experiments on Vision, Hearing, Smell, Touch and Pain, and Their Historical Sources*. Basel and New York, 1970

Slakey, T. J. "Aristotle on Sense-Perception", *The Philosophical Review* 70 (1961), 470-84

Sleeman, J. H. and G. Pollet. *Lexicon Plotinianum*. Leiden, 1980

Smith, A. "Unconsciousness and Quasiconsciousness in Plotinus", *Phronesis* 23 (1978), 292-301

Solmsen, F. "Greek Philosophy and the Discovery of the Nerves", *Museum Helveticum* 18 (1961), 150-67 and 169-97

Sorabji, R. "Body and Soul in Aristotle", *Philosophy* 49 (1974), 63-89
Time, Creation and the Continuum. London, 1983

Strange, S.K. *Plotinus' Treatise "On the Genera of Being": An Historical and Philosophical Study*. Ph.D. dissertation, The University of Texas at Austin, 1981

Taylor, A. E. *Commentary on Plato's Timaeus*. Oxford, 1929

Thillet, P. Introduction to *Traité du Destin* by Alexander of Aphrodisias. Paris, 1984

Todd, R. B. *Alexander of Aphrodisias on Stoic Physics: A Study of the De Mixtione with Preliminary Essays, Text, Translation and Commentary*. Philosophia Antiqua 28. Leiden, 1976

Wagner, M. F. *Concepts and Causes: The Structure of Plotinus' Universe*. Ph.D. dissertation, The Ohio State University, 1979

Wallis, R. T. *The Neoplatonists*. London, 1972

Warren, E. W. "Consciousness in Plotinus". *Phronesis* 9 (1964), 83-97.

Wilson, M. D. "Cartesian Dualism", in M. Hooker (ed.), *Descartes: Critical and Interpretive Essays*, 197-211. Baltimore and London, 1978

Witt, R. E. "The Plotinian Logos and its Stoic Basis", *CQ* 25 (1931), 103-11.

Wittgenstein, L. *Tractatus Logico-Philosophicus*. The German Text with an English Translation by D. F. Pears and B. F. McGuinness. London and New York, 1972.

Zeller, E. *Die Philosophie der Griechen in ihrer geschichtlichen Entwicklung*, vol. 3 part 2. 4th edn. Leipzig, 1903.

Index

Academy, Old 12, 151
act (activity, actuality, *energeia, poiein*), in
perception opposed to affections, 8, 74,
126-33 (*see also* affection, conditions that
sensory affections must satisfy); difference between Plotinus' and Aristotle's
views, 127-9
Aetius, 37,40,157-9,161,165
affection (*pathos*), 6-7, 64-5; progressive,
38-41, 60; and *sympatheia*, 49-50, 56-7
(*see also sympatheia* and vision); sensory
affection: Greek thinkers on, 65-6; Plotinus' views on, 67-73; function of soul
and body in, 67-70; and forms, 71-2; and
assimilation, 70-3; and casual theories of
perception, 73-4; and assimilation as
physical change in the sense-organs, 74-
82, 84-6, rejected as Plotinus' view, 78-
82; as *synaisthêsis*, 75-6; the qualified or
animated body (*to toionde sôma*) as the
subject of, 76; conditions that sensory
affection must satisfy, 82; affections as
sensations, 83-93; sensory affection without perception, 86-8; the sense-organs as
subject of sensory affection, 88-93, 142;
as intermediate between the sensible (extension) and the intelligible, 69, 91-3,
142; account for how we perceive spatial
features of things, 90-2; sensory affection
are not the objects of perception, 142-5
Albinus, 151, 123, 153, 170
Alcmaeon of Croton, 36
Alexander of Aphrodisias, 7, 18, 30, 57, 76,
121-2, 153, 169; on vision and perception

in general, 36-7, 40, 92, 107, 142, 157-60;
and unity of the senses, 96-101, 104-5,
165; *see also* Aristotle and Aristotelianism
Anaxagoras, 4, 20
Antiochus of Ascalon, 151
Aquinas, St Thomas, 33, 104, 156
Aristagoras, 157
Aristarchus, 40, 157
Aristotle (and Aristotelianism), 3-5, 122,
151, 157; on perception as acts, 7-8; and
hylomorphism, 5, 104; on unity, 12; on
actuality, 15, 126-9; on form and matter,
16-17, 20, 52, 153, 166; on Intellect and
intelligibles, 17-18, 30; definition of
man, 26; on the self, 29, 155; on soul and
body, 5, 31-5, 104, 145-6, 156; on the
medium in visual transmission, 39-40,
43, 57, 158-9; on sensory affections, 65,
76-8, 157, 160-2; on the unity of the
senses, 95-100, 104-5, 123, 165; A's notion of the general sense, 107-8; on the
faculty of representation (*phantasia*), 110,
112, 167; on scientific knowledge, 118.
See also Alexander of Aphrodisias.
Armstrong, A.H., 9, 18, 150, 152-4, 157,
163, 167-8
Armstrong, D.M., 162
Arnou, R., 150
assimilation, *see* affection
Augustine, St, 93, 148, 156, 158, 165, 172

Barnes, J., 161
Bazán, B.C., 153-4
Beare, J.I., 157, 159

177

Index

Beierwates, W., 153
being, *see* unity and forms
Berkeley, G., 67
Blumenthal, H.J., 81, 113, 115, 118, 150-6,
    160, 162-3, 167-8
body; nature of bodies in general, 91, 102-6;
    see also soul
Boyer, C., 163, 168
Brentano, F., 161
Bréhier, E., 37, 118, 150, 152, 154, 159,
    162-3, 165, 169
Brisson, L., 150
Burnyeat, M., 161, 164-5

Calcidius, 43, 96, 158, 160, 165
Cherniss, H., 160
Chrysippus, 96-7, 159, 171
Cicero, 151, 158-9, 165, 171
Clark, G.H., 43-4, 150, 158, 168
Cleomedes, 158-9
consciousness, 87, 97, 100, 112
Cooper, J.M., 165
cosmos, 47-9, 59-61
colour, 52-5, 72, 83-91, 121, 142
Cyrenaics, 164

Democritus, 39
Descartes, 8, 32, 145-8, 156, 172
Diels, H., 157
Dillon, J., 153
Diogenes Laertius, 154, 158, 160-1, 165
Dodds, E.R., 152
dualism (of soul and body), 5, 8, 32-4, 69,
    101-6, 145-8
Dubbink, J.H., 150

Ebert, T., 170
Eleatics, 11-12
energeia, see act
Epicurus and Epicureans, 92, 118,
Erasistratus, 105
eye; containing internal light, 43, 48-9; as
    the subject of sensory affections, *see*
    affection

Fielder, J. 139-40, 154, 172
form; and matter, 16-17, 24, 52, 133; realm
    of Forms, 17,30; in visual transmission,
    50-1; different kinds of forms disting-
    uished, 133-4 in perception 71-2, 108-9,
    133-40; *see also* Plato and Aristotle
Frede, M. 160

Galen, 36-7, 43-5, 59-62, 93, 105, 157-8,
    160
Geach, P.T., 156
Greaser, A., 38, 152, 157-8, 163

Hahm, D.E., 157-8,
Hamlyn, D.W., 95, 164-5
Harder, R. 151, 167
Hardie, W.F.R., 167
Harman, G., 170
Hartman, E., 161, 171
hearing, 6, 75-6
Helleman-Elgersma, W. 154, 166
Henry, P., 9, 166
Herophilus, 105
hierarchy; consisting of the One, Intellect,
    and Soul, 10-22; same entities on diff-
    erent levels of 19-29, 25-6, 134-5
hypostasis, *see* hierarchy

Igal, J., 155
image, as a copy of an ontologically prior
    item (*eidôlon*), 119-21; *see logos, and also*
    form, kinds of; as a representation in the
    soul (*phantasma, typos*), 66, 116-21, 145;
    see also typos
Inge, W.R., 150
Intellect (*nous*), 3, 17-21, 23-6, 30, 71-2,
    117-20, 133-8
intelligibles (*ta noêta*), 117-20, 134-5; as
    forms, 17, 71-2, 108-9; opposed to sensi-
    bles, 18-19, 30, 91, 114-15

judgement (*krisis*), 7-8, 74-5, 78-82, 106,
    117, 121-5, 130-1, 145

Kahn, C.H., 165, 167
Kant, I., 4
Kleist, H. von, 167
Krämer, H.J., 152
krisis, see judgement
Kristeller, P.O., 150, 160, 166

Lloyd, A.C., 156, 163, 172
logos, 24, 120-1, 125-6

Mamo, P.S., 155
matter, *see* form
medium (*to metaxy*), meaning of, 38; *see*
    affection, *sympatheia* and vision
Merlan, P., 151-4,
Moore, G.E., 159
Moraux, P., 153-4

noêta, see intelligibles
nous, see intellect

O'Daly, J.P., 155
O'Meara, D., 154, 172
One (hypostasis), 14-20
opinion (*doxa*) 26, 132

178